Politics

and Government

in Japan

SECOND EDITION

THEODORE McNELLY
UNIVERSITY OF MARYLAND

HOUGHTON MIFFLIN COMPANY · BOSTON

NEW YORK · ALANTA · GENEVA, ILL. · DALLAS · PALO ALTO

Library of Congress Catalog Card Number: 74–186377
ISBN: 0–395–12649–5

TO

MY MOTHER

CONTENTS

FIGURES

TABLES

PREFACE

In modern times, no nation has undergone a more dramatic transformation than Japan. An isolated feudal state only a century ago, it has emerged with astonishing rapidity as a leading world power, providing students of politics with a unique source of data for the analysis of political development. In this book I emphasize the fundamental changes that have occurred and are occurring in the Japanese polity, and I use concepts and categories intended to facilitate comparison with other political systems. Most of the chapter titles denote structures involved in the political conversion process. My discussion of interest groups, whose principal function is interest articulation, precedes my description of political parties, whose principal functions in modern polities are interest aggregation and political recruitment. The legislature (function: rule formulation), the judiciary (function: rule adjudication), and the executive (function: rule application) are the topics of succeeding chapters. The two concluding chapters deal with policy outputs.

A principal reason for studying Japanese politics is to gain a better understanding of the foreign policy of one major world power. Although devastated by bombings and disarmed immediately after World War II, Japan today has re-established a respectable military force and boasts of the world's third largest gross national product. Japan's growing foreign trade contributed heavily to the dollar-yen crisis, which was no doubt one of President Nixon's major considerations in announcing in August, 1971, his new economic policy. Citizens and statesmen of other countries are necessarily interested in such a powerful nation's relations with the rest of the world, and one chapter of this book is entirely devoted to the formulation and content of Japan's foreign policy.

I have followed the Japanese practice of putting the family name before the given name of individuals. The Hepburn system of romanizing the Japanese language has been followed, except for Japanese words that have been adopted into the English language according to *Webster's Unabridged Dictionary;* these are given the usual English spelling, without long marks. I have made it a rule to avoid Japanese words and to use standard English translations for Japanese terms, as indicated in *Kenkyusha's New Japanese-English Dictionary.* The official Japanese term is supplied where appropriate.

In Japan, I profited greatly from discussions of Japanese politics and constitutional revision with the late Prime Minister Katayama

Tetsu; Mr. Nishio Suehiro, Chairman of the Democratic-Socialist Party; Professor Satō Isao of Seikei University; Mr. Satō Tatsuo, Chairman of the National Personnel Authority, and the late Dr. Takayanagi Kenzō, Chairman of the Commission on the Constitution. As an Associate of the Columbia University Seminar on Modern East Asia: Japan, I have been privileged to keep abreast of the research of distinguished colleagues in Japanese studies. Further, I am grateful to the General Research Board of the University of Maryland for grants which made it possible to devote the summers of 1961, 1964, 1966, and 1968 to research on various aspects of Japan's political development.

For their various forms of help in writing this book, I wish to thank Professors Chün-tu Hsüeh and Marlene Mayo, Messrs. Charles Schaumburg and Claude Shirai, and Dr. Harold Larson, all at the University of Maryland; Dr. Hattie K. Colton, of the Foreign Service Institute; Professor Kenneth Colton, of Kent State University; Professor David Farquhar, of the University of California at Los Angeles; Professor Dayton McKean, of the University of Colorado; Miss Yoshi Takahashi, of the University of Hawaii; Messrs. Key Kobayashi and Andrew Kuroda, of the Library of Congress; and Messrs. Richard N. Clark and Frank Shelton, of Houghton Mifflin Company. My wife Myra typed the entire manuscript of the first edition and assisted with the preparation of the charts and index. Marsha Grayson, Leslie Speert, and Peggy Zucconi kindly assisted in the typing of the second edition.

The author, of course, must assume responsibility for errors of fact and interpretation.

THEODORE MCNELLY

College Park, Maryland

In the footnotes and at the end of each chapter, the author has listed further readings in English. These lists are far from exhaustive, and for further suggestions the reader is referred to Hugh Borton, Serge Elisséeff, William W. Lockwood, and John C. Pelzel, comp., *A Selected List of Books and Articles on Japan in English, French and German* (Cambridge, Mass.: Harvard University Press, 1954), the *Bibliography of Asian Studies,* published annually by the *Journal of Asian Studies,* and, for material in Japanese, Robert E. Ward and Hajime Watanabe, *A Guide to Japanese Reference and Research Materials in the Field of Political Science,* rev. ed. (Ann Arbor: University of Michigan Press, 1961).

In following research on contemporary affairs, the student may wish to consult *American Universities Field Staff Reports, Asian Survey, Contemporary Japan, Japan Interpreter, Japan Quarterly, Journal of Asian Studies, Monumenta Nipponica, Pacific Affairs,* and *Transactions of the Asiastic Society of Japan.*

The following books of a general nature on Japanese politics will be found of value in addition to those cited elsewhere:

Burks, Ardath W. *The Government of Japan,* 2nd ed. New York: Thomas Y. Crowell, 1963.

Ike, Nobutaka. *Japanese Politics: An Introductory Survey.* New York: Knopf, 1957.

Langdon, Frank. *Politics in Japan.* Boston, Mass.: Little, Brown, 1967.

Maki, John M. *Government and Politics of Japan: The Road to Democracy.* New York: Praeger, 1962.

Quigley, Harold S., and John E. Turner. *The New Japan: Government and Politics.* Minneapolis: University of Minnesota Press, 1956.

Tsuneishi, Warren M. *Japanese Political Style: An Introduction to the Government and Politics of Modern Japan.* New York: Harper & Row, 1966.

Ward, Robert E. *Japan's Political System.* Englewood Cliffs, N.J.: Prentice-Hall, 1967.

Yanaga, Chitoshi. *Japanese People and Politics.* New York: Wiley, 1956.

GLOSSARY

Aikoku-tō	Patriotic Party
Beheiren*	Japan "Peace for Vietnam!" Committee
Burakumin	eta (outcastes)
Chōren	League of Koreans Residing in Japan
Dōmei Kaigi*	Japan Confederation of Labor
DSP	Democratic Socialist Party
Gensuikyō*	Japan Council Against Atomic and Hydrogen Bombs
-ha	faction
JCP	Japan Communist Party
JDA	Japan Defense Agency
Jimin-tō	= Jiyū-Minshu-tō
Jiyū-Minshu-tō	Liberal-Democratic Party
JSP	Japan Socialist Party
Kaishin-tō	Progressive (or Reform) Party
Keidanren	Federation of Economic Organizations
kokutai	national structure (or national polity)
Kōmei-tō	Clean Government Party
Kyōsan-tō	Communist Party
LDP	Liberal-Democratic Party
Minsha-tō	= Minshu-Shakai-tō
Minshu-Shakai-tō	Democratic-Socialist Party
MITI	Ministry of International Trade and Industry
Nikkeiren	Japan Federation of Employers Associations
Nikkyōsō	Japan Teachers Union
saha	left wing
Sambetsu*	Congress of Industrial Unions
SDF	Self-Defense Force
Shakai-tō	Socialist Party
Shimpo-tō	Progressive Party
Sōdōmei	Japan Federation of Labor
Sōhyō*	General Council of Japan Trade Unions
Sōka Gakkai*	Value Creation Society
-tō	party
uha	right wing
Zengakuren*	National Federation of Students Self Government Associations

* Usually not translated.

1

The Political Development of Japan

Nation-Building and Modernization

Japan is particularly appropriate for the study of political develop-ment because the Japanese political system, in one form or another, has existed continuously for over fifteen hundred years. Only once, in 1945, did Japan suffer the humiliation of foreign conquest, but even then, after a brief occupation, the country was permitted to resume its independence with relatively minor alterations in governmental in-stitutions. Japan's political organization has been successively tribal, feudal, monarchical, and democratic, but the symbolic head of the polity since the sixth century has been a monarch drawn from a single dynasty. Change and continuity have existed as complementary themes throughout Japan's political evolution.

Nation-building in the emerging countries of Asia and Africa has recently become a favorite topic of students of comparative politics. However, unlike other Afro-Asian states, Japan is not an emerging or developing country. With the world's third largest gross national product, it is a model of development, not a problem in underdevelop-ment. The political modernization of Japan appears to have been the inevitable concomitant of industrialization and urbanization. The oligarchs of the Meiji era (1868–1912) and the officials of the American occupation (1945–1952), who wrote the 1889 and 1947 constitutions, acted as agents of modernizing social forces. The people's pride in nation, the Confucian tradition of public service, the sense of deference to authority—these elements of political culture which have contributed to the building of a modern state—had been the product of a long development. The purpose of this chapter is to

1

identify the contributions of Japan's prewar political evolution to the modern polity.

Cultural Unity

During the paleolithic era, waves of migration with their accompanying cultural currents reached the Japanese archipelago from the coast of Asia. Once in Japan, migrant tribes could move no further eastward, and, consequently, various ethnic and cultural groups piled up and eventually blended to produce the homogeneous ethnic, linguistic, and cultural pattern of Japan. Thus from its earliest days, the Japanese political system has been free from the kinds of racial, religious, and linguistic conflicts extant in many countries today.

By the fifth century, the kingdom of Yamato had attained dominance in the Japanese islands and the Korean peninsula. The primitive Yamato society was essentially a confederation of clans (uji), each with its own chieftain and ancestral deity. Heading the confederation was the imperial clan, which has provided Japan with all of its Emperors. (The present Emperor is considered the 124th in the dynasty.) The Emperor has sometimes been described as a patriarch of the state, which is thought of as a single united family.[1]

The native Japanese religion, Shinto, was a compound of primitive nature worship, animism, and shamanism and provided the basis for the divine right of the monarch. By the end of the sixth century, Buddhism, with its rich doctrine and ritual and its potentialities for political exploitation, had captured the allegiance of the erstwhile pagan rulers; but Shinto (the "Way of the Gods") has coexisted and sometimes amalgamated with Buddhism in Japanese life down to the present.

Confucian Monarchy

In 604, the Regent Prince Shōtoku promulgated in Chinese his famous "Seventeen-Article Constitution."[2] Shōtoku's Constitution was not an organic law in the modern sense but was a collection of Confucian exhortations emphasizing the need for harmony, for the sub-

---

[1] Hozumi Nobushige, *Ancestor-Worship and Japanese Law* (Tokyo: Maruzen, 1938), p. 103.

[2] Text in Ryusaku Tsunoda, Wm. Theodore de Bary, and Donald Keene, comps., *Sources of the Japanese Tradition* (New York: Columbia University Press, 1958), pp. 49–53.

ordination of inferiors to superiors, and for diligence and honesty in the administration of state affairs. Confucian precepts provided an ideology for the liquidation of rule by clan chieftains and the establishment of a centralized monarchy after the Chinese model.

In 603, Shōtoku, in emulation of the Sui monarchy in China, established a system of "cap-ranks," which would enhance the prestige of the imperial court. There were twelve ranks from top to bottom, each rank being indicated by a silken hat of a different color. While originally the ranks were intended to be hereditary, the merit system made some headway.

The principles of Shōtoku's Constitution were put into effect piecemeal until 645, when a palace revolution resulted in the overthrow of the domineering Soga clan and in the inauguration of the "Great Reform" (Taika).

The Edict of Reform[3] of 646 contained the following provisions:

1. All hereditary guilds are abolished and various local authorities are deprived of the manors and serfs which they have appropriated to themselves.

2. Governors are appointed to the home and outer provinces. The home provinces are to be divided into rural districts, composed of townships, each district to be under the authority of a district governor.

3. Registers of the population are to be drawn up, and land is to be redistributed according to the principle of "mouth-share-field" (i.e., each household is allotted land in proportion to the number of people in the household). The rate of the tax in the form of rice on the land is established.

4. The old taxes and forced labor are abolished, and a system of commuted taxes in kind (e.g., silk) is set up. Contributions are to be made, in a fixed ratio to the number of houses, of post horses, weapons, coolies, and good-looking waiting women for the court. In some cases, these contributions could be replaced with rice.

The primary purpose of the edict seems to have been the redistribution of economic power in favor of the central government. The centralizers cited the Chinese doctrine: "Under the heavens there is no land which is not the king's land. Among holders of land there is none who is not the king's vassal."

[3] An English translation of the reform edict is given in Tsunoda, pp. 74–76.

Borrowing Foreign Institutions

The Taihō Code of 702 set up a central administrative structure adapted from that of the T'ang monarchy in China. Directly under the Emperor was the Department of Worship (Jingi-kan), and below it was the Department of State (Dajō-kan). The former was an ecclesiastical commission which controlled affairs pertaining to the national cult, Shinto. There was no corresponding institution in the T'ang system, the Jingi-kan being a peculiarly Japanese institution. Although Buddhism seemed to eclipse the native "Way of the Gods," the cult of the Sun Goddess, ancestress of the Emperor, was maintained to bolster the Emperor's claim to rule by divine right. The Emperor customarily referred to himself as a "manifest god," though his presumed divinity did not necessarily influence his method of rule. The Confucian idea that the mandate of heaven might be withdrawn from a wicked ruler and that the people might overthrow him was never adopted by the Japanese.

The Department of State was presided over by the Chancellor and included the Minister of the Left, the Minister of the Right, four Great Councillors and three Minor Councillors. The Chancellor served as a kind of moral preceptor to the Emperor, and this post was often vacant. The Minister of the Left (or the Minister of the Right acting in his place) served as the chief administrative officer, and his functions roughly corresponded to those of a modern prime minister. Under the Council were the eight boards or ministries: the Ministries of Central Affairs, Ceremonies, Civil Affairs, Popular Affairs, War, Justice, Treasury, and Imperial Household. These ministries, except Central Affairs and Imperial Household, corresponded roughly to the six ministries of the T'ang administration. The names of these offices were, for the most part, self-explanatory. The Ministry of Central Affairs was concerned with transmitting the Emperor's decrees to the appropriate authorities and memorials to the Emperor. The Ministry of Ceremonies determined promotion and degradation of officials. Civil Affairs was concerned with noblemen, ecclesiastics, and aliens; Popular Affairs with land, people, taxes, and forced labor. There was finally an Office of Censorship, which corrected evil customs and punished the misbehavior of officials.

The transplantation of Chinese institutions to Japanese soil necessarily resulted in dilution, compromise, and sometimes improvement. The Japanese court could not afford to antagonize the clan chieftains and local gentry whose privileges would be wiped out by the principle of imperial centralization. Therefore, from the very beginning of the reform movement, although the clan nobles were replaced by imperial governors, the imperial governors and high ranking court officials were as a rule drawn from the traditional aristocracy.

The custom of the Yamato court was to maintain no fixed residence but to move from one place to another, but when missions to the T'ang court returned with dazzling descriptions of the Chinese capital, a permanent Japanese capital was erected in 710 at Nara, near the present city of Kyoto; the capital included a university where sons of the nobility could study the teachings of Confucius. The wholesale borrowing of Chinese institutions in the seventh and eighth centuries later served as a precedent for the adoption of foreign legal and constitutional models in the Meiji and the post–World War II periods.

Divine Right

In 712 the court published the *Kojiki* (Record of Ancient Things) and in 720 the *Nihongi* (Record of Japan). These were compilations of oral legends concerning the Age of the Gods and the founding of Japan. According to these accounts, Amaterasu, the Sun Goddess, gave a mandate to her Heavenly Grandchild, Ninigi-no-Mikoto: "The Country of Goodly Grain with the promise of one thousand five hundred mellow autumns to come is the land where Our descendants shall become Sovereigns. The prosperity of the Imperial Throne shall be coeval with heaven and earth."[4] Ninigi-no-Mikoto took with him on his descent to the divine land the Three Sacred Treasures: the sacred jewels, the sacred mirror, and the sacred sword. The Sacred Treasures are even today in the possession of the Japanese Imperial Family and have throughout the ages served as the Imperial Regalia and as evidence of the legitimacy of the claim to the throne. Thus the compilation of the early histories by the court increased the prestige of the Yamato state and the imperial clan by asserting the supernatural creation of the country and the divine origin of the dynasty.

Diarchy

With the decline of the T'ang dynasty in the ninth century, the direct influence of China on Japanese institutions came to an end; native traditions of clan privilege and local autonomy were reasserted.

[4] Fujii Shinichi, *Tenno Seiji* (Tokyo: Yuhikaku, 1944), p. 8.

The Fujiwara clan became increasingly powerful in the capital. Although the positions of Chancellor, Minister of the Left, and Minister of the Right continued, the Fujiwara set up more powerful posts in the court which they managed to monopolize.

This powerful clan saw to it that Emperors abdicated soon after reaching their majority, so that a Fujiwara Regent (Sesshō) would be the effective ruler on behalf of a child Emperor. When the monarch became of age, the Regent would become Civil Dictator (Kampaku). The Emperor was required to marry a Fujiwara lady, so that his offspring were quite as much the descendants of the Fujiwara as they were of the Sun Goddess.

The Fujiwara monopoly of high position in the court continued until the Restoration of 1867. This great family firmly established the principle of diarchy, or dual government, according to which the Emperor ruled in name only and another exercised actual authority. In the sense that he reigns but does not rule, the Emperor has, with rare exceptions, been a "constitutional monarch" for 1300 years.

The spread of tax-exempt manors and the rise of a military nobility in the provinces helped to destroy the power of the imperial court. The lands of Shinto shrines, Buddhist temples, and powerful officials were exempted from taxation. As more areas became exempt, the burden of taxation on the nonexempt small-holders increased. These subjects often found it to their advantage to commend their lands to exempt neighbors, thus avoiding their obligations to the Son of Heaven. Often minor nobles would commend their lands, including land commended to them, to greater nobles. Thus, hierarchical structures of vassals—commendors and commendees—came into being, laying the basis for feudalism. As the court became incapable of enforcing its will and protecting its subjects in the provinces, country gentry found it expedient to maintain small armies for protection. With increasing frequency the court commissioned one or another of the provincial nobles to punish recalcitrant vassals. In the latter half of the twelfth century, the greatest of the territorial barons were engaged in wars to determine the fate of entire provinces. Finally, in 1192, Minamoto Yoritomo emerged as the ultimate victor and was formally recognized as the feudal overlord of all of Japan.

In concluding the discussion of the fate of Chinese institutions on Japanese soil, we note that (1) the Confucian merit system did not permanently displace the Japanese traditions of hereditary privilege and divine right, (2) the system of individual small-holders paying taxes to the imperial court gave way to a hierarchical feudal structure, (3) dual government (diarchy) in which the Emperor ruled only in name while clan leaders ruled in fact became an established principle, and (4) the central administration was, for all practical purposes, gradually superseded by military feudal barons.

Feudal Institutions and Values

In 1192, the imperial court conferred upon Minamoto Yoritomo the title of Barbarian-Subduing Generalissimo (Sei-i Tai Shōgun). The Shogunate became hereditary in the Minamoto clan. Although Emperors and court nobles continued to perform ceremonies in Kyoto, the ruler of Japan for the next 675 years was the Shogun, a military dictator, who maintained his own feudal capital removed from the influence of the imperial court. Under the new diarchy, successive clans of barons rather than court nobles would rule on behalf of the Emperor.

The chief organs of the early Shoguns' administration were: (1) the Samurai Council (Samurai-dokoro), an administrative and judicial body concerned with the affairs of the military class such as rewards and punishment, promotion and demotion, allocation of military duties, and criminal matters, (2) the Administrative Office (Mandokoro) concerned with the administration of the domains of the Minamoto, and (3) a High Court (Monjū-sho), the final court for appeals of suits concerning rights of feudal tenure. The law applied was the precedents and feudal contracts which had developed during the preceding two centuries, more frequently than the Chinese-inspired codes of the earlier periods. Throughout the country, newly established provincial constables and local stewards enforced the Shogun's authority.

After the extinction of Yoritomo's line, the government of the Shogunate was taken over by a line of Regents (Shikken) of the Hōjō clan (1226–1333), who governed on behalf of child Shoguns appointed from the court nobility in Kyoto. The Regency in 1232 issued the famous Formulary of Jōei, a compilation of feudal law based upon precedent.

One great accomplishment of the Hōjō Regents was the repulse of two attempted invasions of the land by the Mongols in 1274 and 1281. The Japanese defense was aided by the prayers of the people to the Buddhist and Shinto deities and by the "Wind of the Gods" (kamikaze), which on both occasions destroyed the enemy invasion fleets. The result of this experience was a conviction, inbred in succeeding generations, that the divine land of Japan enjoyed the special protection of the deities.

In the fourteenth century, fief-hungry barons found an opportunity to satisfy their ambitions in a succession war between competing claimants to the imperial throne. The war between the rival northern and southern courts accompanied the establishment of a new dynasty of Shoguns—the Ashikaga. The Ashikaga period (1338–1573) was one of unremitting civil war among feudal lords for more fiefs, and the power of the Ashikaga Shoguns scarcely went beyond their own immediate domains. The Ashikaga have been excoriated by patriotic historians because they declared themselves kings of Japan, subject to the Chinese emperor. Their motive seems to have been primarily commercial, because the Shoguns' tribute missions to China were actually trading enterprises.

The period of the "Country at War" was brought to an end by the great military unifiers, Oda Nobunaga, Toyotomi Hideyoshi, and Tokugawa Ieyasu. Tokugawa Ieyasu obtained from the Emperor the title of Shogun in 1603.

Feudalistic Monarchy

Tokugawa Ieyasu was an administrator of the first order as well as a great general, and he established a regime which, under fifteen successive Tokugawa Shoguns, ensured unprecedented peace and political stability for Japan. The policies that account for the success of the Tokugawa were stringent control over the feudal barons and the Emperor, the isolation of Japan from the outside world, and the suppression of Christianity. In 1638, a peasant revolt led by Christian samurai was put down with great severity. The Catholic Church, regarded as the vanguard of Spanish and Portuguese imperialism, was ruthlessly extirpated, and the Catholic states of Spain and Portugal were forbidden to send missionaries or traders to Japan. Only the Dutch, who swore not to proselytize, and the Chinese were allowed to trade in Japan. An upper limit was placed on the size of Japanese ships, so that no subject of the Shogun could carry on foreign trade or travel abroad.

Those barons who had recognized Ieyasu as their overlord before the battle of Sekigahara (1600) were designated "vassal lords" (fudai daimyō), while those who had been neutrals and Ieyasu's enemies and belated allies before the crucial battle were designated "outside lords" (tozama daimyō). The new Shogun redistributed the fiefs in the land in such a way as to isolate the outside lords from one another. The outside lords were not permitted to serve as Elders or Junior Elders, who advised the Shogun on the administration of the country. The new regime maintained a highly effective spy system to report any suspicious plotting or intrigue. The daimyo were not to be permitted to have contacts with the Emperor. The barons, as a rule, were required to spend every other year with their families at Edo (present Tokyo), the Shogun's capital, and every other year at their fiefs, leaving their families as hostages in Edo. The cost of maintaining sumptuous residences both in Edo and in their own domains, of processions to and from Edo, and of salaries (paid in rice) to samurai retainers was ultimately ruinous to the feudal lords.

The trouble with the Tokugawa system of maintaining internal peace was that it worked all too well. The long period of domestic stability favored the expansion of the money economy at the expense of the rice economy and the rise of the commercial classes at the expense of the agrarian feudal classes. As the merchants in Edo and Osaka grew richer, the daimyo and samurai grew poorer.

Not only was the economic basis of the feudal regime subverted, but its ideology was undermined. The Bakufu had sponsored the conservative Chu Hsi form of Confucianism, which emphasized obedience and loyalty, but Wang Yang-ming Confucianism, which emphasized intuition and action, became increasingly influential and was a potential encouragement to rebellion. Much more important, however, was the school of national literature. As scholars revived the study of the *Kojiki* and *Nihongi,* impoverished samurai learned that Japan, far from being ruled by the divine Emperor as decreed by the Sun Goddess, was actually being controlled by a usurper in the form of the Shogun. The Shinto revival thus provided the ideological basis for revolt.

In 1853, Commodore Matthew Calbraith Perry left a message to be delivered to the Emperor calling for the opening of Japan and promising that he would return the following year for a reply. Clearly, the Shogun's duty as Barbarian-Subduing Generalissimo was to reject Perry's demands, but he possessed neither the military strength nor the support of the daimyo necessary to repel the American barbarian. After the Shogun negotiated a treaty with Perry, his enemies rallied around the Emperor under the slogan: "Revere the Emperor; expel the barbarian!" In 1867, beset with difficulties on all sides, Tokugawa Keiki declared the Shogunate at an end. He assumed that he would be named a leading councillor in the "restored" imperial regime. When the western clansmen excluded him, he and his followers resorted to war but were promptly defeated.

The feudalistic monarchy of the Tokugawa had made substantial contributions to the political modernization of Japan. The Shogunate had pacified the nobility, consolidated the administration, and kept Western imperialism at bay. The peace enforced by the last dynasty of

Shoguns had fostered the commercial revolution and encouraged the formation of a class of effective bureaucrats. The Tokugawa regime had unified the nation and prepared it for the centralized bureaucratic regime which was to follow.

Bureaucratic Monarchy

The men who had engineered the "Restoration" of the Emperor Meiji were samurai from the southern and western fiefs, or clans (han), of Chōshū, Satsuma, Tosa, and Hizen. Members of these clans were destined to monopolize effective political authority in Japan until the close of World War I. To dramatize the transfer of political authority from the Shogun to the Emperor, the imperial capital was moved from Kyoto, where it had been located since 794, to Edo, the capital of the former Tokugawa Shoguns. Edo was renamed Tokyo, "Eastern Capital," and the Shogun's palace was taken over by the Emperor.

A basic law was promulgated in 1868 providing for a resuscitation of the Chinese-inspired institutions of the prefeudal epoch. In 1869, the daimyo transmitted their registers of land and of people to the Emperor to formalize the end of feudalism and the restoration of imperial rule. The fiefs of the *ancien régime* were replaced by prefectures (ken), administered by governors appointed by the Emperor, and the daimyo were granted liberal pensions. The samurai, also pensioned off, were deprived of their privileges, including the right to wear two swords.

The sweeping changes from the Tokugawa form of feudalism to bureaucratic monarchy were subjects of bitter disputes. The government determined to concentrate on internal economic and political reform rather than engage in military adventures on the Asiatic continent, as was strongly urged by some leaders. This reform policy alienated samurai who wished to cover themselves with glory in a war with Korea. When the government commuted the samurai pensions to niggardly lump-sum payments, the warriors felt betrayed. In 1877, discontented samurai in Satsuma rebelled. The Emperor's newly organized conscript troops, trained by Western methods and equipped with modern weapons, put down the uprising, and the new regime survived its first great test.

When the clan leaders Itagaki of Tosa and Ōkuma of Hizen were forced out of the councils of the new regime, which fell increasingly under the domination of samurai from Chōshū and Satsuma, they demanded the establishment of a representative parliament and organized political parties. The authorities met the demands of the opposition with nominal concessions and police repression. In 1881, the government promised that a constitution providing for an elective parliament would be established in 1890. The Liberal Party (Jiyūtō), formed by Itagaki in 1881, called for a constitution based on the principle of popular sovereignty. Ōkuma's Progressive Party (Kaishintō), inaugurated in 1882, advocated the English form of parliamentarianism. (The present-day Liberal-Democratic Party is the lineal descendant of the parties of Itagaki and Ōkuma.) The government organized the Imperial Party (Teiseitō) in 1882 and charged the opposition parties with disloyalty to the Emperor. These early parties were formed primarily to support the ambitions of oligarchic leaders. From the beginning they were shot through with opportunism and personal factionalism. Political parties in Japan did not then and do not now represent grassroots movements.

The government charged Itō Hirobumi, a Chōshū leader, with the formulation of a constitution. He was convinced that a basic law like that of autocratic Prussia would best suit Japan. Aided by a German adviser, he and his close associates, working in deepest secrecy, produced a constitution which obtained the approval of the Privy Council, of which Itō was President. On February 11, 1889, the Meiji Emperor promulgated the Constitution of the Empire of Japan and the Imperial House Law, together with implementing ordinances. Itō hailed the new Constitution as the "Emperor's gift to the Japanese people" and published his own *Commentaries on the Constitution of Japan,* an article-by-article interpretation of the new basic law.

The 1889 Constitution was in part a manifesto of the Shinto revival.[5] Article I provided, "The Empire of Japan shall be reigned over and governed by a line of Emperors unbroken for ages eternal." "The Emperor," Article III stated, "is sacred and inviolable." The Constitution did not provide that the Cabinet be answerable to the Diet. To make the Ministers of the Emperor responsible to the parliament would, Itō held, deny the principle that the Emperor rules. Lest the power of the purse be used by the Diet to control the executive, Itō's Constitution provided that when the Diet failed to enact the budget, the Government would carry out the budget of the preceding year.

The upper chamber of the Imperial Diet consisted of a House of Peers made up of high-ranking peers, representatives of lower-ranking peers, representatives of the highest taxpayers, and imperial appointees. (The peerage had been created in 1884 by Itō to rally former daimyo,

[5] For the text of the Meiji Constitution, see Theodore McNelly, comp., *Sources in Modern East Asian History and Politics* (New York: Appleton-Century-Crofts, 1967), pp. 57–64.

court nobility, leading samurai, and wealthy merchants to the support of the new regime.) The members of the lower house, the House of Representatives, were elected by a relatively small electorate which met minimum taxpaying requirements. Japanese subjects enjoyed freedom of speech, press, and assembly "within the limits of law." The Constitution could be amended only upon proposal of the Emperor and with the approval of two-thirds of the members present in each house. The Imperial House Law, which regulated the succession to the Throne, could not be modified by the Diet.

The Privy Council, established by an Imperial Ordinance in 1888, was made up of a President, Vice President, and twenty-five Councillors, all appointed by the Emperor on the advice of the Cabinet. The Constitution provided that they would "deliberate upon important matters of state when they have been consulted by the Emperor."

A principal characteristic of the Meiji Constitution was the predominance of the executive branch. Normally, the most that the Diet could do was oppose, and its independence was weakened by the need to support the government during the Sino-Japanese War (1894–1895) and the Russo-Japanese War (1904–1905).

Government by the clan oligarchs (hambatsu) meant that the samurai clansmen who had brought about the Meiji restoration were the effective rulers of Japan and prevented the political parties from establishing an executive responsible to the majority in the national legislature. The men who advised the Emperor on the choice of Prime Minister were an extraconstitutional group known as the genro, or elder statesmen.[6] With a single exception, the genro were drawn from the Chōshū and Satsuma clans, and they saw to it that the prime ministership normally alternated between the samurai aristocracy of the two clans. After 1924, only one member of the genro remained, Saionji (d. 1940). The jūshin (senior statesmen), i.e., former prime ministers, took the place of the genro in the 1930s and early 1940s. They and the Lord Keeper of the Privy Seal advised the Emperor on the appointment of prime ministers and on other important questions.

Relations between the Cabinet and Diet were normally poor. The Diet represented predominantly agrarian interests that balked at appropriating the substantial funds which the government demanded for expanding the armed services and establishing model industrial enterprises. Often the Cabinet would meet the recalcitrance of the lower house with a prorogation (suspension of the session) or a dissolution, and frequently the Cabinet itself would resign immediately following a

[6] The genro should not be confused with the Genrō-in, a kind of senate created in 1875 which existed until the enforcement of the Meiji Constitution.

dissolution. The lives of Cabinets and of Houses of Representatives usually did not exceed two and a half years. Nevertheless, the First Sino-Japanese War and the Russo-Japanese War enabled the Cabinet to bring great pressure to bear on the Diet to cooperate in times of national emergency.

During World War I, inflation drove up the price of rice in Japan, and in 1918, riots in which peasants seized rice stores broke out throughout the country. The situation was too serious for the genro to cope with, and Hara, the leader of the Seiyūkai party, was appointed the first commoner to serve as Prime Minister of Japan. A Cabinet made up predominantly of members of the majority party was established. The power of the clan oligarchs was broken.

Parliamentarianism

Japan was not immune to the worldwide enthusiasm for democracy which had been kindled by the Allied victory in World War I and Wilsonian idealism. Liberal intellectuals and businessmen hoped that the accession of Hara, the party politician, would end rule by an elite and inaugurate a period of responsible cabinet government after the British model. They coined the expression "normal constitutional government" (kensei no jōdō) to designate the parliamentary-cabinet system which they wished to see established in Japan. The cabinets from 1918 to 1922 and from 1924 to 1932 were headed by leaders of the majority party or majority coalitions in the Diet. On May 5, 1925, a universal manhood suffrage law was passed which gave the right to vote to all male citizens over twenty-five years of age, increasing the electorate from three to thirteen million. A week later, however, the Diet passed the Peace Preservation Law which banned societies or parties advocating alteration of the Constitution, of the existing form of government, or of the system of private ownership of property. The party cabinets were no more tolerant of socialism and the labor movement than the oligarchic cabinets had been.

The rise of Chinese nationalism, which threatened Japanese interests in the Asiatic continent, and the world depression created problems apparently too great to be resolved in the framework of Japan's nascent parliamentarianism. In 1928, a Chinese boycott of Japanese goods forced a Japanese retreat in north China and the resignation of the Seiyūkai Cabinet of Baron Tanaka, which had favored a "positive" policy towards China.

The succeeding Minseitō Government of Hamaguchi won an absolute majority in the election of 1930. Hamaguchi made himself unpopular by practicing financial retrenchment and outraged the Navy by accepting an inferior naval ratio for Japan at the London Disarmament Conference. The Prime Minister was shot in November, 1930, by an ultranationalist and died the following year.

On September 18, 1931, a minor bomb explosion on the Japanese-operated South Manchurian Railway was used as a pretext by the Japanese Army to seize all of Manchuria. The Army acted on its own initiative, without consulting either Prime Minister Wakatsuki or Foreign Minister Shidehara.

The last of the party governments was that of Inukai, whose Seiyūkai won an overwhelming majority in the 1932 elections for the House of Representatives. However, ultranationalists tried to overthrow the government on May 15, 1932, and assassinated the Prime Minister. Although party members participated in the succeeding cabinets, the executive branch ceased to be responsible to parliament and was dominated by the military and bureaucracy until the end of World War II.

Military Ascendancy

The Manchurian Incident and the assassination of Inukai brought an end to party government and began a new period of "transcendental" cabinets. "Dual government," in which the military was able to act independently of the civil branch, became the rule.

The constitutional basis for the autonomy of the military was the "independence" of the military prerogative of the Emperor in the Meiji Constitution. Articles 11 and 12, which provided that the "Emperor has the supreme command of the Army and Navy" and "determines the organization and peace standing of the Army and Navy" were interpreted by the services to mean that the supreme command and the service ministries had a right equal to that of the Prime Minister to direct access to the Emperor. Since the Emperor, as a constitutional monarch, was expected to follow the counsel of his advisers, the right of direct access was very important.

An Imperial Ordinance of 1898 required that the Minister of Army and the Minister of Navy be a general (or lieutenant general) and an admiral (or vice admiral) respectively on the active list. The Army or Navy would not permit its officers to serve in a cabinet unless it approved the composition and policies of the cabinet. Since cabinets had to have service ministers, the Prime Minister had no choice but to meet the demands of the Army and Navy at least part way. The services could cause the resignation or prevent the formation of cabinets unacceptable to them. In 1912, the Saionji Cabinet, which enjoyed the support of a majority in the lower house, refused a demand by the Army for two additional divisions. The War Minister, on orders from his military superiors, resigned in protest. Because of the Army's attitude no successor was made available, and the Saionji Cabinet fell.

After the assassination of Prime Minister Inukai in 1932, cabinets dominated by the military became the rule. An attempted coup d'état on February 26, 1936, by young army officers resulted in the assassination of a number of members of the Okada Cabinet. Although the ringleaders were forced to surrender and were summarily executed, the effect of the incident was further to strengthen the control of the Army over the state. After the Army had brought about the resignation of the Hirota Cabinet in 1937, the "moderate" General Ugaki was granted the mandate (Taimei) of the Emperor to form a cabinet. The Army, however, found him unacceptable and refused to participate so that he was forced to admit his failure to form a government. Public interest in the matter was great, and it was suggested that Ugaki request the Emperor to command the Army to recommend a War Minister. Such a step "would have been constitutional though not politic."[7] General Hayashi Senjūrō, the Army's choice, became the new Prime Minister.

In the subsequent elections, the Minseitō and Seiyūkai made common cause against militarism and fascism and won three-fourths of the seats in parliament. Nevertheless, they were not represented in the first Cabinet of Prince Konoye, who was made Prime Minister in order to achieve unity among the financial, industrial, military, and naval elements who ruled Japan.

The clash between Japanese and Chinese troops at Marco Polo Bridge, near Peking on July 7, 1937, rapidly developed into a full-scale, though undeclared, war. In November, the Imperial Headquarters was established to coordinate and centralize all Japanese military efforts in China. It would have direct access to the Emperor. The Diet in 1938 enacted a National Mobilization Law conferring sweeping powers on the Cabinet.

In 1940, Prince Konoye devoted his full energies to the establishment of a unified political structure. In July and August, the political parties voted themselves out of existence, and in October, Konoye announced the inauguration of the Imperial Rule Assistance Association, of which he was President. Apparently Konoye regarded the

---

[7] Chitoshi Yanaga, *Japan Since Perry* (New York: McGraw-Hill, 1949), pp. 529–530.

IRAA as a device for controlling the Army and terminating the war in China, and he did not originally intend the new organization to become a totalitarian political party. However, the IRAA, with prefectural and local branches and affiliate organizations, became increasingly totalitarian under the domination of bureaucrats and the military and was used by Prime Minister Tōjō during World War II to indoctrinate the population with war propaganda and Shinto ideology and to control the Diet. In the House of Representatives election of 1942, 381 of the 466 successful candidates were nominees of the Tōjō Government.

Why had the promising liberal tendencies of the 1920s given way to military rule in the 1930s? In the early '30s, intellectuals, liberal businessmen, and party politicians supported parliamentary government. They failed, however, to convince much of the public, particularly the peasantry, of their interest in the welfare of the people. Party politicians in the Diet and Cabinet were frequently depicted in the press as corrupt self-seekers, using their authority to benefit monopolists at the expense of hard-working peasants and laborers. Many of the officers and men in the Army were of rural background and believed that only a military take-over would bring about relief from their hardships and high taxes. Some hoped that by conquering Manchuria, the Army could establish a base for reforming the social order in Japan. At their trials, political assassins justified their actions to the public on the grounds of their patriotic aspirations to eliminate the corrupt influences in the capital and establish direct rule by the Emperor.

There was no charismatic fuehrer like Adolf Hitler in Japan, but Nazi (National Socialist) ideas appealed to many military men. As the depression worsened, as military and diplomatic involvements in north China escalated, and as rightists in the military threatened to get completely out of control, military government increasingly seemed necessary and inevitable. Not only bureaucrats and politicians, but even some intellectuals and labor leaders reconciled themselves to the new order, sometimes in the hope that they could check or at least influence the military.

After World War II, all Japanese were keenly aware of the frightful consequences of rampant militarism at home and aggression abroad. Progressives especially were determined that history should not repeat itself, and that the democratic freedoms and rights guaranteed by the 1946 Constitution would not be endangered by large-scale rearmament and political and military adventures on the Asian mainland. Thus the postwar military alignment with the United States was regarded with suspicion at least or bitter hostility at most. In the 1960s the unhappy experience of the Americans in Vietnam confirmed many Japanese in their view that militarism and imperialism were no better solutions to Japan's problems in the '60s than they had been in the '30s.

Japan's Political Heritage

The political heritage of Japan before 1945 included the following traditions:

1. aristocratic, rather than democratic, government
2. dispersion of political authority among elite groups
3. strong family, clan, and local loyalties
4. provincialism
5. emphasis on loyalty and discipline rather than on individual self-expression
6. diarchy
7. close association of religion with politics
8. divine right monarchy
9. patriotic pride in a long history of national independence under a single dynasty
10. militarism
11. willingness to borrow useful political ideologies and institutions from abroad
12. ability to adapt borrowed institutions to local conditions

The following are weak or absent in Japan's political heritage:

1. the ideal of limited government
2. belief in the right of revolution, conspicuous in the Chinese and Western liberal traditions
3. political and economic individualism
4. strong representative institutions
5. subjection to alien rule
6. monarchical absolutism (except in theory)
7. charismatic leadership
8. rationalism
9. the cult of material well-being

Although most of Japan's traditions developed under and were supportive of feudal institutions, obviously some of them could be mobilized for the economic and political modernization of the country, possibly even for the democratization of Japan. Some might prove antagonistic to modernization or democratization. The Japanese themselves are keenly aware of these historical themes and are prompt to cite them when explaining political phenomena to foreign observers. For example, during student demonstrations and teachers' strikes, Japanese conservatives note the apparent inability of otherwise intelligent people to think for themselves as individuals and their strong propensity to act in groups. The willingness of individuals to sacrifice their own interests for group interests contributes greatly to the power of groups in Japanese politics. Partly because the individual is so often deprecated, charismatic leadership in the form of absolute monarchy or political dictatorship has failed to emerge. Politics takes the form of confrontations of groups, and the national government, including the Prime Minister and his Cabinet, normally consists of career bureaucrats rather than popular leaders.

The thesis of this author is that the Japanese are not inscrutable and that their political institutions are not wholly unique, as some Japanese and Western scholars would have us believe. The view that Japanese politics are what they are because the people are "Orientals" begs the question and discourages intelligent analysis. Japanese feudalism was not greatly different from European feudalism, and the establishment of a centralized state and the industrialization of Japan occurred at about the same time as similar developments in Germany and Italy. In terms of political culture, social dynamics, political parties, and governmental institutions, the Japanese political system resembles Western European polities more than it resembles other Asian polities. The superficially exotic features of Japan which are the special subject of tourist propaganda should not blind the student to the fact that for over 100 years Japan has been an active participant in Western civilization and has reached about the same level of scientific and industrial development and political sophistication as the more advanced nations of Europe.

Political Change in Japan

Recurring themes of this book will be the modernization and democratization of Japan's political institutions. Chapter 2 is concerned with changes initiated by the Occupation, and, at appropriate points in the other chapters, prewar and postwar institutions will be compared and contrasted, and structural changes will be identified and explained. It would be appropriate here, however, to make some general comments about political change in Japan.

The subdiscipline of comparative politics has recently been much concerned with political development. This topic is much more complicated than it first appears, partly because of terminological difficulties. The term *development* implies some kind of improvement, so that it should not be applied indiscriminately to any kind of political change. Political *decay* as well as political development has characterized the politics of many recently emerged nations. Economic modernization does not always favor political modernization. Economic development fosters the growth of economic groups whose demands overload the existing political system. This results in a breakdown of the traditional polity or the overthrow of a newly established democracy, and its replacement by a military or communist dictatorship. The concepts of development and decay require not only a knowledge of the facts of a situation, but also normative judgments.

In the case of Japan, the political system was centralized and consolidated before industrialization was well under way. Far from being overwhelmed by economic development, the Meiji regime fostered industry and was in turn strengthened by it. Unlike the postwar emerging nations, Japan's political system, resembling those of Britain, America, and Western European powers, was already well developed before modern industry existed. The Meiji Restoration, of course, had largely been made possible by the prestige of the ancient imperial institution and the sense of common Japanese nationality among the population. Nation-building, the prerequisite of political modernization, had thus been largely accomplished long before the Meiji Restoration. Many of the emerging nations of today, on the other hand, are as yet incapable of significant political development because of a lack of a sense of national unity and common destiny among the population.

Much of the scholarly fascination with the study of Japan's political modernization stems from the idea that Japan's success in modernizing might serve as a model for underdeveloped countries. This line of thought is largely stimulated by the awareness that Japan, like the emerging nations, is part of the Afro-Asian world. But the relevance of the Japanese model for the developing countries is highly debatable in the light of the long history of the Japanese state as contrasted with the relatively short-lived institutions of the emerging countries.

Another problem arises with the relationship between political modernization and democratization. Some scholars define political modernization simply to mean that the political institutions are effective instruments for the authoritative allocation of values in an industrial society. Thus the political systems of the Soviet Union and the United States are equally modern. Other scholars, including most Japanese, insist that a truly modern state must be democratic. These different definitions of modernization lead to different evaluations of the Meiji Restoration. The Meiji period witnessed the creation of a *modern* (i.e., effective) polity which presided over Japan's industrialization and its rise to the status of a world power. On the other hand the Meiji regime was authoritarian, failed to encourage popular participation in politics, and launched Japan on policies of militarism and aggression which led to the catastrophic defeat in 1945. A debate between Japanese officials and the leading societies of historians raged in 1967 regarding the evaluation of the Meiji Restoration, whose centennial was approaching. The officials stressed the positive side of the Restoration; the historians the negative side. In the narrow sense, the Meiji Restoration was modernizing because it created stable and effective government. In the broad sense it was not, because it did not contribute adequately to the democratization of the country.

Suggested Reading

Akita, George. *The Foundations of Constitutional Government in Modern Japan, 1868–1900.* Cambridge, Mass.: Harvard University Press, 1965.

Beckmann, George M. *The Making of the Meiji Constitution: The Oligarchs and the Constitutional Development of Japan, 1868–1891.* Lawrence: University of Kansas Press, 1957.

Bellah, Robert N. *Tokugawa Religion: The Values of Preindustrial Japan.* Glencoe, Ill.: Free Press, 1957.

Benedict, Ruth. *The Chrysanthemum and the Sword: Patterns of Japanese Culture.* Boston, Mass.: Houghton Mifflin, 1946.

Borton, Hugh. *Japan's Modern Century,* rev. ed. New York: Ronald Press, 1970.

Brown, Delmer M. *Nationalism in Japan: An Introductory Historical Analysis.* Berkeley and Los Angeles: University of California Press, 1955.

Byas, Hugh. *Government by Assassination.* New York: Knopf, 1942.

Dore, R. P., ed. *Aspects of Social Change in Modern Japan.* Princeton, N.J.: Princeton University Press, 1967.

Duus, Peter. *Party Rivalry and Political Change in Taishō Japan.* Cambridge, Mass.: Harvard University Press, 1969.

Earl, David M. *Emperor and Nation in Japan: Political Thinkers of the Tokugawa Period.* Seattle, Wash.: University of Washington Press, 1964.

Eisenstadt, S. N. "Transformation of Social, Political and Cultural Orders in Modernization," *American Sociological Review* Vol. XXX, No. 5 (1965), 659–673; reprinted in Cohen, Ronald, and John Middleton, eds. *Comparative Political Systems: Studies in the Politics of Pre-Industrial Societies.* New York: The Natural History Press, 1967.

Fujii Shinichi. *The Essentials of Japanese Constitutional Law.* Tokyo: Yuhikaku, 1940.

THE POLITICAL DEVELOPMENT OF JAPAN 21

Hall, John Whitney, and Richard K. Beardsley. *Twelve Doors to Japan.* New York: McGraw-Hill, 1965.

Holt, Robert T., and John E. Turner. *The Political Basis of Economic Development: An Exploration in Comparative Political Analysis.* Princeton, N.J.: D. Van Nostrand, 1966.

Ike, Nobutaka. *The Beginnings of Political Democracy in Japan.* Baltimore, Md.: Johns Hopkins University Press, 1950.

Ito Hirobumi. *Commentaries on the Constitution of the Empire of Japan.* Translated by Ito Miyoji. Tokyo: Insetsu [sic] Kyoku, 1889.

Jansen, Marius B., ed. *Changing Japanese Attitudes Toward Modernization.* Princeton, N.J.: Princeton University Press, 1965.

Lockwood, William W., ed. *The State and Economic Enterprise in Japan.* Princeton, N.J.: Princeton University Press, 1965.

Mayo, Marlene, ed. *The Emergence of Imperial Japan: Self-Defense or Calculated Aggression?* Lexington, Mass.: D. C. Heath, 1970.

McLaren, Walter Wallace. *A Political History of Japan during the Meiji Era: 1867–1912.* London: Allen and Unwin, 1916.

McNelly, Theodore. "The Role of Monarchy in the Political Modernization of Japan." *Comparative Politics,* Vol. I, No. 3 (April, 1969), 366–381.

McNelly, Theodore, comp. *Sources in Modern East Asian History and Politics.* New York: Appleton-Century-Crofts, 1967.

Miller, Frank O. *Minobe Tatsukichi: Interpreter of Constitutionalism in Japan.* Berkeley: University of California Press, 1965.

Morley, James, ed. *Dilemmas of Growth in Prewar Japan.* Princeton, N.J.: Princeton University Press, 1971.

Morris, Ivan, ed. *Japan, 1931–1945: Militarism, Fascism, Japanism?* Boston: D. C. Heath, 1963.

Norman, E. Herbert. *Japan's Emergence as a Modern State: Political and Economic Problems of the Meiji Period.* New York: Institute of Pacific Relations, 1940.

Quigley, Harold S. *Japanese Government and Politics.* New York: D. Appleton-Century, 1932.

Scalapino, Robert A. *Democracy and the Party Movement in Prewar Japan.* Berkeley: University of California Press, 1953.

Shively, Donald R., ed. *Tradition and Modernization in Japanese Culture.* Princeton, N.J.: Princeton University Press, 1971.

Tobata Sei-ichi, ed. *The Modernization of Japan.* Tokyo: Institute of Asian Economic Affairs, 1966.

Totten, George O., ed. *Democracy in Prewar Japan: Groundwork or Facade?* Boston, Mass.: D. C. Heath, 1965.

Totten, George O. *The Social Democratic Movement in Prewar Japan.* New Haven, Conn.: Yale University Press, 1966.

Ward, Robert E., ed. *Political Development in Modern Japan.* Princeton, N.J.: Princeton University Press, 1968.

Ward, Robert E., and Dankwart A. Rustow, eds. *Political Modernization in Japan and Turkey.* Princeton, N.J.: Princeton University Press, 1964.

Yanaga, Chitoshi. *Japan Since Perry.* New York: McGraw-Hill, 1949.

2

The Occupation and Democratic Reforms

The Potsdam Proclamation and the Occupation of Japan

After Germany surrendered in May, 1945, American policy makers sought to induce Japan to surrender without a bloody invasion of the main islands. Because Japan's defeat seemed inevitable, the American leaders hoped that, if the Allies published tolerable peace terms, Japan's leaders might be willing to halt the war, thus saving their country from continuing devastation and sparing many thousands of lives. On July 26, 1945, in Potsdam, Germany, President Truman and Prime Minister Churchill, with Chiang Kai-shek's concurrence, issued a Declaration (or Proclamation) which stated the terms for a Japanese surrender.[1] Fourteen days later, when the Soviet Union entered the war against Japan, it announced its support of the Potsdam principles.

The Japanese, in negotiating the end of the war, "accepted" the terms of the Potsdam Declaration. The announced purpose of the Allied Occupation was to enforce the provisions of this Declaration and to ensure that Japan would never again menace world peace. The present chapter describes how Allied and Japanese authorities carried out the Potsdam terms and assesses the results of their efforts.

The Potsdam Proclamation required the elimination of the authority

---

[1] On the history of the Potsdam Declaration see Herbert Feis, *Japan Subdued: The Atomic Bomb and the End of the War in the Pacific* (Princeton, N.J.: Princeton University Press, 1961), pp. 15–27, and Department of State, *Foreign Relations of the United States, the Conference of Berlin (The Potsdam Conference) 1945* (2 vols.) (Washington, D.C.: Government Printing Office, 1960), Vol. I, 884–903; Vol. II, 1265–1298.

and the influence of those who had misled the Japanese people into embarking on world conquest. War criminals would have to be punished. Japanese sovereignty would be limited to the four main islands and such minor islands to be determined by the Allies. The Japanese military forces would be disarmed and returned to their homes. The Japanese government would "remove all obstacles to the revival and strengthening of democratic tendencies" among the people. "Freedom of speech, religion, and thought, as well as respect for the fundamental human rights" would be established. Until such time as these objectives had been accomplished and there had been "established in accordance with the freely expressed will of the Japanese people a peacefully-inclined and responsible government," Japan would be occupied by Allied forces.

Shortly before Japan's final offer to surrender, the Soviet Foreign Minister suggested that two Allied supreme commanders remain in Japan: Marshal Vasilevski and General MacArthur. The American Ambassador to the Soviet Union protested that while the United States had been at war with Japan for over three and a half years, the Soviet Union had fought Japan only two days, and it was unthinkable that any but an American should be Supreme Commander in Japan. Stalin later concurred with President Truman in the appointment of Mac-Arthur as Supreme Commander, and on September 2, Allied and Japanese representatives signed the Instrument of Surrender aboard the U.S.S. *Missouri* in Tokyo Bay.

The United States planned to have the deciding voice in the Occupation of Japan while the other Allies would be permitted only to air their views in the Far Eastern Advisory Commission. The Soviet Union, however, refused to participate in this Advisory Commission because of its purely consultative character and declined an invitation to send occupation forces to Japan to serve under an American general. Japan was not divided into occupation zones to be administered by the different victorious powers, as were Germany, Austria, and Korea but was occupied by American and British Commonwealth forces under the supreme command of a single American general. The virtual nonparticipation of the Soviet Union and the overwhelming predominance of the United States in Japan were thus established from the beginning. American policy and the autocratic temperament of General Douglas MacArthur, Supreme Commander for the Allied Powers (SCAP), were to preserve and enhance American predominance.

For four months, following the surrender ceremony, the victorious powers were unable to agree on the organization of Allied control machinery for Japan. Thus General MacArthur was able to interpret and apply American interpretations of the Potsdam Declaration[2] largely as he saw fit.

The Sections of SCAP Headquarters, staffed almost exclusively by American military and civilian personnel, issued directives to the Japanese Government for the enforcement of the Potsdam Declaration.

Because Japan had surrendered before her homeland was invaded, the Imperial Japanese Government (IJG) was intact and operating at the inception of the Occupation. Previous American plans for the establishment of military government in Japan (such as had been set up in Germany) were scrapped, and instead the Potsdam provisions were enforced by the Imperial Japanese Government under orders from SCAP. (The abbreviation SCAP was used to indicate either General MacArthur personally or his Headquarters generally.) SCAP's written directives, known as SCAPINs, were sent to the Central Liaison Office (CLO) of the IJG for implementation by the appropriate agency in the government. Often SCAP officials would suggest a program to Japanese officials, with the hint, stated or implied, that if the Japanese did not undertake the program on their own initiative, a SCAPIN would be forthcoming. Following the termination of the Occupation on April 28, 1952, a spate of memoirs and exposés was published in Japan detailing the hitherto confidential relations between Japanese and American officials.

The Japanese government of the day would translate the SCAP order or suggestion into a bill which would be passed by the Diet, or the government might, when Diet approval was too slow or uncertain, issue the SCAP-inspired measure in the form of an Imperial Ordinance (before May 3, 1947) or a Cabinet Order (after May 3, 1947). Some 520 such "Potsdam Ordinances" were issued by the government during the course of the Occupation. The conservative Governments of Shidehara and Yoshida were often unenthusiastic about SCAP's reform policies and often sought to delay and water down their enforcement. After SCAP began to turn its back on reform in favor of political stability, economic recovery, and rearmament, the conservative second, third, fourth, and fifth Yoshida Cabinets proved quite cooperative. So-called Military Government teams attached to the U.S. Eighth Army in the prefectures were assigned the sole task of *reporting* to higher headquarters cases in which the SCAP policies were not being carried out. However, military government in the usual

---

[2] "U.S. Initial Post-Surrender Policy for Japan," in Supreme Commander for the Allied Powers, *Government Section, Political Reorientation of Japan: September 1945 to September 1948,* 2 vols. (Washington, D.C.: Government Printing Office, n.d. [1949?]), Vol. II, 423–426.

sense did not exist because of the SCAP procedure of working through the Imperial Japanese Government centered in Tokyo.

The United States could not indefinitely stave off British and Soviet demands for a greater voice in the Occupation. The December, 1945, meeting of Big Three Foreign Ministers in Moscow established a Far Eastern Commission (FEC) made up of eleven nations: Australia, Canada, China, France, India, the Netherlands, New Zealand, the Philippines, the Soviet Union, the United Kingdom, and the United States. (Burma and Pakistan joined when they gained their independence.) The Far Eastern Commission, meeting in Washington, would formulate Allied policy for the Occupation of Japan. It was intended that the Allied Council for Japan (ACJ), made up of China, the British Commonwealth, the United States, and the U.S.S.R., would advise SCAP and act as a watchdog in Japan for the Far Eastern Commission. Early in its existence, the American and Soviet representatives in the ACJ engaged in little else than propaganda and mutual recrimination, so that the Council had virtually no influence over the course of the Occupation.

The United States, like the United Kingdom, the U.S.S.R. and China, enjoyed the power to veto proposed decisions of the Far Eastern Commission. The United States also had the power to issue interim directives to the Supreme Commander, pending action by the Commission, whenever urgent matters arose which were not already covered by the Commission's policies. However, any directives dealing with fundamental changes in the Japanese constitutional structure or in the regime of control, or dealing with a change in the Japanese Government as a whole could be issued only following consultation and the attainment of agreement in the Far Eastern Commission. Thus it would appear that constitutional reform in Japan could not be unilaterally carried out by American Occupation authorities.

The "Japanese Bill of Rights"

The first great task of the Allied Occupation was to supervise the demobilization of over five million Japanese troops scattered throughout Manchuria, Korea, and Southeast Asia as well as in Japan. The Emperor, on August 17, appointed his uncle, Prince Higashikuni, as Prime Minister so that the prestige of the imperial family would help to ensure an orderly surrender by the Army and Navy. On October 16, 1945, General MacArthur was able to announce that the Japanese Armed Forces throughout Japan had completed their demobilization and as such ceased to exist.

On October 4, MacArthur's Headquarters forwarded to the government a memorandum on "Removal of Restrictions on Political, Civil, and Religious Liberties" (SCAPIN 93).[3] This directive, styled the "Japanese Bill of Rights" by SCAP officials, ordered the government to abrogate and suspend all laws and ordinances which restricted freedom of thought, religion, assembly, and speech including discussion of the Emperor, the Imperial Institution, and the Imperial Japanese Government. All persons detained or imprisoned because of their thought, speech, religion, or political beliefs were to be released. All secret police organs and departments in the Home Ministry and the Police concerned with censorship and thought control were to be abolished. The Home Minister and the Chiefs of Metropolitan and Prefectural Police were to be dismissed. The enforcement of the "Bill of Rights" seemed too difficult a task for the Higashikuni Cabinet, and it announced its resignation the following day.

On October 11, General MacArthur informed the new Prime Minister, Shidehara: "In the achievement of the Potsdam Declaration the traditional social order under which the Japanese people for centuries have been subjugated will be corrected." Specifically the reforms which MacArthur "expected" the government to institute were: (1) the emancipation of women by their enfranchisement, (2) the encouragement of the unionization of labor, (3) the opening of the schools to more liberal education, (4) the abolition of "systems which through secret inquisition and abuse have held the people in constant fear," and (5) the "democratization of economic institutions" by curbing monopoly and widening the distribution of income and ownership of the means of production and trade.[4] In close consultation with SCAP Headquarters, the Shidehara Government began drafting laws to enforce the sweeping social and political reforms demanded by Allied policy.

The ideological basis of ultranationalism and militarism had been the cult of the Emperor, as elaborated by the state religion, Shinto. On December 15, 1945, SCAP Headquarters ordered that the state religion be disestablished. SCAPIN 448[5] distinguished between State (or Shrine) Shinto, which was to be abolished altogether, and Sect Shinto, represented by thirteen officially recognized privately supported sects, which would be allowed to continue in existence. All financial support from public funds and all official affiliation with Shinto and Shinto shrines were to cease immediately. Private individuals would be permitted to contribute on a voluntary basis to the support of shrines

[3] Text in *ibid.*, Vol. II, 463–465.
[4] *Ibid.*, Vol. II, 741.
[5] SCAPIN 448, in *ibid.*, Vol. II, 467–469.

hitherto maintained by the government. No Shinto doctrines could be taught in public-supported educational institutions. Shinto teachings would be deleted from public-school textbooks and teachers' manuals. "No official of the national, prefectural, or local government, acting in his public capacity" would be permitted to visit any shrine to report on his assumption of office or conditions of government or to participate as a representative of government in any Shinto ceremony or observance.

In addition to disestablishing the state religion, the SCAP directive also forbade the propagation by schools or any religious group of militaristic and ultranationalistic ideology. The forbidden ideology was defined as embracing teachings which advocate Japan's mission to rule over other nations by reason of the divine or special origin of the Emperor, the divine origin of the Japanese people, the divine origin of the Japanese islands, and any other doctrine which might delude the Japanese people into embarking on wars of aggression or which glorified the use of force as an instrument for the settlement of disputes with other peoples.

Two weeks after the Shinto directive, the Emperor, in his 1946 New Year's Message, stated that the ties between the Throne and the people had always stood on mutual trust and affection:

> They do not depend upon mere legends and myths. They are not predicated on the false conception that the Emperor is divine and that the Japanese people are superior to other races and fated to rule the world.[6]

The American-inspired Constitution of 1947 was intended to perpetuate the religious freedom introduced by SCAPIN 448. Article 20 of the new Constitution guaranteed freedom of religion to all and forbade the state from engaging in religious education or any other religious activity or giving privileges to any religious organization.

The Great Purge

The Potsdam Declaration had required the removal from public office of the leaders who had led Japan to ultranationalism and war and who were therefore unfit to lead the nation in the paths of democ-

---

[6] Theodore McNelly, comp., *Sources in Modern East Asian History and Politics* (New York: Appleton-Century-Crofts, 1967), pp. 175–176. Concerning the original drafting in English of this rescript by an American Occupation official, see Harold G. Henderson, "The 'Secret History' of the Japanese Emperor's Renunciation of his 'Divinity' 1946," in Wilhelmus H. M. Creemers, *Shrine Shinto after World War II* (Leiden: E. J. Brill, 1968), pp. 223–225.

racy and peace. In January, 1946, SCAP directed the Japanese government to plan for the removal and exclusion from office of persons who fell in the following categories: (A) those arrested as suspected war criminals, (B) commissioned officers in the Imperial Japanese Regular Army and Navy, all persons who had served in the Military or Naval Police or in secret intelligence, and high-ranking civilians in the Ministry of War and Navy, (C) influential members of ultranationalisic, terroristic, or secret patriotic organizations, (D) the leaders of the Imperial Rule Assistance Association and its related organizations, (E) officials of financial and development organizations involved in Japanese expansion, (F) governors of occupied territories, and (G) additional militarists and ultranationalists.[7]

The actual purge was administered by the Japanese Government under the direction of SCAP. Holders of and candidates for important offices were required to fill out comprehensive questionnaires in both English and Japanese (English version prevailing) concerning their past political activities and affiliations. The purge ultimately involved the examination of literally millions of questionnaires and the purging of over 200,000 individuals. The enforcement of the purge was simplified by the fact that it was primarily an administrative rather than a judicial task. Individual motives and intentions were not delved into, so that while certain individuals might not have been in sympathy with the prevailing aims of the militaristic organization to which they had belonged, they were nonetheless automatically disqualified. Much of the confusion such as attended the administration of denazification in Germany was thus avoided.

SCAP's purge orders came in three waves. The first order (January, 1946) primarily concerned persons holding office in the central government, the second (January, 1947) concerned local and prefectural governments, information media, and business. The third important SCAP order came in the form of a letter from General MacArthur to Prime Minister Yoshida on June 6, 1950, in which he ordered the removal of the Central Committee of the Japan Communist Party from public office.[8] A short time later the purge of the editorial staff of the Communist newspaper *Akahata* was ordered. Of all the political leadership in Japan the Communists bore the least responsibility for Japan's aggressions, but they were resorting to violence to disrupt the Occupation.

[7] SCAPIN 550, in *Political Reorientation,* Vol. II, 484–488. *Ibid.,* 482–564, includes SCAPIN and government ordinances from 1946 to 1948 relating to the purge.

[8] Hans Baerwald, *The Purge of Japanese Leaders under the Occupation* (Berkeley and Los Angeles: University of California Press, 1959), p. 19.

Many prominent postwar politicians were disqualified from office at one time or another. Before becoming Prime Minister, Hatoyama, Ishibashi, and Kishi, had been purged and depurged. The purge kept the political parties in constant turmoil, since the purge status of party leaders was a crucial factor in factional politics. It was widely believed that the purge of some individuals, such as Hirano Rikizō, Minister of Agriculture in 1947, was politically motivated. The case of Hatoyama Ichirō was the most sensational. As president of the Liberal Party, which won a plurality of seats in the 1946 lower house election, Hatoyama was on the verge of becoming the new Prime Minister. On the eve of Hatoyama's appointment, however, General MacArthur issued a formal directive banning Hatoyama from office because his past praise of Hitler's labor policies and Tanaka's foreign policy, among other things, meant that he fell under the vaguely worded Category G of the January 4 directive.[9]

Opinions vary about the effect of the purge. It worked a hardship on many innocent individuals. It is said that "political bias had affected the work of the screening committees, slowing the progress of democracy and damaging the prestige of the Occupation."[10] As the Occupation policies became more conservative, a depurge was in full swing, and with the end of the Occupation, SCAP directives no longer applied. The application of the purge to Communists in 1950 suggested that the policy had become a weapon of the Cold War. Nevertheless, the purge helped to clear the way for new leadership.[11]

The Tokyo War Crimes Trial

The Potsdam Declaration had provided that "stern justice shall be meted out to all war criminals," and the Allies agreed that the major Japanese war criminals would be tried by an international court. Thus the war crimes trials were carried out separately from the purge, which was administered by an agency of the Japanese government under SCAP supervision. The International Military Tribunal for the Far East (IMTFE) was composed of eleven justices, one from each of the powers represented on the Far Eastern Commission. The principal charge against the twenty-eight "Class A" war criminals was the

[9] SCAPIN 919, *Political Reorientation,* Vol. II, 494–495.
[10] Harold S. Quigley and John E. Turner, *The New Japan: Government and Politics* (Minneapolis: University of Minnesota Press, 1956), p. 109.
[11] Kazuo Kawai, *Japan's American Interlude* (Chicago: University of Chicago Press, 1960), p. 95.

commission of "crimes against the peace." The indictment included numerous violations of international law on the part of Japan for which the suspects were held responsible. As in the case of the Nuremberg trials, which received much more attention in Europe and America, there were controversial legal questions regarding the responsibility of individuals for state acts.

The court met almost daily from May 3, 1946, to November 12, 1948. Two defendants died during the trial; Ōkawa Shūmei was declared insane and not brought to trial. All twenty-eight defendants, save Ōkawa, an ultranationalist philosopher, had held high government and military offices. All were found guilty. Seven, including former Prime Ministers Hirota and Tōjō, were hanged, sixteen committed to prison for life, and two given shorter prison terms. After his release from prison, Shigemitsu Mamoru became President of the Progressive Party (1952) and Foreign Minister in the three Hatoyama Cabinets.

There was some criticism because the Emperor was not indicted and tried. The reason usually given was that the Emperor was not constitutionally responsible in the Japanese system—he was simply a figurehead, and in spite of his personal views he had to do as his advisers told him. It was widely believed that the Americans spared the Emperor because his authority was necessary for administering the country and because his indictment might arouse popular opposition to the Occupation.

The Democratization of the Economy

In December, 1945, SCAP directed the government to initiate a land reform to end the abuses of absentee landownership. Before the war, 46 percent of the cultivated land was farmed by tenants.[12] Of the total number of farmers, 70 percent were nonowners of part or all of the land that they tilled.[13] Under the land reform program carried out under the supervision of MacArthur's staff, owners who were not themselves cultivating their land were required to sell it to the government in exchange for bonds. The government resold the land to tillers who paid for it in annual installments. The monetary inflation during the early Occupation meant that the purchasers bought their land cheaply. Locally elected land commissions assisted in the administration of the program. By the end of 1950, only 10 percent of the farm land was cultivated by tenants, while 90 percent was cultivated by

---

[12] SCAPIN 441, *Political Reorientation*, Vol. II, 575–576.
[13] *Agriculture in Japan* (Tokyo: Japan FAO Association, 1958), p. 53.

owners.[14] The land reform was one of the most durable accomplishments of the Occupation.

In order to end the control of the great monopolies over the Japanese economy, SCAP Headquarters ordered the dissolution of the Mitsui, Yasuda, Sumitomo, and Mitsubishi (Iwasaki) holding companies (zaibatsu) in the fall of 1945. A Holding Company Liquidation Commission was set up to take over the securities of the monopolies and resell them to the general public. Before the program had gotten well under way, however, American policy shifted from reform to recovery. Financial circles in the United States were highly critical of zaibatsu dissolution, and by 1949 it was feared that the economic disorganization which it would entail could sabotage the economic rehabilitation of Japan just when the Cold War was becoming more intense. The reform legislation was permitted to lapse, and before the Occupation was over the prewar forms of financial and corporate organization had partially revived.

The Allied policy of encouraging the unionization of labor had startling results. At the end of the war, unions were virtually nonexistent in Japan; in October, 1945, only six labor unions existed, with a total of 3,866 members. Under SCAP stimulus, by October, 1946, 15,172 unions claimed a membership of 4,168,305.[15] The new unions rapidly fell under extreme leftist leadership and began to engage in political strikes. To check Communist labor leaders, General MacArthur issued an order calling off a general strike scheduled for February 1, 1947, which would have paralyzed the Japanese economy and threatened to overthrow the Yoshida government.

In the face of a new labor offensive in 1948, MacArthur's Headquarters directed the Ashida Cabinet to issue an ordinance denying the right of all government employees—national or local—to bargain collectively or to resort to strikes. The ordinance was later embodied in amendments to the National Public Service Law. Since most of the railroads as well as communications systems were government owned, the number of workers denied the right to strike was substantial. The change of SCAP policy from strengthening unions to weakening them increased the militancy of the Communists and at the same time strengthened the hands of the more moderate labor leaders.

By 1949, it was evident that the Occupation had shifted its emphasis from democratic reform to defense against communism. When General Matthew Ridgway in 1951 succeeded MacArthur as Supreme

[14] *Ibid.*, p. 55.
[15] Oka Yoshitake, ed., *Gendai Nihon no Seiji Katei* (The Course of Contemporary Japanese Politics) (Tōkyō: Iwanami Shoten, 1959), p. 10.

Commander, he ordered a review of SCAP directives in order to eliminate those that had been too drastic. The Occupation officially ended on April 28, 1952, when the Japanese Peace Treaty became effective.

The Reform of the Japanese Constitution

The Potsdam Declaration had called for the establishment of a "peacefully inclined and responsible government" in accordance with the "freely expressed will of the Japanese people." In October, 1945, General MacArthur urged Prince Konoye Fumimaro, "Vice Prime Minister" of the Higashikuni Cabinet, to take the leadership in liberalizing the Japanese Constitution, and Konoye obtained a commission from the Emperor to investigate constitutional reform. Mr. George C. Atcheson, Jr., SCAP's Political Adviser, indicated to Konoye the points in the Japanese Constitution which the Americans felt needed revision but did not demand the elimination of the Emperor system.[16]

Critics in Japan and America charged that Konoye, because of his alleged war guilt, should not direct constitutional revision. Furthermore, Konoye's efforts had no democratic basis since the Office of the Lord Privy Seal, with which Konoye was now connected, was not responsible to either the Diet or the Cabinet. SCAP Headquarters on November 1 announced that MacArthur had not chosen Konoye to reform the Japanese Constitution. In December, Konoye was indicted as a war criminal, and he committed suicide just before his arrest. Konoye's efforts to revise the Constitution, like his efforts to bring about a peace earlier in 1945, were primarily intended to preserve the Japanese throne.

Just as Konoye was beginning his investigations, General MacArthur also directed the new Shidehara Cabinet to reform Japan's system of government, insisting that this would "unquestionably involve the liberalization of the Constitution." However, Prime Minister Shidehara publicly stated that altering the text of the Imperial Constitution to achieve democracy was unnecessary, holding that suitable legislation enacted by the Diet, such as laws expanding the franchise, would be sufficient. In response to MacArthur's prodding, Shidehara appointed a committee of scholars and bureaucrats headed by Minister of State Matsumoto Jōji to investigate "whether the Constitution needed to be revised and if so to what extent."

[16] For a detailed account of the revision of the Japanese Constitution, see Theodore McNelly, "The Japanese Constitution: Child of the Cold War," *Political Science Quarterly*, Vol. LXIV, No. 2 (June, 1959), 176–195.

The MacArthur Draft Constitution

In January, 1946, the State-War-Navy Coordinating Committee (SWNCC), composed of representatives of the Departments of State, War, and Navy in Washington, drew up a policy on "The Reform of the Japanese Governmental System" (SWNCC-228). The purpose of the paper, which was sent to MacArthur, was to "determine the constitutional reforms which the Occupation authorities should insist be carried out in Japan."[17] The fourteen-page SWNCC document specified, among other things, that "The Japanese should be encouraged to abolish the Emperor system or reform it along more democratic lines."

At the same time, the newly organized Liberal and Progressive Parties were advocating constitutional amendments to enhance the powers of the Diet without altering the principle that sovereignty resided in the Emperor. The Communists demanded the trial of the Emperor as a war criminal and advocated the establishment of a Japanese People's Republic. Cabinet Minister Matsumoto and his committee on constitutional reform began to work overtime, and on February 1, a Tokyo newspaper published a version of the very conservative Matsumoto proposals.

General MacArthur found the Matsumoto proposals too conservative to be acceptable. On February 3, he directed his Government Section to prepare immediately a constitution to serve as a guide for the Shidehara Cabinet as the most effective method of instructing the Japanese government on the principles he considered basic.

The Supreme Commander directed that the "guide" provide that the Emperor be "at the head of the state" and that his powers be "exercised according to the will of the people." The draft was also to state that:

> War as a sovereign right of the nation is abolished. Japan renounces it as an instrumentality for settling its disputes and even for preserving its own security. It relies upon the higher ideals which are now stirring the world for its defense and its protection.
>
> No Japanese Army, Navy, or Air Force will ever be authorized and no rights of belligerency will ever be conferred upon any Japanese force.[18]

[17] The text of SWNCC-228 is printed in McNelly, *Sources,* pp. 177–186.
[18] The text of MacArthur's famous "Three Points" is given in *Political Reorientation,* Vol. I, 102. The lawyers in Government Section did not include "even for preserving its own security" in their draft of February 13, 1946, nor did this phrase appear in subsequent versions. According to

The Government Section worked in extreme secrecy between February 4 and 10 to produce its draft Constitution.[19] On February 13, 1946, General Courtney Whitney, Chief of the Section, presented the draft Constitution to members of the Japanese Cabinet with the understanding that if they did not accept its essential principles, MacArthur would present it over their heads to the Japanese people. Whitney also said that if the Cabinet refused to adopt the principles of the MacArthur Constitution, the Americans could not guarantee "the person of the Emperor."

The Cabinet was afraid that if it did not adopt the SCAP draft, the Far Eastern Commission might force it to adopt a republican constitution abolishing the throne. Cabinet members also feared that if they did not accept the MacArthur draft, SCAP Headquarters would publish it, the newspapers would approve it, and the Cabinet might be forced to resign. A Cabinet which supported the MacArthur Constitution would then come into being and politics in Japan would veer sharply to the left.

Minister of State Matsumoto brought an adaptation of the American draft to SCAP Headquarters on March 4. There ensued a hectic thirty-six-hour overnight session of Japanese and American officials to produce a text acceptable to General MacArthur. The most important concession to Japanese views was that the Diet would consist of two

General MacArthur, the constitutional ban on war and arms was suggested to him by Prime Minister Shidehara on January 24, 1946. A prevailing view among Japanese authorities, however, is that Shidehara advocated a pacifist policy for Japan but did not necessarily desire that a ban on war and arms be inserted as a provision of a new Constitution. Cf. Inumaru Hideo, "Nihonkoku Kempō daikyūjō hatatsusha ni tsuite," in *Bōei Daigakkō Kiyō,* No. 19 (September, 1970), 1–80, and Theodore McNelly, "The Renunciation of War in the Japanese Constitution," in *Political Science Quarterly,* Vol. LXXVII, No. 3 (September, 1962), 350–378.

[19] The original mimeographed text of the Whitney draft Constitution, as presented to the Japanese Cabinet on February 13, 1946, was published in *Kokka Gakkai Zassi* (The Journal of the Association of Political and Social Sciences), Vol. LXVIII, Nos. 1, 2 (September, 1954) and in *Contemporary Japan,* Vol. XXIV, Nos. 4–6, 7–9 (1956). A draft Constitution prepared by a group of prominent Japanese liberals (Kempō Kenkyūkai) had a great influence on Government Section officials, especially in the formulation of Chapter I of the SCAP-draft Constitution. See Theodore McNelly, "The Role of Monarchy in the Political Modernization of Japan," *Comparative Politics,* Vol. I, No. 3 (April, 1969), 366–381. The debates within Government Section during the constitutional drafting are described in considerable detail in the papers of Milo E. Rowell, translated and annotated in Japanese: "Raueru shozō bunsho: Nihonkoku kempō no seitei ni kansuru Makkāsa sō shireibu no kiroku," in *Jurisuto* (December, 1965, through January, 1967).

chambers rather than one. The proposed Constitution would deprive the Emperor of all of his prerogatives and vest sovereignty in the people. It was replete with New Deal philosophy and was more radical than any of the proposals of the leading parties except the Communists. It reduced the Emperor's role to that of "the symbol of the State and of the unity of the people."

Prime Minister Shidehara told his cabinet concerning the draft Constitution:

> We are making an extremely grave commitment in accepting such a Constitution as this. Perhaps this commitment will also bind our posterity. When this draft is made public, some will applaud and others will keep silence. The latter will undoubtedly be highly indignant at bottom towards us. However, I believe that we are following the only possible course in view of the situation confronting us.

Some ministers wiped tears from their eyes.

On March 6, 1946, the Cabinet published the American-inspired Constitution as its own proposal and made public an imperial rescript indicating the Emperor's approval of the democratic principles of the draft and implying that the Shidehara Government had drawn up the proposal on his orders. General MacArthur also published his "emphatic approval" of the document. The Far Eastern Commission was now faced with the *fait accompli* of a draft Constitution sponsored by the Japanese Cabinet and the Emperor and approved by the Allied Supreme Commander.

During the critical food shortage of May, 1946, a series of leftist-led mass demonstrations in Tokyo induced General MacArthur to issue a public "Warning Against Mob Disorder and Violence." The Supreme Commander had been initially instructed by the United States government not to intervene in any efforts by the Japanese people to change their form of government by force, unless the security of Allied forces was endangered. Nevertheless, he abhorred the thought of civil war in Japan, and his actions made it clear that any change in Japan's form of government would have to come about through nonviolent methods.

In June, the Yoshida Cabinet presented its Constitution Revision Bill to the Diet. The Communists were the only political party to oppose the draft Constitution; they continued to advocate the trial of the Emperor as a war criminal and the establishment of a Japanese People's Republic. The Japanese Communists had an ally in the FEC: the Soviet representative, who also criticized the MacArthur Constitution.

Conservatives feared that the proposed Constitution would impair the traditional "national structure" by transferring sovereignty from the Emperor to the people, and that the no-arms clause would endanger Japan's security. However, Diet members seemed to believe that the passage of the democratic Constitution was necessary to bring an early end to the Allied Occupation, and they approved the draft Constitution (Constitution Revision Bill) by nearly unanimous majorities in both houses. The Emperor promulgated the new Constitution on November 3, 1946, and it became effective on May 3, 1947.

The struggle over the drafting and adoption of the Japanese Constitution was actually a three-way affair. The conservative Japanese officials strove to preserve the imperial institution essentially unchanged. The Americans, both in Tokyo and in Washington, endeavored to preserve and reform the throne as a basis for stability and democracy. International communism, represented by the Japan Communist party and the Soviet Union, sought to abolish the throne and establish a Japanese People's Republic.

Basic Principles of the New Constitution

Popular Sovereignty

Japanese commentators stress three basic principles in the new Constitution: (1) popular sovereignty, (2) human rights, and (3) pacifism. Human rights and pacifism will be discussed in detail in subsequent chapters, and we shall confine our discussion here to popular sovereignty.

The most fundamental difference between the old Constitution and the new is that the former was based upon the principle of the rule of the Emperor by divine right, while the latter is based upon the principle of popular sovereignty.

In the Preamble to the Constitution of the Empire of Japan (1889), the Emperor Meiji declared, "The rights of sovereignty of the State, We have inherited from Our Ancestors, and We shall bequeath them to Our descendants."[20] Chapter I of the same Constitution provided that "The Empire of Japan shall be reigned over and governed by a line of Emperors unbroken for ages eternal," and that "The Emperor is the head of the Empire, combining in Himself the rights of sovereignty, and exercises them, according to the provisions of the present Constitution."

The new Constitution signifies the transfer of sovereignty from the Emperor to the people. Its Preamble states, "We, the Japanese people, . . . do proclaim that sovereign power resides with the people."

[20] Text in McNelly, *Sources*, pp. 57–65.

Government is "a sacred trust of the people, the authority for which is derived from the people, the powers of which are exercised by the representatives of the people, and the benefits of which are enjoyed by the people. This is a universal principle of mankind upon which this Constitution is founded." The Emperor no longer inherits authority from his divine ancestors, but, according to Article 1 of the new Constitution, derives his position "from the will of the people with whom resides sovereign power."

There was no popular referendum in Japan concerning the retention of the monarchy such as was held in Italy in June, 1946; the will of the people to keep the Emperor was expressed by the enactment of the new Constitution by the people's representatives in the Diet. Presumably the Throne could be abolished by simply amending the Constitution.

Amendment Procedure

One of the most distinctive attributes of sovereignty is the constituent power, i.e., the authority to enact and amend the Constitution. The Meiji Emperor, on his own authority as occupant of the "Throne of a lineal succession unbroken for ages eternal," promulgated the 1889 Constitution as "a fundamental law of the State."[21] The Meiji Constitution was known as the *kintei kempō*, a "Constitution granted by the Emperor." Under Article LXXIII of that basic law, the Constitution was amended when a project to that effect was submitted to the Diet by Imperial Order and two-thirds of those present (two-thirds of the whole number of members were required to be present) in each House passed the project. Only the Emperor possessed the power to initiate constitutional amendments. Actually, until 1946, no serious effort was made to amend the Meiji Constitution, since it was almost universally regarded as perfect. The postwar Constitution was enacted as a constitutional amendment in accordance with Article LXXIII of the Meiji document.

Under the new Constitution, the people, rather than the Emperor, exercise the constituent power. "We, the Japanese people, acting through our duly elected representatives in the National Diet, . . . do firmly establish this Constitution."[22] Amendments to the new Constitution are initiated by the Diet, through the concurring vote of two-thirds or more of all the members of each house, and then submitted to

---

[21] Constitution of the Empire of Japan, Preamble.
[22] *Ibid.* The text of new Constitution is printed at the end of this book.

the voters for ratification, which requires the affirmative vote of a majority of the votes cast.[23]

Separation of Powers and Checks and Balances

Since classical times, advocates of constitutional government have extolled the principle of separation of powers as a barrier against tyranny. The Constitution of the United States, of course, provides a classic example of the application of this idea, and it is not surprising to find the principle embodied in the new Constitution of Japan. In its purest form, separation of powers implies that the executive, legislative, and judicial branches are each supreme and independent in its respective sphere. The new Japanese system of government, however, is primarily patterned after that of Britain, where *fusion* rather than separation of powers between the legislative and executive branches is the rule. In Japan today, as in Britain, the executive (Cabinet) is composed entirely or almost entirely of members of the legislature and is responsible to the lower house; the Cabinet is the executive committee of the parliament and is dependent upon the support of the parliament ("the highest organ of state power") for its continued existence. On the other hand, the Japanese system bears a similarity to the American system in that the judicial branch may declare acts of the legislative and executive branches unconstitutional.

Figure 1, adapted from a Japanese high school textbook, illustrates the system of separation of powers and checks and balances as it exists in Japan. Note how the Emperor, who has no "powers related to government," is conspicuously absent from the chart.

Although the new Constitution includes a chapter on local self-government, ever since the Meiji Restoration, local government has been relatively weak. In a federal system such as that found in the United States and in Switzerland, constituent states exercise important constitutional powers which cannot be usurped by the central government. "States' rights" provide protection for minority and sectional interests against the encroachments of the central authority. The Japanese system, on the other hand, is essentially unitary rather than federal. Prefectural governments do not have constitutions of their own, and they exercise authority largely subject to central direction. The lack of a federal system and the lack of thorough-going separation of powers after the pattern of presidential democracy help to make possible centralization and executive domination.

[23] Constitution, Article 96.

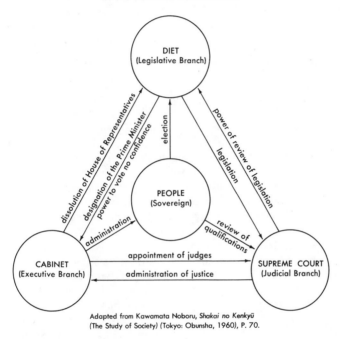

Figure 1

**SEPARATION OF POWERS AND CHECKS AND BALANCES
IN THE JAPANESE CONSTITUTION**

Adapted from Kawamata Noboru, *Shakai no Kenkyū*
(The Study of Society) (Tokyo: Obunsha, 1960), P. 70.

Prospects for the New Constitution

How, in practice, the American-inspired Constitution affected the Japanese political process will be discussed on numerous occasions in the chapters which follow, but a few general comments are appropriate at this point. Occupation officials professed to have great faith that the new Constitution would prove to be a powerful influence on Japan's future. However, the successful transplantation of Anglo-American law to a foreign country would seem to require a hospitable social and political environment. Even among the drafters of Japan's

Constitution were some who doubted that it would outlast the Occupation. Once the American troops were removed, the Japanese would, they thought, cast off the foreign-inspired document and revert to their old ways. Indeed, in the mid 1950s, the movement to revise the Constitution seemed bound to succeed. Prime Ministers Hatoyama and Kishi were prominent advocates of revision, and in 1955, the Diet passed a law creating a Commission on the Constitution whose mission was to report on the formulation, operation, and possible revision of the Constitution. The Commission was nonpartisan in form, but the majority of its members were conservative. The Socialists, suspecting a scheme to revise the Constitution, refused to accept seats on the Commission.

During the life of the Commission, the Liberal Democratic Party suffered some erosion of its strength in the electorate and in the two houses of the Diet. The prospects of ever commanding the two-thirds majority in each house necessary to pass a revision bill became dim. At the same time, the government was able to proceed with step-by-step rearmament without amending the disarmament clause.

The electorate was generally suspicious of the conservative designs on the democratic Constitution, but as other issues became more salient, the conservative prime ministers were reluctant to endanger their political lives by making an issue of constitutional revision. By 1971, nineteen years after the end of the Occupation, the new Constitution seemed less in danger than ever before. Not a single word had been changed in it, and the constitutional revision movement was apparently dead. The Constitution enjoyed some degree of support from nearly every section of the political spectrum. The precise reasons for this support will be discussed in the concluding chapter. It seems to this writer in hindsight that the 1946 Constitution was a far less radical document than it first appeared to be. The symbolic position of the Emperor was in accord with the historical and political facts. The parliamentary-cabinet system of government prescribed in the new basic law was well suited to the governance of an educated public in an industrial society.

The Evaluation of the Occupation

The declared general purposes of the Occupation were to ensure that Japan would never again menace world peace and to enforce the terms of the Potsdam Declaration. How the specific objectives were carried out has been the topic of this chapter.

Some critics held that the Americans who dominated the Occupation were too lenient with the Japanese. The Emperor and capitalists, they feared, were let off too lightly. Thus Japan might again become an imperialist power in Asia, with the tacit, if not the overt, support of the United States. Japan, however, still maintains a low posture in world politics.

The land reform greatly equalized land ownership, but the low productivity of agriculture relative to industry has stimulated suggestions that larger farms would be more efficient. Recently farmers have used their political influence to ensure that the government pay them inflated prices for their rice, which they have been producing in excess of the country's need. Thus the problem of farm tenantry, which was corrected by the Occupation, has been succeeded by new problems in agriculture.

The labor movement was greatly stimulated by the Occupation and became a force to be reckoned with in postwar Japan. The zaibatsu, of course, were dissolved by the Occupation but have been replaced by much larger and more efficient oligopolies. The purge became a part of history the moment the Occupation ended.

The image of the Occupation suffered from the so-called reverse course, when American policy shifted from the democratization of Japan to the rebuilding of that country in order to contain communism.[24] The conservative tendencies of the Occupation after 1947 embittered the labor movement and progressives against the United States.

Much of the ultimate success of the Occupation depends on its most notable monument, the Constitution. Ironically, the new basic law, because of its liberal features, has seemed to enjoy more support from the anti-American progressive elements in Japan than from the pro-American conservatives. Although the disarmament clause has been greatly watered down by the elastic interpretations of successive governments, the new democratic Constitution now seems more firmly established than ever, a great credit to the Occupation.

Some writers insist that the shortness of the Occupation and its reversal of direction in mid-course meant that it could not possibly have a lasting influence on Japan. They would assert that social forces, rather than well-intended laws such as were passed during the Occupation, determine political change. On the other hand, conservatives who deplore the nefarious effects of the Occupation reforms and

[24] For the role of George F. Kennan, the author of America's containment policy, in bringing about a change of policy in Tokyo, see Frederick S. Dunn, *Peace-Making and the Settlement with Japan* (Princeton, N.J.: Princeton University Press, 1963). For a refutation of the contention that there was a reverse course, see Justin Williams, "Completing Japan's Political Reorientation, 1947–1952: Crucial Phase of the Allied Occupation," in *American Historical Review*, Vol. LXXIII, No. 5 (June, 1968), 1454–1469.

progressives who support the new Constitution seem to agree that the Occupation made a big difference.

Given the vastness and complexity of the data and the ethical and ideological issues involved, evaluation of the Occupation must of necessity be subjective. This author believes that General Douglas MacArthur had the necessary charisma to administer the Occupation with great effect. He and his staff enforced sweeping, and for Japan, radical reforms largely because the highly disciplined Japanese, having accepted the Potsdam principles, carried them out in good faith. These reforms had a profound, ineradicable and, on the whole, beneficial effect on the Japanese political system.

Suggested Reading

Baerwald, Hans H. *The Purge of Japanese Leaders under the Occupation.* Berkeley and Los Angeles: University of California Press, 1959.

Ball, W. Macmahon. *Japan: Enemy or Ally?* New York: John Day, 1949.

Bisson, T. A. *Prospects for Democracy in Japan.* New York: Macmillan, 1949.

Bisson, T. A. *Zaibatsu Dissolution in Japan.* Berkeley: University of California Press, 1954.

Blakeslee, George H. *A History of the Far Eastern Commission.* Washington, D.C.: U.S. Department of State, Publication 5138, Far Eastern Series 60, 1953.

Borton, Hugh. *Japan's Modern Century,* rev. ed. New York: Ronald Press, 1970.

Borton, Hugh. *American Presurrender Planning for Postwar Japan.* New York: East Asian Institute, Columbia University, 1968.

Braibanti, Ralph, J. D. "Administration of Military Government in Japan at the Prefectural Level," *American Political Science Review,* Vol. XLIII (1949), 250–274.

Brines, Russell. *MacArthur's Japan.* Philadelphia, Pa.: J. B. Lippincott, 1948.

Cohen, Jerome B. *Japan's Economy in War and Reconstruction.* Minneapolis: University of Minnesota Press, 1949.

Costello, William. *Democracy vs. Feudalism in Post-War Japan.* Tokyo: Itagakishoten, 1948.

Coughlin, William J. *Conquered Press.* Palo Alto, Calif.: Pacific Books, 1952.

Creemers, Wilhelmus H. M. *Shrine Shinto after World War II.* Leiden: E. J. Brill, 1968.

Dore, Ronald P. *Land Reform in Japan.* New York: Oxford University Press, 1959.

Gayn, Mark. *Japan Diary.* New York: William Sloane Associates, 1948.

Gibney, Frank. *Five Gentlemen of Japan: The Portrait of a Nation's Character.* New York, Farrar, Straus & Giroux, 1953.

Hadley, Eleanor M. *Antitrust in Japan.* Princeton, N.J.: Princeton University Press, 1969.

Hall, Robert King. *Education for a New Japan.* New Haven, Conn.: Yale University Press, 1949.

Haring, Douglas G. *Japan's Prospect.* Cambridge, Mass.: Harvard University Press, 1946.

Hewes, Lawrence I. *Japan: Land and Men.* Ames: Iowa State College Press, 1955.

Johnstone, William C. *The Future of Japan.* New York: Oxford University Press, 1945.

Jones, F. C., Hugh Borton, and B. R. Pearn. *The Far East, 1942–1946.* London: Oxford University Press, 1955.

Kawai, Kazuo. *Japan's American Interlude.* Chicago, Ill.: University of Chicago Press, 1960.

Kelley, Frank, and Cornelius Ryan. *Star Spangled Mikado.* New York: McBride, 1947.

Martin, Edwin M. *The Allied Occupation of Japan.* New York: American Institute of Pacific Relations, 1948.

Mears, Helen. *Mirror for Americans: Japan.* Boston, Mass.: Houghton Mifflin, 1948.

Montgomery, John D. *Forced to be Free.* Chicago, Ill.: University of Chicago Press, 1957.

Passin, Herbert. *The Legacy of the Occupation: Japan.* New York: East Asian Institute, Columbia University, 1968.

Rosecrance, R. *Australian Diplomacy and Japan, 1945–51.* Cambridge: Cambridge University Press, 1962.

Roth, Andrew. *Dilemma in Japan.* Boston, Mass.: Little, Brown, 1945.

SCAP, Government Section. *The Political Reorientation of Japan.* Washington, D.C.: Government Printing Office, 2 vols., n.d. [1949?].

Sebald, William. *With MacArthur in Japan: A Personal History of the Occupation.* New York: Norton, 1965.

Textor, Robert B. *Failure in Japan.* New York: John Day, 1951.

Wakefield, Harold. *New Paths for Japan.* New York: Oxford University Press, 1948.

Ward, Robert E. "The Origins of the Japanese Constitution," *The American Political Science Review,* Vol. I, No. 4 (December, 1956), 980–1009.

Whitney, Courtney. *MacArthur: His Rendezvous with History.* New York: Knopf, 1956.

Wildes, Harry Emerson. *Typhoon in Tokyo: The Occupation and Its Aftermath.* New York: Macmillan, 1954.

Williams, Justin. "Completing Japan's Political Reorientation, 1947–1952: Crucial Phase of the Allied Occupation." *American Historical Review,* Vol. LXXIII, No. 5 (June, 1968), 1454–1469.

Williams, Justin. "Making the Japanese Constitution: A Further Look,"

The American Political Science Review, Vol. LIX, No. 3 (September, 1965), 665–679.

Woodard, William P. *The Allied Occupation of Japan, 1945–1952, and Japanese Religions.* Leiden: E. J. Brill, forthcoming.

Yoshida Shigeru. *The Yoshida Memoirs: The Story of Japan in Crisis.* Boston, Mass.: Houghton Mifflin, 1962.

3

Interest Groups

Groups in the Political System

Political scientists have devoted much attention in recent years to the identification and classification of interest groups and theories of their role in politics. Some interest groups are self-conscious and well organized and engage overtly and continuously in political activity. These are readily identifiable as "pressure groups." Conversely, other interest groups are not self-conscious, not well organized, and seldom engage in political activity. There may be a question as to whether or not it is appropriate to identify the latter as interest groups, especially if the members of the purported group fail to perceive and support strongly the common interest involved. Groups which do not articulate their interests are sometimes referred to as latent interest groups, but identification of such latent groups poses a theoretical problem; they may be merely the product of an academic theory.

Categories of interest groups and systems of classification which have varying degrees of theoretical utility have been suggested. The population may be divided into occupational and economic groups, age groups, religious groups, racial groups, language groups, and so on, so that theoretically it would be possible to list a great number of interest groups whose memberships would often overlap. An individual might be the member of two or more groups, and when the claims of these groups on him conflict, he may be confused about his proper role, and his behavior will be difficult to predict. If politics is, as one theory holds, the struggle among interest groups for political power, the group theory would seem to overemphasize the importance of group interests and underemphasize the importance of regional and national interests.

Most writers insist on a distinction between interest groups and political parties. An interest group is concerned with bringing about the enactment and enforcement of policies which advance the economic or social interests of the group. A political party is concerned with acquiring political *office* and political *power* for its members. An interest group often may influence and lend electoral and financial support to a political party, and the latter may become highly dependent on the former. Or a political party may organize interest groups designed primarily to support the political party. A given individual may be a member of both an interest group and a political party. Thus, in practice the textbook distinction between interest group and political party sometimes seems to break down. In Japan, the Socialist Party is extremely dependent on the Sōhyō labor confederation, and the Liberal-Democratic Party is heavily dependent on big business. Thus, the two leading Japanese parties, which serve largely as mouthpieces of particular interests, cannot exist independently. The relationship of interest groups to political parties will be a particular concern of this chapter and the next.

In the present chapter, the author has tried to identify some of the more conspicuous interest groups in Japanese politics. Some of these groups overlap and, with social and economic change, some groups will change in importance, and new groups, possibly some not yet identified, may come to the fore.

In the late 1930s and early 1940s, the military was the dominant group in Japan. After the war, the military was liquidated and a great many groups emerged, some of which have been highly articulate. However, since 1950, the influence of business has overwhelmed that of all the other groups combined.

Interest Groups and Demographic Change

The distribution of population has massively shifted from farm villages to cities since World War II; thus the background and outlook of many city dwellers are rural. One of the consequences of this shift, as will be noted later, is the emergence of the Sōka Gakkai. Another important recent change is in the age distribution of the population. The life expectancy in Japan is now one of the world's highest, higher than in the United States. With fewer babies born each year and with people living longer, the old people greatly outnumber the young. The demands for more medical care and for better pension systems seem to be a result of both the shifting age distribution and the decline of the self-sufficient farm, where aged parents continued to live on their farm cared for by their son and daughter-in-law.

The "generation gap" has been a popular topic of conversation in Japan for several decades—even before it became a common preoccupation in the United States. The Confucian tradition in Japan had long taught respect for and deference to the opinions and the authority of elders. However, the rapid modernization of Japan's economic and social orders has placed a premium on energy and innovation, qualities most often associated with youth. How do these conflicting factors affect the political orientations of Japanese youth? Recent research indicates that youths' party identifications correlate with the party identifications of their parents, especially where Liberal-Democratic or Communist parents are involved.[1] The school, one's workday peers, and the public media certainly influence a person's political orientations, but the family in Japan evidently remains the most important agent of political socialization.

A majority, or at least a plurality, of voters of nearly all age groups favor the Liberal-Democratic Party, while the Socialist Party finds the bulk of its support among youth and labor. Older people are more predominantly Liberal-Democratic in party identification than are younger people, and as a Japanese gets older, he becomes more apt to identify with the Liberal-Democratic Party.

The mode of production, it is often contended, in large measure determines the class composition of a society. In turn, the class composition has much to do with the development of ideologies and political parties. In recent Japanese history we note two tendencies: (1) between 1868 and 1945 the rise of the secondary, or industrial, sector of the economy, at the expense of the primary, or extractive (agricultural, fishing, and forestry) sector of the economy, and (2) between 1945 and 1970 the rise of the tertiary, or service sector (education, administration, information services, commerce, and entertainment) at the relative expenses of the other sectors. Put simply, the relative decline of agriculture and the rise of industry and services have brought about the urbanization and the increased education of the population. Society has become pluralized in contrast to the former homogeneity in which both the rulers and the ruled were overwhelmingly committed to agricultural economy.

Political scientists have pointed out that political stability is more easily maintained when people who take one side on any given political issue take differing sides on other political issues. Thus individual issues are decided on their respective merits, and a struggle for power between permanently opposing groups is avoided. Reasoned argument rather than ideological confrontation tends to prevail.

Before Japan's defeat in World War II, Japan had what appeared to

[1] Akira Kubota and Robert E. Ward, "Family Influence and Political Socialization in Japan," paper read at the American Political Science Association meeting in New York, September 2–6, 1969.

be a homogeneous political culture in which the people were united in their willingness to sacrifice their lives for their country and Emperor. Since the war, there has been an ideological confrontation between conservatives, who would like to revive the spirit of patriotism and nationalism, and progressives who advocate pacifism and socialism. Nearly every individual political issue is perceived as impinging directly or indirectly upon the struggle between the political right and left.

Ethnic Minorities

Discrimination based upon race, caste, or creed is a fairly universal phenomenon. However, because of the linguistic and ethnic homogeneity of the Japanese one might easily conclude that discrimination is not an issue in Japan. The Japanese are aware of the problem of race relations in the United States and elsewhere and often criticize racial discrimination. Discriminatory policies aimed against Japanese residing in America before World War II affronted the national pride and were a cause of much bad feeling between the two countries. Article 14 of the 1946 Constitution makes the sweeping statement that "All of the people are equal under the law and there shall be no discrimination in *political, economic, or social relations* because of race, creed, sex, social status or family origin" (emphasis added).

Political equality is partially ensured by Article 44 of the Constitution, which provides that the qualifications for members of both houses of the Diet and for their electors shall not discriminate on the basis of race, creed, sex, social status, family origin, education, property, or income. However, the extent to which the state is required to enforce nondiscrimination in the economic and social spheres and how this might be accomplished are not indicated in the Constitution. The possibility always exists in a democracy that the majority may use its votes to trample on the rights of minorities. Americans are particularly aware of the problems involved in ensuring that minorities will not be discriminated against in the economic and social spheres. How a country treats its minorities is an indicator of its commitment to the democratic ideal of human equality. That is why the topic of discrimination in Japan is dealt with here, although it has received relatively little attention from foreign observers. Perhaps the most effective form of discrimination is the refusal to perceive that the problem exists.

The principal non-Japanese groups in Japan are Koreans, Chinese, Americans, English, Europeans, and Southeast Asians. The Americans are generally military and business people who regard their sojourn in Japan as temporary although pleasant. They have their own clubs and work for the American government or American business. They do not compete as individuals with the average Japanese for jobs and status. Much the same is usually true of the Europeans in Japan who also contribute to the transient foreign colony. The Americans and Europeans normally do not learn to speak more than a few words of Japanese and almost never learn to read it. Their acquaintance with the Japanese is confined to their English-speaking business counterparts or with servants. The illegitimate offspring of American white and black GIs, however, are too often identifiable by their racial features, are rejected by both Orientals and Occidentals, and are unable to get decent jobs or marriage partners. The fact that the girls who work in the bars and honky-tonks surrounding American bases often marry GIs cannot be taken as evidence that upper-class Japanese approve of interracial marriages. The Chinese community (about 50,000 in 1970) is fairly permanent and learns the Japanese language, which is written with Chinese characters, but confines itself largely to the restaurant and night-club industries.

The over 600,000 Koreans, by far the largest foreign group, are the only aliens who present Japanese society with serious problems. The unequal treatment traditionally suffered by Koreans in Japan stems historically from the Japanese annexation of Korea in 1910, the partial assimilation of Koreans as Japanese subjects, and the immigration of Koreans into Japan as laborers. Koreans are usually readily identifiable as such because of their accent when speaking Japanese, their Korean names, or the cut of their clothes. At the end of World War II, there were about 2,400,000 Koreans in Japan, a large portion of whom had been conscripted during the war to work in factories and mines.[2]

Those who wished were permitted to return to Korea with only a tiny amount of money and property. The half-million Koreans remaining sometimes claimed to be exempt from Japanese law and sometimes, like many Japanese, engaged in blackmarketing. Many who returned to Korea managed to return to Japan illegally, after experiencing the difficult living conditions at home.

Koreans residing in Japan are organized in two rival groups. The Chōsōren, the General Confederation of Korean residents in Japan, supports the Communist government of North Korea. It is by far the larger and more influential of the two groups. The smaller Mindan, the Community of Korean Residents in Japan, supports South Korea. The predecessor of the former organization had close ties with the Japan Communist Party during the Occupation, and both groups were

[2] Richard Hanks Mitchell, *The Korean Minority in Japan* (Berkeley: University of California Press, 1967), p. 102.

a constant source of concern for the Japanese police and Occupation authorities. Although the Koreans were Japanese nationals before the end of World War II, they were regarded as "liberated" at the end of the war. By 1949, the Occupation had made it clear that the Koreans still in Japan were under the jurisdiction of the Japanese government.

The Koreans complain of job discrimination, while Japanese often criticize the apparently dishonest ways in which Koreans make their livelihoods. Many were voluntarily repatriated to North Korea in the 1950s, although the South Korean government bitterly protested that sending people to the North was the equivalent of enslavement and evidence that Japan continued to mistreat the Korean people. In 1965, most of the outstanding issues between Japan and her former colony were settled when the Japan–South Korea treaty was signed. The Korean residents who sympathize with the North Korean regime, with which Japan does not have diplomatic relations, live in a limbo akin to statelessness. The Koreans have demanded their own schools where the language of instruction is Korean and in 1968, the governor of Tokyo, over the bitter opposition of the Ministry of Education, which feared the possibility of anti-Japanese indoctrination, permitted Koreans to establish their own university in Tokyo.

The unequal treatment complained of by Koreans in Japan is usually not regarded as a moral problem or a question of human rights so much as a diplomatic problem. The obvious solution for Koreans who do not like Japan is to go to Korea, so that their difficulties in Japan are either of their own making or the fault of one or several governments—North Korean, South Korean, or Japanese—which are caught up in the tensions of the Cold War. Aside from their involvement in leftist riots during the Occupation and their foreign affiliations,[3] Koreans have not been significant factors in the Japanese political process. They do not identify or cooperate with the only other oppressed minority in Japan, the Burakumin.

The Burakumin and Their Politics

From ancient times there has existed in Japan a caste of untouchables formerly known as Eta, a word written with Chinese characters meaning "full of filth." The contemporary descendants of the Eta are referred to as Burakumin. Their hereditary occupations, in addition to farming, were preparing corpses for burial or cremation, executions,

---

[3] Kim Ch'ŏn-hae (Kin Ten-kai), the president of the leftist Chōren (League of Koreans Residing in Japan) in Occupation days, was a leading member of the Central Executive Committee of the Japan Communist Party.

slaughtering animals, tanning hides, and making leather, fur goods, and sandals. During the Tokugawa era, these occupations were their monopolies. The Buddhist and Shinto taboos concerning death meant that these trades and those who engaged in them were ritually unclean. Furthermore, the Eta, unlike other Japanese, ate meat, a practice forbidden by Buddhist teaching. The Eta and a few other marginal classes were not normally counted in censuses.

In 1871, upon the overwhelming recommendation of the then existing national lower house, the Council of State issued the Eta Emancipation Edict. Eta emancipation was apparently part of the general policy of the new imperial regime to abolish the whole system of inherited status, caste, and privilege (except the Imperial Family). Emancipation was a mixed blessing for the Eta caste, which lost its monopoly privileges and exemption from the land tax. As other Japanese entered previously Eta-connected industries and later as machine production became widespread, the plight of the former Eta worsened. The edict was not enough to eliminate the feeling of fear and revulsion which the Eta evoked among the majority Japanese, and emancipation could not provide respectable geneologies for the Eta, who became known as "new commoners." Because family background is an extremely important factor in contracting marriage in Japan, it remains almost impossible for people of Eta ancestry to marry outside of their caste.

Physiologically, the new commoners were identical with other Japanese, and although traditions hold that they are of alien (usually Korean) origin, no evidence substantiates this claim. The new commoners could be identified only by the particular hamlets in which they lived; they have come to be euphemistically referred to as Burakumin ("hamlet people").

In the 1920s, the leaders of the Burakumin organized the Levellers Society (Suiheisha), which articulated their demands for equal treatment. The Suiheisha leaders were often bitterly divided about the tactics to be followed in relation to the government and to the leftist political parties. In 1935, three Suiheisha leaders were elected to the Fukuoka Prefectural Assembly, and in February, 1936, Suiheisha Chairman Matsumoto Ji-ichiro won election to the national House of Representatives. Matsumoto had distinguished himself in a successful nationwide struggle to quash a legal verdict that made it a crime for a Burakumin not to publicly label himself as such. In April, 1937, Matsumoto was reelected, and the Socialist Masses Party, with which he had cooperated (although he ran as an independent), received thirty-seven seats in the lower house. Following the outbreak of war with China in 1937, the Suiheisha became inactive.

The postwar Constitution banned discrimination in political, economic, and social relations because of race, creed, sex, social status, or family origin. However, the Burakumin continued to be discriminated against and to suffer from poverty, disease, and unemployment in their miserable ghettoes. The Suiheisha was reorganized and became the National Committee for Buraku Emancipation. In 1947 Matsumoto, running as a Socialist, was elected to a seat in the House of Councillors. He won the seat with 400,000 votes, the fourth largest number of votes won by a candidate in the national constituency. Nine other Burakumin were elected to the House of Councillors and the House of Representatives.[4]

Matsumoto was elected Vice President of the House of Councillors, and in 1948 refused to bow to the Emperor in the traditional manner at the formal opening of the Diet. As a result of this gesture, the tradition of formal obeisances to the Emperor was dropped from parliamentary procedure. In the following year, Matsumoto was purged from public office on the grounds of his membership in a wartime patriotic society. A million signatures, including those of two-thirds of the members of both houses of the Diet, were obtained for a petition demanding revocation of the purge, and in 1951, Matsumoto was reinstated. MacArthur's original acquiescence in Matsumoto's purge solidified the anti-American orientation of the Burakumin movement.

Although the Buraku Emancipation League estimates that there are three million Burakumin in Japan, other informed sources place the figure at about two million. Thus, between 2 and 3 percent of all Japanese belong to this underprivileged group. They live in about six thousand hamlets, some urban, others rural. The Emancipation League has local chapters in about half of the hamlets. Local League officers are regarded as spokesmen for the inhabitants of the ghetto and are often active in municipal and prefectural politics.

The Buraku Emancipation League capitalized handsomely on the publication of a sensational story on Buraku by an officer of the Kyoto City Health Department in 1957. The Committee was unsatisfied with the firing of the author of the article, and successfully demanded that the city finance the building of low-rent apartments, public toilets, sanitary water supplies, bath houses, community centers, parks, and nurseries in the Buraku.

Before his death, Matsumoto Ji-ichiro headed the leftist Heiwa Dōshikai faction of the Socialist Party. Within the policy affairs research council of the Liberal-Democratic Party, there is a special

---

[4] George de Vos and Hiroshi Wagatsuma, *Japan's Invisible Race: Caste in Culture and Personality* (Berkeley: University of California Press, 1966), p. 69.

conciliation committee whose specialty is the problems of the Burakumin. In addition, there exists an official Council on Integration
Policy which is an advisory organ of the Prime Minister. In 1968 it
asserted that the solution of integration problems was the responsibility
of both the national and local governments and proposed legislation
for the improvement of living environment, of the farming, fishing and
forestry industries, and of education. The negative attitude of the
government towards these proposals sparked the establishment of a
four-party council and a petition movement led by the Buraku Emancipation League to support the proposed legislation.[5] In the same
year, evidently as the result of the Emancipation League's protests, the
Ministry of Justice ordered restrictions on public access to census
registers covering the years 1872–1886, because some of them contained outcaste designations.[6]

In 1970, the Buraku Emancipation League launched a nationwide
movement to (1) realize the enactment of the integration special
measures law and (2) overturn the decision in the Sayama case. The
latter concerned the conviction of a Burakumin for murder in Sayama,
Saitama-ken, near Tokyo, in 1963. The Buraku leaders insisted that
the local police in their eagerness to achieve a conviction in the brutal
killing of a high school girl, tortured an innocent Burakumin into
signing a fabricated confession. The Buraku leaders asserted that the
arbitrary decision to accuse a Burakumin in a locality where much
prejudice existed followed the failure of the police through incompe-
tence to apprehend a prime suspect before the latter committed suicide.
Meetings, demonstrations, and marches were held in various places in
Japan to articulate the Buraku demands, including a meeting in Tokyo
in June, 1970, attended by 5,000 people, to which the governors of
Tokyo, Osaka, and Kyoto and other political leaders sent messages.[7]

The plight of the Burakumin and their reactions to it are similar to
those of American blacks. Although it is possible for an educated, well-
dressed Burakumin to pass as a majority Japanese because he is
racially similar, it is very difficult to hide his family origin in the close-
knit Japanese society. If his Buraku background is revealed to his
employer or his non-Buraku associates he may be economically or
socially ruined. The poor and uneducated Burakumin depend on the
Buraku for their livelihood and do not have a real chance to escape.

[5] *Asahi Nenkan, 1969,* p. 298.
[6] *Ibid.,* p. 328.
[7] Hijikata Tetsu, "Sayama sabetsu saiban o kyūdan suru" (We censure the
discriminatory Sayama decision), *Asahi Jānaru,* Vol. XII, No. 26 (June 28,
1970), 105–109; Hijikata Tetsu, *Sabetsu Saiban* (Discriminatory Decision)
(Tokyo: Shakai Shimpō, 1970).

The leftist political parties blame the plight of the Burakumin on capitalism, and, like the conservatives, often think improvement of ghetto housing and education are solutions. Public expressions of prejudices are illegal, and flagrant incidences are made examples by the Buraku Emancipation League. The plight of the Burakumin seems basically to result from the age-old hateful image of the Eta which Burakumin as well as the general public hold. This image sometimes evokes self-fulfilling expectations of immorality, crime, and poverty among the Burakumin.[8] The problem of a negative self-image is the same social-psychological phenomenon found among underprivileged minorities in other parts of the world.[9]

The New Religions and the Sōka Gakkai

At the end of World War II, when Japan was faced with dire shortages of food and housing and was under foreign military occupation, people's faith in the future of their families and their country was at low ebb. Some Americans believed that just as there was a possibility for the introduction of democratic ideals and institutions to fill the spiritual gap, there might also be an unparalleled opportunity to Christianize Japan. Missionaries were encouraged to return to the wartorn country, but the results of their efforts were, on the whole, as unimpressive as they had been in the past. Instead, a rash of "new religions" sprang up in the postwar environment. The new sects were led by charismatic personalities whose teachings were often a conglomeration of traditional religious or ethical beliefs, Buddhist, Shinto, and Confucianist. Faith-healing was often a conspicuous feature of these sects. Sometimes a long-established sect, such as Tenrikyō, showed a sudden spurt of growth under dynamic new leadership.

The best known among the "new religions" has been the Sōka Gakkai, the layman's organization affiliated with the Nichiren Shōshū (sect) of Buddhism. The Sōka Gakkai has been particularly popular among the urban lower middle classes. The rise of big business and powerful labor unions has placed their small enterprises at a competitive disadvantage. They have suffered from inflation, unemployment, inadequate medical care, and a feeling that society and the state have been unresponsive to their needs. Many of them have recently migrated from the country to the city, have difficulties in adjusting to urban life, and feel lonely. The traditional Buddhist elements in Nichiren Shōshū appeal to their nostalgia for a simpler age.

[8] Cf. de Vos and Wagatsuma, pp. 149–150.
[9] *Ibid.*, pp. 353–384, concerns the cross-cultural psychology of caste behavior.

The Sōka Gakkai is organized along hierarchical, military lines. Its leaders, all of whom are laymen, are unusually aggressive and resourceful. Included in the organization are women's groups, student groups, youth groups, musical and gymnastic organizations, etc. Huge rallies, featuring mass calisthenics, and the building of massive, costly sanctuaries take up much of the time of the members in organization and fund raising. The high pressure evangelistic techniques of the Sōka Gakkai have brought it under much criticism, but its membership reportedly grew to 6,600,000 families in 1968.

Since its founding by the Buddhist monk, Nichiren, in the thirteenth century, Nichiren Shōshū has been one of the main sects of Buddhism in Japan. Nichiren was a fanatical evangelist who insisted that his interpretation of the scriptures was the only correct one and that all other teachings were heretical and should be banned by the state. He claimed that the only security from natural catastrophies and the attempted Mongol invasion of Japan lay in the propagation of his doctrine of salvation. The key to happiness in this world and the next lay in faith in the Lotus Sutra and in the constant repetition of the chant, "Nam-myōhō Renge-kyō" (Devotion to the Lotus Sutra).

In the 1930s, the Sōka Gakkai (Value Creation Society) was organized as an educational layman's auxiliary of the Nichiren Shōshū. During World War II, its leaders challenged the military-dominated government over the special position enjoyed by Shinto, and some of them were imprisoned. After the war, under the leadership of the dynamic Toda Jōsei, the Sōka Gakkai enjoyed phenomenal growth. In 1956, the Political Department of the Sōka Gakkai sponsored six candidates to the upper house of the Diet; three won seats. In 1959 they sponsored six candidates to the upper house, all of whom were successful. In 1962, the Sōka Gakkai organized the Clean Government League (Kōmei Seiji Remmei) as its political arm. In 1964, the Political Department was abolished and the Clean Government League was converted into the Clean Government Party (Kōmeitō). By 1970 the Kōmeitō was the third largest party in both houses of the Diet.

The "Rightists"

In contemporary Japan, the extreme right is remarkably similar in spirit to what it was in the prewar era. In the 1930s the military, supported by the ultranationalists, succeeded in establishing political hegemony over the nation, but today the violent right is numerically small, having no significant political influence. Nevertheless, the "rightists" (uyokusha), by assuming a strongly patriotic and anti-

Communist pose, are still a potential threat to democratic institutions. In the event of a severe economic depression or a gross deterioration of Japan's international relations, it is conceivable that influential conservative elements in the country would be tempted to condone violent rightist attacks on radical students, socialist politicians, and labor leaders. It has happened before, and many Japanese today are keenly aware that it could happen again.

The first important rightist incident after the war was the attack by members of the "New and Powerful Masses Party," a band of extortionists pretending devotion to democracy, on the life of Kikunami Katsumi, in January, 1947. Kikunami was a Communist member of the Diet and Chairman of the Congress of Industrial Unions, which was planning a general strike. The stabbing of Kikunami was hailed by the rightists as a patriotic act and cited by the left as evidence of a revival of prewar fascism. In July, 1948, a member of the All-Japan Anti-Communist League attempted to assassinate Tokuda Kyūichi, secretary-general of the Japan Communist Party. The terrorist threw a stick of dynamite at the speaker's platform during an address Tokuda was giving. Tokuda was hospitalized for a week but recovered. Another unsuccessful attempt on his life was made a year later.[10]

During the 1960 Security Pact struggle, a number of instances of rightist terrorism occurred. On April 2, ten members of the Matsubakai, a rightist organization, tore up the main office of the moderate *Mainichi Shimbun* and threw sand into the rotary presses. On June 15, right-wing thugs drove a truck into a line of leftist student demonstrators near the Diet and injured some of the students. The excited students then attacked the police in protest of their failure to protect them and stormed the gates of the Diet compound. Hundreds of students and police were ultimately hurt, and a coed was killed. As a consequence, the Kishi Government cancelled a scheduled visit by Eisenhower. Although the left received most of the blame for the fracas, it is nevertheless true that the rightists had provoked the riot, probably deliberately. Two days after the June 15 incident, Kawakami Jōtarō, the Socialist leader, was stabbed while he was collecting signatures for a petition near the Diet. In the following month, at a party to celebrate the election of Ikeda Hayato as President of the Liberal-Democratic Party, Prime Minister Kishi was stabbed in the leg by a right-wing fanatic who had had a long prewar record of affiliation with terrorist organizations.

The most notorious terrorist deed in the postwar era was the Asanuma stabbing. The NHK national television network, no doubt

[10] Ivan Morris, *Nationalism and the Right Wing in Japan: A Study of Post-War Trends* (London: Oxford University Press, 1960), p. 91.

prompted by the example of the Kennedy-Nixon television debate, sponsored a debate among the heads of the three major political parties in October, 1960, in Hibiya Public Hall in Tokyo. When Asanuma Inejirō, Chairman of the Socialist Party, rose to speak, a seventeen-year-old youth in a black student's uniform leaped onto the stage and before a terrified audience plunged a dagger into the speaker. The boy was immediately captured and, while awaiting trial, hanged himself.

The assassin was Yamaguchi Otoya, son of a Ground Self-Defense Force colonel. He had been arrested more than ten times during the year for his fanatical antileftist rioting but was each time released because of his youth. After being expelled from the Great Japan Patriotic Party, a rightist group led by Akao Bin, he joined the All-Asia Anti-Communist League, another group of rightist storm troopers. He told police that he had perpetrated the assassination single-handedly and without the help of collaborators. He said that he had been overwhelmed by a sense of danger concerning the future of his fatherland in light of the disturbances over the United States–Japan Security treaty. Since July he had planned to kill one of the three spokesmen of the leftist movement—Asanuma, Nosaka, a Communist leader, and Kobayashi Takeshi, Chairman of the Japan Teachers Union. The boy was an admirer of Yoshida Shōin and Saigō Takamori, patriotic leaders of the Meiji era, and of Adolf Hitler. Japanese custom required that someone in the government assume responsibility for acts of political violence, and the Autonomy Minister resigned.

The Socialists, of course, made political capital of the incident. Mass demonstrations were held by Sōhyō and the Zengakuren. The left accused the Liberal-Democrats of condoning and encouraging right-wing terrorism. At a funeral ceremony held near the scene of the killing political leaders of all parties, including Prime Minister Ikeda, spoke. Asanuma's widow ran for the Diet seat vacated by her martyred husband and won.

In December, 1961, the police discovered an elaborate plot to assassinate the Ikeda Cabinet. One of the ringleaders was Mikami Taku, a former naval lieutenant who had been imprisoned for his connection with the assassination of Prime Minister Inukai in 1932. Also involved were a former lieutenant general in the Imperial Army and a businessman who had helped to finance the effort. These rightists called themselves the Society for Japanese History and had gathered together 300 helmets, 150 gas masks, and much other equipment similar to that used by the Self-Defense Forces. They had attempted unsuccessfully to enlist the support of members of the Forces.

The plotters had reportedly planned not only to assassinate Prime

Minister Ikeda and the sixteen members of his Cabinet, but also to bomb police headquarters and the headquarters of the Sōhyō and the Communist Party. They were said to believe that the Ikeda Government was incapable of preventing a Communist revolution in Japan and could have been encouraged to act by the military coup d'état in Korea in May, 1961.

In September, 1971, a day laborer, who had once studied for the Buddhist priesthood, stabbed the Chairman of the Kōmeitō, Takeiri Yoshikatsu, who had recently visited Communist China and advocated closer ties with that country.

Perhaps the most serious right-wing incident since the war was the suicide in 1970 of the internationally famous novelist and playwright Mishima Yukio. Mishima in his writing had deplored the materialism and spiritual emptiness of postwar Japan. In 1966 he wrote a film play which extolled the sincerity and selflessness of the young officers who had attempted the February 26, 1936, coup d'état. In the film, Mishima himself acted the part of an officer who committed seppuku (harakiri) after the failure of the coup. In November, 1970, he and several of his aides tried to persuade the soldiers at the Self-Defense Forces headquarters in Tokyo to carry out a coup in order to accomplish the repeal of the disarmament clause (Article 9) of the Constitution. His speech was met with jeers. After this rebuff, he committed suicide in traditional samurai fashion. While Mishima cut himself in the abdomen, he kept his head bowed so that his aide could decapitate him. His associate, in turn, committed suicide in the same fashion, but the person who carried out the second decapitation remained alive in order to explain to the world the significance of the self-immolations.

Mishima's death came as a great surprise and shock to the Japanese people, the more so because his type of feudalistic thinking did not seem to enjoy much support in twentieth-century Japan. However, Mishima's suicide deeply impressed Japanese youth, many of whom, although leftist rather than rightist, were similarly alienated by the modern materialistic ethic. Also, the Mishima suicide, like the May 15, 1930, incident and the attempted 1936 military coup, coincided with a period of national crisis. In 1970, as in 1930, Japan had become a leading power and was seeking outlets for her energy and ambition. In 1930 and 1970, the urgent problem facing the Japanese was to define an enlarged role for their nation in world politics. Coming at this time, the Mishima incident may have an important influence on the attitudes of many Japanese.[11]

---

[11] Cf. Noma Hiroshi, "Sakugo ni michita bungaku: Seiji no tanraku," *Asahi Jānaru,* Vol. XII, No. 48 (December 6, 1970), 4–6. The suicides of the famous General Nogi and his wife upon learning of the death of their

Such "incidents" (jiken) take on special political and ideological significance for the Japanese. Both before and after the war, incidents have been exploited by extremist parties and have found their way into political mythology. Some become causes célèbres. An incident may be an assassination or attempted assassination, an attempted coup d'état, or a bombing. The authors of incidents are usually obscure and unbalanced individuals who have been highly agitated by rightist (or occasionally leftist) propaganda. Each conceives of his act as one which may save the nation or Emperor from political corruption, treason, or communism. The public figures singled out for assassination are often little known personally to the assassins; the victim is a symbol. An assassination by a rightist is seized upon by the political left as evidence that the conservative government is indifferent to the threat of fascism and is willing to see its political opponents terrorized, beaten up, or killed. The political right, on the other hand, is prone to deplore the incident but at the same time point out leftist excesses which may have provoked the act.

The present-day ultranationalist groups are not as generously financed as were some of the prewar groups. They have thus far failed to elicit support among the masses as they did before the war when they gave expression to the discontent of the poor peasantry. The postwar Japanese military is under civilian control and does not support rightist activists. Japanese conservatives working through the Liberal-Democratic Party already rule Japan and have no reason to wish for a coup d'état by the extreme right. At the same time, the highly sophisticated police keep close tabs on extremist activities, both on the left and on the right.

Students

In Japan, about one-fifth of all college-age youths attend college. Although this figure is smaller than that for the United States, it is far in excess of the proportion of youths in college in most other industrialized countries. About 1,670,000 students attended college in 1970. It is extremely important to a young man that he be admitted to the right university; his career for the rest of his life will be largely determined by the prestige of his college. Entrance examinations are highly

---

beloved Emperor in 1916 were widely admired and made a profound effect on the public. "To rush into the thick of battle and to be slain in it," says a Prince of Mito, "is easy enough, and the merest churl is equal to the task; but," he continues, "it is true courage to live when it is right to live, and to die only when it is right to die." (Inazo Nitobe, *Bushido: The Soul of Japan,* 19th ed. [Tokyo: Teibei, 1902], p. 26.)

competitive, and the Japanese often refer to their country as an "examination hell." But once admitted to a school, the academic requirements are not demanding. As a consequence, the best schools are full of bright students, many of whom have a great deal of time available for political activities.

The students do suffer from many real and imaginary deprivations. Housing and eating facilities for students are inadequate, classes are overcrowded, and the universities do not provide as many recreational and other extracurricular facilities for their students as do American schools. Beginning in the early 1950s, demonstrating, sometimes violently, has been a conspicuous feature of student activity in Japan and a powerful political weapon as well. The United States is twenty years behind Japan in this respect. The students and faculty are over-whelmingly leftist and antiestablishment in their political orientation, perennially opposed to the government, which has been consistently conservative since 1948. Most of the students, however, are usually apathetic, but when a popular issue arises it is not difficult for the well-organized radical students to mobilize their normally passive class-mates. In 1960, student demonstrations that resulted in the death of a coed were the principal reason for the cancellation of President Eisenhower's visit to Japan and the resignation of Prime Minister Kishi later that year.

In Japan, as in the United States and France, student turmoil in 1968 through 1970 reached the proportions of a national crisis. The objectives of the radical Zengakuren (All-Japan Federation of Students' Self-Governing Associations) were the termination of the United States–Japan Security Treaty, the return of Okinawa to Japanese rule, the removal of American military forces from Japanese soil, and the withdrawal of the American "imperialists" from Vietnam. The most radical students evidently hoped to exploit these issues in order to take control of the universities for use as bases in carrying out a leftist revolution.

In 1969, violence erupted on over one hundred campuses, and at various times students occupied all twenty buildings of the main campus of prestigious Tokyo University. The Zengakuren had long been divided into factions, and in 1969, there were two rival groupings, the Yoyogi group connected with the Japan Communist Party, and the anti-Yoyogi groups of Maoists, "Trotskyites," and anarchists to the left of the Japanese Communists. In early 1969, the JCP-oriented students advocated nonviolence and played the strategic role of mediating between the extreme leftists and the Tokyo University officials. In January, 1969, during a conference between university administrators and students, hundreds of anti-JCP radicals, armed with staves and helmets, clashed head-on with hundreds of pro-JCP students, similarly equipped for battle. University officials in Japan, concerned for the protection of academic freedom from governmental interference, had traditionally opposed the intrusion of police into the campus. However, in this situation, Tokyo University officials asked for police help. For two days, 400 militant students inside and on top of the Yasuda Hall of Tokyo University withstood a siege by the police, who used high pressure water and dropped tear gas from helicopters. During the struggle, about 200 policemen and thirty students were injured, and over 500 students were arrested.

The adverse reaction of the general public and of the politicians to student violence and the inability of university officials to restore order led to government efforts to exercise greater supervision of the universities. Concessions made by Tokyo University officials to the radical students were regarded as of doubtful legality by the government. The public was gravely shocked when in January, 1969, the University announced the cancellation of entrance examinations for the year. Most top governmental and many business leaders had graduated from Tōdai (Tokyo University). The highest aspiration of parents was to see their children accepted by Tōdai; now that great school was, for the time being at least, closed to them. In the spring of 1969, sixteen of the national universities failed to hold classes.

The government was concerned not only with the breakdown in the educational process but also with the prospect that the campuses would be used in 1970 as bases in the struggle against the United States–Japan Security Treaty. The Satō administration proposed a university control bill which would empower university authorities to suspend classes for nine months in order to settle campus disputes on their own; if they failed the Education Ministry could take over, using police if deemed necessary. The university control bill was bitterly resisted in the Diet, and in order to overcome the opposition's delaying tactics, the government finally passed the measure by blocking debate in the upper house. The governing Liberal-Democratic Party had a majority of seats in both houses of the Diet, and was able to enact the bill notwithstanding the protests of the opposition. Among intellectuals, the feeling was that the government had gravely abused the parliamentary process and that democracy was in danger. Although the purpose of the university bill was to calm the campuses, the immediate effect of its passage was to intensify the political passions of the students and professors, who went on a nationwide protest strike.

Campuses cooled off considerably by the fall of 1969, when most of those closed managed to reopen. The public and students had been antagonized by the violent minority who were more devoted to revolution than to scholarship. In the spring of 1970, however, a band of revolutionary students hijacked a Japan Airlines passenger plane and forced the pilot to take them to Pyongyang, North Korea.

The student movement has had notably small success in combining on a continuous basis with the labor movement. The workers tend to regard the students as part of the bourgeoisie which, after a youthful fling at revolution, will join the managerial class upon graduating from college. The students' preoccupations are usually not those of the workers, and labor is unwilling to become identified with the unpopular tactics of physical violence which the more radical students favor. For the most part, the political parties have little influence among the students, and the Socialist Party, it is said, did badly in the 1969 lower house election because of its inability to restrain the violence-prone Socialist Youth League.

The Peace Movement

The potentialities of the peace movement in Japan must be viewed against the background of a basically pacifistic, isolationist attitude toward world affairs to which the people have been historically conditioned by their catastrophic defeat in World War II and their experiences with atomic weapons at Hiroshima and Nagasaki. The burden of proof is imposed on those who advocate rearmament and the presence of foreign military bases, not on those who advocate peace. This historical perspective is elaborated upon at the conclusion of this discussion.

Peace became a leading political issue in the 1950s when United States forces in Japan became involved in the war in Korea. The Japanese Peace Treaty and the accompanying Security Treaty with America (1951) were bitterly criticized by the opposition as involving Japan in the Cold War. In 1952, the Socialist Party split in half over the question of supporting the Peace Treaty with the United States and the other non-Communist states. The Left Socialists insisted on an "overall" peace treaty that the Soviet Union and Communist China as well as the non-Communist states would adhere to. Not until 1955 did the party reunite. The question of the reversion of Okinawa to Japanese rule became involved with the peace issue because American reluctance to give back the island was justified on the grounds of the Communist military threat in the Far East. The escalation of the Vietnam War in the 1960s reminded the Japanese of their own disastrous involvement on the Asian mainland thirty years before and aroused fears of a similar new involvement. The Socialist and Communist opposition, whose ideological appeal had been largely limited to organized labor and intellectual circles, early discovered that the peace issue in one form or another was a particularly effective one with which to belabor the pro-American conservative government.

The Ban-the-Bomb Movement

The Gensuikyō (Japan Council Against Atomic and Hydrogen Bombs) was formed as a multipartisan group in 1954. It was customary for the Gensuikyō to hold several meetings in August each year in Hiroshima, Nagasaki, and Tokyo. Some of these were billed as world congresses, and delegations from foreign countries played conspicuous roles. By 1958, the Gensuikyō had been firmly taken over by the Sōhyō, the Japan Socialist and Communist Parties, the Zengakuren, and the front organizations affiliated with them. In 1958, at its fifth World Congress in Hiroshima, it insisted not only on outlawing nuclear weapons but also on opposing Japan's rearmament and the revision of the United States–Japan Mutual Security Treaty.

At the Gensuikyō's 1961 Congress, the Japanese Communists, backed by delegates from other Asian Communist parties, were able to dominate the meeting and pass resolutions closely corresponding to the international Communist line. With full Soviet approval, the JCP-dominated Congress passed a resolution stating, "Today the government which first resumes nuclear testing is to be censured as the enemy of peace and mankind." However, in the same month, the Soviet Union itself resumed nuclear testing. This placed the JCP in the extremely embarrassing position of having to defend the Soviet tests in spite of the Gensuikyō position. At an April, 1962, Gensuikyō conference in Tokyo, mainstream (anti-JCP) Zengakuren demonstrators disrupted the meeting shouting slogans against the Soviet testing.

During the August, 1962, Congress, the Soviet Union set off a massive nuclear explosion in Siberia. The Japanese Communists resisted Sōhyō proposals to send protests to Moscow as well as to Washington. Fighting broke out between the Socialist Youth League and the Communist-sponsored Democratic Youth League, and the Congress ended in chaos.

As the Gensuikyō had been a principal vehicle for united front activity with the rest of the Japanese left, the JCP made efforts to restore the unity of the organization before the 1963 World Conference. However, at the last minute, when it appeared that the Communists were going to dominate the meeting, the Socialists and Sōhyō boycotted it. The Communist-run Ninth Congress in Hiroshima proved as stormy as its predecessors. Ten days before the meeting, the United States, the Soviet Union, and Great Britain signed the partial nuclear test-ban treaty. The treaty was bitterly opposed by Communist China, which charged Khrushchev with revisionism and capitulationism. The Sino-Soviet dispute came out into the open at the Hiroshima meeting, and bitter words were exchanged between the Soviet and Chinese delegates.

In 1964, the Sōhyō and Socialists attacked the Gensuikyō as dominated by a single political party and organized their own Hiroshima conference. A Soviet delegation arrived in Japan in July with the declared intention of attending both the Tenth Gensuikyō Conference and the Socialist-sponsored meeting. However, the Gensuikyō directors ruled that supporters of other peace movements could not be elected to leading posts in the international session. The Russians and pro-Soviet delegates therefore withdrew, leaving the Gensuikyō completely under the control of the JCP and the Chinese Communist bloc. The Soviet Union and its friends figured prominently in the Socialist-sponsored Hiroshima International Conference, which supported the nuclear test-ban treaty.

In 1965, Sōhyō, the Socialists, and their affiliates formally organized the Gensuikin (Japan Congress Against Atomic and Hydrogen Bombs). Its establishment was greeted by messages from the Soviet-sponsored World Council of Peace and the United States National Committee for a Sane Nuclear Policy. The Gensuikin International Conference included a number of Soviet-bloc delegations. The Soviet Union did not send a delegation to the Eleventh World Congress of the Gensuikyō in 1965, and that Congress was completely dominated by the JCP and other Peking-oriented groups. Both the Gensuikin and the Gensuikyō opposed the United States–Japan Security Treaty, the Japan-Korea normalization talks and American aggression in Southeast Asia.

In 1966, relations between the Japanese and Chinese Communist Parties began to deteriorate badly. Gensuikyō officials permitted the World Federation of Democratic Youth, a Soviet-bloc organization, to register for the Twelfth Congress. This move outraged Peking, and the Chinese delegation and its supporters, who included over one-half of the foreign delegates, withdrew from the Congress.

The Gensuikyō had served successively as an arena for a leftist take-over, a Communist-Socialist confrontation, the Sino-Soviet split, and the break between the Japanese and Chinese Communists. Beginning in 1966, three major groups sponsored international antibomb conferences in Japan, the newest comer being the Kakkin Kaigi (People's Conference for the Banning of Nuclear Weapons and the Establishment of Peace), an organization sponsored by the non-Communist Dōmei labor-union confederation, the Democratic-Socialist Party and some Liberal-Democrats. Efforts to bring about a reunification of the antibomb movement were without success. The Gensuikyō and Gensuikin agreed on the need to terminate the United States–Japan Security Treaty, the immediate reversion of Okinawa, and the immediate withdrawal of American troops from Vietnam. However, they could not reunify because of their failure to agree to condemn nuclear testing by Communist as well as by non-Communist states. The strongly anti-American lines of both of these leftist groups were unacceptable to the Kakkin Kaigi.

The Vietnam Peace Movement

The problems of the surviving victims of the atomic bombings and the threat of fall-out and war from persistent testing continued to concern the public. However, the political parties and foreign countries were so obviously exploiting these issues for their own selfish ends that the trifurcated antibomb movement evoked widespread disgust. In the meantime, the Vietnam War became a salient issue. To many Japanese, the United States appeared to be making the same kind of mistakes on the Asian mainland that Japan had made with disastrous results in the 1930s. Japanese newspapers sent reporters to both North and South Vietnam, and the suffering to Asians caused by American bombings got full play in the newspapers and on television. Partly because of a distrust of the political parties and the ban-the-bomb organizations, much of the struggle against the Vietnam War was carried out by private groups and individuals.

On October 21, 1966, under the auspices of Sōhyō, there was a nation-wide strike for peace in Vietnam. This was the first of the numerous large-scale peace strikes and demonstrations held in Japan in the late 1960s. Appeals, petitions, and declarations by ad hoc groups of scholars, scientists, students, etc., for peace in Vietnam became commonplace. All of this was in addition to the antiwar propaganda issued by the labor unions, the leftist political parties and the antibomb groups.

There was organized in 1967 a three-day Vietnam War Crimes Tribunal in Tokyo, headed by the president of Ritsumeikan University and including the leftist critic Hani Goro among its twenty-three justices. It heard testimony from an investigating team which twice visited Vietnam and considered as evidence weapons collected there. The verdict was that the governments of United States and Japan, which provided a logistical base for the American effort in Vietnam, were guilty. The trial, of course, was the Japanese edition of the famous Stockholm trial, but the Tokyo war crimes trial of Occupation days was an obvious precedent.

Notable was the emergence of a new organization, headed by the author Oda Makoto, appealing to individuals and the general public: the Beheiren (Japan "Peace for Vietnam!" Committee). This group first attracted international attention in 1967 when it aided the desertion of four American airmen from the aircraft carrier, *Intrepid*. At a news conference, the Beheiren showed motion pictures and played tapes of the voices of the four men. The organization also published the airmen's statement that it was criminal for a developed nation to bomb systematically an impoverished agricultural country and that America should stop all of the bombing and withdraw from Vietnam. The Beheiren continued its moral and legal aid to American deserters and encouraged the underground peace movement among American troops stationed in Japan. It also raised funds for a ship to send medicine to North Vietnam and the National Liberation Front in South Vietnam.

On October 10, 1969, the Beheiren cooperated with the principal anti-JCP radical student groups in organizing a nationwide demonstration involving rallies in fifty-three cities. This group of organizations, not under the control of established political parties and labor unions, was regarded by journalists as the "New Left" in Japanese politics. Beheiren activists, including Oda, have visited the United States and coordinated some of the peace demonstrations in Japan with those in America and in other countries.

Although the American public was scarcely conscious of the breadth and intensity of the peace movement in Japan—the problem was worldwide—American diplomats feared that Japanese-American relations were being gravely jeopardized by the continuation of the unpopular war in Vietnam. President Nixon's promise to Prime Minister Satō in November, 1969, to return Okinawa to Japan facilitated a lower-house electoral victory by the Liberal-Democrats that year. The opposition, however, claimed that the price for Okinawa's reversion was Satō's assurance that American bases in Japan and Okinawa could be more freely used than in the past in order to support American military ventures in Asia. The Okinawa question, the American military and naval bases in Japan, the United States–Japan Security Treaty, like the atomic weapons issue and the Vietnam War, all lent immediacy to the peace issue for the Japanese people, and these questions were usually lumped together among the slogans of demonstrators.

Japanese Pacifism in Historical Perspective

Japan's defeat in World War II, which was brought on by militarism at home and aggression abroad, discredited the military establishment and the policies of imperialism. The Japanese were the only people ever subjected to atomic attacks, and they are very conscious of the suffering of the victims and their families. The frightful conventional air raids on Tokyo, Yokohama, and many other cities during the war made the Japanese aware, even before the invention of atomic weapons and long-range missiles, of the extreme vulnerability of their cities to air attack. Another war was unthinkable. Article 9 of the postwar Constitution renounces armaments and war, and this provision enjoys wide support.

Because the Japanese peace movement has sometimes appeared to be anti-American and pro-Communist, it has often been misunderstood in the United States. For purposes of analysis, the peace movement might be said to present several aspects. First, it appears that one of the negative results of the protection which America has extended to Japan throughout the Cold War has been the lack of defense consciousness among much of the population of that country. Since the Japanese people and leadership did not perceive the spread of communism as a threat to them, they could avoid facing up to hard questions concerning rearmament and taxation for national defense. The intellectuals could afford to be highly idealistic about peace versus war, and the businessmen could avoid high taxes for defense, while American soldiers fought in Korea and Vietnam and American taxpayers paid the bill for Japan's "free ride."

Second, there is a widespread feeling in Japan that America's problems in the Far East are the result of a failure to understand Asians. The American fear of the Chinese Communists, for example, seems almost pathological to many Japanese. To Japanese with experience in Asia, the Chinese seem backward, unbusinesslike, and incapable even of self-government. Japan has little to fear from China; if anything, as shown in the 1930s, the converse is true. Japanese intellectuals, feeling guilty for Japan's aggression in China, tend to excuse the belligerence of Peking's rhetoric as an expression of a legitimate fear of American and Japanese threats. China's atomic capability, which the Japanese could easily surpass if they chose to, is explained as a defensive reaction against the danger from the United States and the Soviet Union. Because of their Asian culture and geographic location, Japanese of varying ideological persuasions have been intrigued by the notion that Japan might serve as a bridge between America and China. However, in the 1970s, it seems likely that Japan would favor a more positive role in world affairs than that of a buffer.

Third, it might be said that, perhaps because of their own experience with the horrors of war on their own territory and the extreme vulnerability of their cities, the Japanese assign an unusually high priority in their foreign policy to the maintenance of peace. To Americans, the wars in Korea and Vietnam, like the Berlin airlift and the intervention in Lebanon, seem distant, limited, military actions necessary to prevent the spread of international communism, to maintain the balance of power, and to forestall a nuclear confrontation between the United States and the Soviet Union. To the Japanese, Korea and Taiwan (former Japanese possessions) and Vietnam are awfully close to home, and Japanese territory is being used as a base in supporting American military activities in that area. Most Japanese, including conservatives, are fearful of even a small escalation of warlike activities by the Americans because it might involve Japan and provoke attacks on her territory and population, a point about which Americans often seem completely insensitive. Things look very different from Tokyo than they do from Washington. Because Japanese conservatives appreciate the need for an American presence in the western Pacific to maintain a balance of power for world peace and because they value their commercial ties with the United States, they are reconciled to American bases in Japan as a necessary evil. Americans are sometimes prone, because the Japanese politely refrain from arguments, to confuse philosophical resignation with positive enthusiasm.

Fourth, the American bases in Japan provide opportune targets for pacifist activities. Because of the rapid expansion of Japanese cities, bases which once were in the country are now surrounded by suburban and industrial developments. The aircraft noise, the automobile and airplane accidents, and the bars associated with military bases are public nuisances. If a violent incident occurs between a foreign soldier and a Japanese, or if violence breaks out during an antibase demonstration, it can be plausibly asserted that such unpleasant events could be avoided in the future by eliminating the base. If the Chinese Communists or Viet Cong maintained military bases in Japan, there would no doubt be demonstrations against them; but they do not. The bases are American, and America must bear the brunt of emotional feelings against the Cold War and the war in Vietnam. American deserters and antiwar GIs are lionized by political activists, and their cases become causes célèbres. While on Japanese soil, their human rights under the protection of the Japanese Constitution are asserted against the cruel and arbitrary claims of an alien military establishment.

Agriculture

Nearly every Japanese farmer belongs to an Agricultural Cooperative Association, and these associations are vital to the fortunes of individual conservative politicians and the Liberal-Democratic Party as a whole. The Agricultural Problems Association, operated by leaders of various agrarian organizations, collects and disburses campaign funds for the Liberal-Democrats. The Government fixes the price of rice, determines support for agriculture research, and is able in many ways to determine policies affecting agriculture, so that the farmers have a real interest in the outcome of elections. Since the Liberal-Democrats are the permanent ruling party, they are in a much stronger position than the opposition parties to solicit funds from interest groups.

It must be noted, however, that agriculture is becoming a less important factor in the nation's economic and political life. In 1900, almost two-thirds of Japan's population lived in rural areas, and only one-third in urban areas. By 1965, the situation was reversed, and 68 percent of the population lived in the cities. As people move from the farms to the cities, the predominantly agricultural prefectures suffer a relative loss of population while the predominantly urban prefectures show substantial increases. Some agricultural prefectures have actually suffered an absolute decrease in population. The political consequences of these changes are obvious. Agriculture has less political clout than it once did. The basis for the rise of the Liberal and Progressive Parties in the 1890s was agriculture, whose advocates strenuously objected to the high land taxes being imposed by the government and tried to use their organized strength in the Diet to resist the government. Today, agriculture tends to be conservative, and the political opposition to the government is based in the labor and student movements. The Socialists have had little success in organizing support among the farmers. The land reform carried out during the Occupation virtually eliminated absentee landlordism and tenantry, so that farmers in Japan are not susceptible to calls for revolution in the countryside. In recent years, landlords who were forced to sell their land at extremely low prices during the land reform put great pressure on the Liberal-Democratic party to reimburse them for their losses and as a result received a generous settlement from the government.

Japanese agriculture has changed a great deal since World War II. Increasingly farmers are moving towards commercial crops. Recently, improved seeds, chemical fertilizers, insecticides, and greater use of machinery have greatly increased crop yields. Not too long ago, Japan had to import rice to supplement its own production. Since 1966, however, Japan has been producing more rice than her population can consume. The excess of rice production is partly the result of the price of rice which was originally set by the government in the immediate postwar period in order to protect the consumer. The official price of rice now encourages overproduction, but it cannot be lightly tampered with by a government which relies heavily on agriculture for its electoral support.

Japan's tiny farms do not provide sufficient income for most farm households, and farming yields little pay for long hard work. Only one out of five farm families engages in full-time farming.[12] The rest obtain much if not most of their incomes from other pursuits. Farmers, therefore, are likely to identify less with agriculture and more with other segments of the economy.

The electoral system for the two houses of the Diet, which will be discussed in detail in a later chapter, has not kept up with the movement of the population from the country to the city. Thus rural districts, which vote predominantly for Liberal-Democrats, are overrepresented in proportion to their population as compared with urban districts. The problem is particularly acute for the minor parties in the prefectural constituencies of the upper house. In some rural prefectures, only one councillor is elected in a given election, making it almost a foregone conclusion that a Liberal-Democrat will be elected and that minor party candidates have no chance. The minor parties have been demanding reapportionment to give greater weight to the urban vote, but they do not control the necessary number of seats in the Diet to enact an electoral reform. The problem of rural overrepresentation, of course, is one which Japan shares with nearly every other modern state.

Labor

The lot of the Japanese worker has never been an easy one. In the past, the oversupply of labor in Japan enabled employers to hire workers at low wages, and Japan's need to export and compete in world markets was a powerful argument to keep wages down. In the

[12] *Statistical Handbook of Japan, 1969* (Tokyo: Bureau of Statistics, 1969), p. 28.

prewar era, labor unions and proletarian political parties were intermittently suppressed by the government, which normally sided with the
employers. The labor movement has been and remains constantly rent
with disputes over theoretical and practical questions. In 1936, the
peak year of the labor movement in prewar Japan, labor unions
included only 420,000 members, 6.9 percent of the nonagricultural
workers. A period of decline set in because of government interference
and repression, and by the end of the Pacific War, labor unions were
virtually nonexistent.

In the first year of the Occupation, MacArthur's Headquarters,
especially the Labor Division of the Economic and Scientific Section,
fostered the expansion of labor unions as part of its democratization
program. The Trade Union Law of 1945 was patterned after the
Wagner Act (1935) of the American New Deal, which gave labor the
rights to organize, to strike, and to bargain collectively. By the end of
1946, there were in Japan two large national federations of labor: the
Congress of Industrial Unions (Sambetsu) and the All-Japan Federation of Labor (Sōdōmei). To the American observer, these corresponded to the CIO and the AFL in the United States.

From the very beginning, the Supreme Commander was seriously
embarrassed by the Communist and pro-Communist leadership of
some, though not all, of the labor movement. A common tactic used
by labor unions early in the Occupation was "production control" in
which strike leaders took over the complete management of enterprises
involved in labor disputes. The radical politics of the Japanese labor
leaders should not have been surprising since many of them had been
hounded by the police or imprisoned during the prewar period. The
frequent political strikes to bring about the fall of the first Yoshida
Cabinet showed that the labor movement in Japan was not politically
"neutral" in the tradition of the American labor movement and that
organized labor's commitment to parliamentarianism was doubtful.
The great general strike planned for February 1, 1947, was called off
by a direct order of General MacArthur. Toward the end of March,
1948, the Communications Workers Union organized a movement for
a nationwide strike for better wage standards for government workers,
but the strike was banned by General Marquat, of the Economic and
Scientific Section (ESS). In July, 1948, General MacArthur informed
Prime Minister Ashida that strikes of government employees would
henceforth be forbidden. The Chief of the Labor Division in ESS,
James S. Killen, resigned in protest against the new attitude of SCAP
towards labor.

In 1949, SCAP pressured the Japanese Government into revising the
Trade Union Law to follow more closely the restrictive provisions of

the Taft-Hartley Act, enacted in the United States in 1947. By 1950, MacArthur's Headquarters had assumed a posture of apparent hostility towards organized labor, which resulted in distrust and resentment of the Occupation and the United States.[13] Aside from measures of suppression, SCAP merely lectured the workers and infiltrated union organizations with "Democratization Leagues," which were essentially SCAP-sponsored anti-Communist cells.[14]

In June, 1970, 8,944,000 workers were members of unions with affiliations as follows:[15]

Sōhyō	4,282,000
Dōmei	2,060,000
Shinsambetsu	75,000
Chūritsu Rōren	140,000
Unions unaffiliated with above	1,127,000

The principal affiliates of Sōhyō are public workers unions such as the All-Japan Government and Public Workers Union, National Railways Workers Union, and Japan Teachers Union (Nikkyōso). The Sōhyō is closely affiliated with the Socialist Party. It nominates most of the Socialist candidates and provides the bulk of their campaign funds and votes. If the policies of the Socialist Party fail to reflect adequately the party's debt to Sōhyō, there is the danger that Sōhyō may assume a "neutral" position in politics, i.e., support Communist as well as Socialist candidates.

The Sōhyō leadership throws its support to many leftist movements. As in the 1960 Security Pact struggle, it has called widespread strikes, even among the National Railway workers, who legally may not strike, and can pay small subsidies to its demonstrators. But notwithstanding the large numbers of people it can mobilize, the general level of ideological consciousness among the workers, even those demonstrating, is relatively low. Its most notable political successes have been the defeat of the Police Duties Revision Bill in 1958, and the cancellation of the Eisenhower visit and resignation of Kishi in 1960. The Anti-Violence Bill, sponsored by the Democratic-Socialists and Liberal-Democrats in 1961, was largely aimed at preventing recurrences of Sōhyō-organized mob pressure on the Diet.

The Socialists, in 1961, supported the principle of "structural reform," which seems to imply the achievement of socialist aims by evolutionary means and without socialist revolution. The Sōhyō main-

---

[13] Kazuo Kawai, *Japan's American Interlude* (Chicago: University of Chicago Press, 1960), p. 165.

[14] *Ibid.*, p. 166.

[15] *Asahi Nenkan, 1971*, p. 478.

stream, on the other hand, has attacked structural reform as a form of "revisionism." Notwithstanding this doctrinal difference, in which Sōhyō stands slightly to the left of the Socialists, Sōhyō usually supports the Socialist Party rather than the Communist Party. Sōhyō also opposes the "rationalization," i.e., technological modernization, of industry, because of the fear of unemployment. In Japan, where underemployment and job insecurity have long been serious problems for the workers, featherbedding is regarded with greater tolerance than in the United States.

The Dōmei Kaigi (formerly Zenrō) federation supports the anti-Communist Democratic-Socialist Party and favors rationalization of industry in order to advance the welfare of the people.

Japanese unionism has a number of weaknesses. Most unions are "enterprise" unions, i.e., based upon single enterprises, although not company controlled. Unions often include a high proportion of white collar workers, who have affiliations with management but whose organizational skill is needed by the workers. The great national labor federations are actually loosely articulated federations of federations. The relation of the top leadership to the rank and file is tenuous. The labor federations, like the political parties, are plagued with rivalries among leaders and disputes over ideology and tactics. Workers in government industries, which include most of the railroads and communications, are not legally permitted to strike; when they do so they are subject to punishment. About one-third of organized labor is made up of government employees, most of whom belong to Sōhyō-affiliated unions. Much energy which might be concentrated on obtaining concrete economic benefits for the workers is expended on political strikes.

The weaknesses of the labor movement are in part traceable to the bifurcation of the Japanese economy. On the one hand, the great zaibatsu enterprises are engaged in efficient, automated, mass production. In these modern industries, labor is concentrated and readily organized, and management can afford to pay relatively good wages. On the other hand, in the vast number of small enterprises, often little more than household shops, the ties between employer and employee are close and paternalistic, and because of undercapitalization and inefficiency, wages are necessarily low. Furthermore, until recently a labor excess in the country impelled workers to accept low wages in industry and agriculture. For Japan to compete in world markets, the cost of labor had to be kept low, especially in those industries which were not adequately mechanized. At the same time, the tradition that when an employer hires a man, the man is hired for life provided job security for the employee, partly offsetting the problem of low pay.

During the economic boom of the 1960s, an apparently permanent shortage of workers arose, strengthening the bargaining position of organized labor. There remains the problem of the unorganized "temporary employees." In many large enterprises, the salary and security of the unionized workers are relatively good. At the same time, however, management, which once may have been concerned with possible slack seasons and recessions, employs many temporary workers. These temporary workers have in effect become permanent employees but are paid much less and enjoy fewer benefits than the permanent employees, who belong to labor unions. The unions are primarily concerned with the interests of their own membership, and tend to neglect the temporary workers, who have become forgotten men in Japan's affluent society.

One source of the political influence of organized labor in America has been its lack of permanent commitment to a single political party. By making both political parties bid for its support, labor is in a strong bargaining position to get what it wants from the government. In Japan, on the other hand, labor is committed to the Socialist, Democratic-Socialist, and sometimes the Communist Parties. These parties are apt nearly always to do labor's bidding, but they cannot win control of any of the branches of the national government. The Liberal-Democratic Party controls the government and it can win elections without catering to organized labor, which is an electoral minority in Japan. As a consequence, the political influence of labor in Japan is weak except when it engages in extraparliamentary tactics. Labor will perhaps exercise more political influence only when the Socialists reunite into a single party and broaden their appeal to agriculture and the middle class so as to win a parliamentary majority. This broadening of the Socialist base would probably lessen union domination over the Socialists, an occurrence which the unions are reluctant to allow. Organized labor in Japan, therefore, seems to be caught in a vicious circle making for political impotence and frustration. This frustration helps to account for its propensity to political strikes and demonstrations.

Business

By far the most powerful interest group in Japan is big business, which has long been well organized for collective activity. The families which made up the prewar zaibatsu were largely removed from control of their financial, industrial, and commercial complexes when the Occupation ordered the dissolution of the trusts and the public sale of their stock. A large zaibatsu complex might typically include a chain of banks, wholesale and retail stores, and light and heavy industries, all capped off by a holding company, the stock of which was held by the family. The house law of the family sometimes dictated the manner in which company shares and administrative posts were allotted to heirs. Although peak holding companies and control by certain families were largely ended during the Occupation, the firms formerly belonging to former zaibatsu complexes have retained their profitable connections. A new managerial class has arisen, owing its position to proven merit rather than family connections, and ownership and management are now largely separated. As in America, ownership of the stock of the leading corporations and investment companies is widespread, and the middle class follows with keen interest the fluctuations of their securities in the stock market.

In most major industries, a few large corporations dominate. For example, only four or five automobile manufacturers contribute to making Japan the world's second largest producer of automobiles and trucks. These few large enterprises also exercise substantial influence over the 100 major trade associations, such as the Shipbuilding Industry Association, and the Coal Association. The "Big Six" (Yawata, Fuji, Nihon Kokan, Kawasaki, Kobe, and Sumitomo), for example, largely control the policies of the Japan Iron and Steel Federation. The Japanese government, like its European counterparts, often favors the formation of cartels, which are believed to improve efficiency in production and distribution and to strengthen Japan's competitive position in the world market.

The peak associational interest groups in Japanese business are the "Big Four": the Federation of Economic Organizations, the Japan Committee for Economic Development, the Japan Federation of Employers' Associations, and the Japan Chamber of Commerce and Industry. The most important is the Federation of Economic Organizations (Keidanren). The Keidanren was organized in 1946 with the encouragement of the government and the Occupation. Its membership includes over 100 major national trade associations and 750 large corporations. It excludes small and medium enterprises, speaking exclusively for big business and using its close ties with the government to influence their interests. Cabinet ministers attend some of its general meetings, and large public and quasi-public corporations, including the Japan National Railways, Japan Air Lines, and the Bank of Japan, are members. The Keidanren's twenty standing committees and its special committees cover every aspect of the national economy and maintain continuous liaison with the government bureaucracy. The president of the Keidanren occupies one of the most responsible and prestigious positions in the Japanese power structure, and his public statements on the economy and politics receive much attention.

The Japan Committee for Economic Development, or Keizai Dō-yūkai, was organized in 1946 by middle-echelon progressively-minded business executives. It has about 1500 individuals as members. Like the Committee for Economic Development in the United States, with which it sometimes cooperates, it constantly reminds business of its responsibility to society at large. The Japan Federation of Employers Association, or Nikkeiren, was founded in 1948 to bring about industrial peace and increase productivity and is still primarily concerned with these objectives. As part of its effort to convey the employers' point of view to the public, it finances a daily newspaper (*Sankei Shimbun*), a television outlet (Fuji Television), and a radio broadcasting company (Bunka Hōsō).

The Japan Chamber of Commerce and Industry was founded in 1878 largely as the result of government prodding. Today it is a federation of 445 local and regional chambers throughout the country, and it represents small industrial, commercial, and financial enterprises as well as big business. Like the other business associations, it is engaged in disseminating the views of business and in lobbying activities with government agencies.

The term *zaikai,* which literally means financial world, is widely used to designate big business in Japan, and has largely superseded the term *zaibatsu,* which connotes the prewar economic structure in which the holding companies of certain families dominated. Often zaikai merely refers to the executives of the big four business associations. The zaikai is regarded as presiding over Japanese society, and it is generally believed that no one can become or remain Prime Minister without at least its tacit approval.[16]

In the United States, the two houses of Congress are largely made up of lawyers. In Japan, businessmen make up the largest occupational group in the Diet. Anywhere between 25 to 35 percent of the members of the House of Representatives are businessmen. Ninety percent of these businessmen are Liberal-Democrats.[17] Thus the business point of view is well represented in the Diet. In this way, the roles of businessman, conservative politician, and Diet member may all be performed by the same individual.

While in the United States it is not uncommon for a businessman to be a political appointee in the bureaucracy, in Japan the reverse is more often the case. When they reach retirement age, bureaucrats

[16] Chitoshi Yanaga, *Big Business in Japanese Politics* (New Haven, Conn.: Yale University Press, 1968), p. 33.

[17] *Ibid.,* p. 78.

often choose to become managing directors, vice presidents, and presidents of big businesses. The move from government to business is referred to as "descent from heaven" (amakudari), reflecting the Confucian tradition that business is a much less exalted calling than public service.[18] As executives of private or public corporations or trade associations, these former bureaucrats are expected to make use of their intimate contacts with the bureaucracy. They serve as effective links between private enterprise and government. Personal friendships and family ties between economic leaders and politicians and small exclusive clubs of the business and political elite are very important informal vehicles by which big business channels its support and demands to the state. "Tea-house politics" and the fund-raising activities of groups organized to support individual politicians have been the legitimate concern of journalists and political scientists.[19] Conflicts of interest are often obviously involved when businessmen, bureaucrats, and politicians engage in overt and covert cooperation. The protection of the public interest and honesty in government are impossible to enforce where face-to-face private relationships of the business and political elite are concerned. The opportunities for political bribery, intrigue, and corruption are ample in Japan. Enterprising newspapermen constantly seek to expose instances of dishonesty, and when these come to light the opposition party makes the most of them. In 1967, following a number of scandals nicknamed the "black mist," the conservative candidates for the House of Representatives for the first time since the war failed to win a majority of the votes cast. Some Socialist politicians have been accused of personally profiting from their connections with firms engaged in trading with Communist China. The widespread belief that neither the conservatives nor the Socialists are primarily concerned with the advancement of the interests of the majority of the people partly accounts for the appeal of the Kōmei (Clean Government) Party sponsored by the Sōka Gakkai.

In spite of its dominant position in Japanese society, business is not monolithic. Competition does exist, though in varying degrees. Small protection. The business community in Osaka struggles for its share of profits, a disproportion of which find their way to Tokyo. Although business is solidly anti-Communist in its ideology, a debate has long been waged within the business-dominated LDP concerning diplomatic and trade relations with Communist China. The government's long-

[18] *Ibid.*, p. 108.
[19] See the excellent discussion of small units, clubs, cliques, and associations in Frank Langdon, *Politics in Japan* (Boston, Mass.: Little, Brown, 1967), pp. 97–126.

standing formula of separation of politics and economics (trade without diplomatic relations) has been the subject of much dispute. China has historically been Japan's principal trading partner, and, if only to assure a potential future market in China, Japanese business must establish its foothold there before the opportunity is closed by other industrial nations.

Japan's phenomenal postwar economic growth is partly the result of the state's responsiveness to the demands of big business. The expansion of production has taken priority over nearly everything else, and in the early 1970s it was widely agreed that more attention must be given to the cleaning up of water, air, and sound pollution, to slum clearance and better housing, the modernization of education, the expansion of social security, and foreign aid. The government's economic policies will be the topic of a later chapter in this book, and we shall not expatiate on these matters here. In examining the relationship of government and business in Japan, several questions inevitably arise: (1) whether big business will permit the state to shift the nation's priorities from high productivity to social welfare and the environmental clean-up, (2) how business will respond to such a shift in priorities if it occurs, and (3) whether Japan's burgeoning military-industrial complex, a by-product of the Vietnam War, will ultimately pose a threat to peace and democracy in Asia as it did in the 1930s.

Each of the Liberal-Democratic candidates in the 1960 election reportedly spent an average of 10,000,000 yen[20] on his campaign, and the Socialist candidates spent an average of 2,500,000, Democratic-Socialists an average of 5,000,000, and Communists an average of 1,-000,000. Possibly over three-fourths of the total funds spent by all parties on campaigns are disbursed by the Liberal-Democrats. The individual candidates get money from their party headquarters, faction leaders, and personal supporters.

In 1955, in order to regularize contributions to political parties, big business established the Conference on Economic Reconstruction whose primary function was to subsidize the Liberal-Democrats, although some aid was to be given to other parties. The organization contributed 20,000,000 yen monthly to the Liberal-Democratic Party, and at election time granted a large sum, amounting in the 1960 election to about 800,000,000 yen. During the six years of its existence, the organization contributed about 3,800,000,000 yen to the Liberal-Democratic Party.[21] In addition, business circles subsidized the various factions of the party. Obviously, since much government activity is concerned with business, it is sometimes difficult to differ-

[20] At the then official exchange rate of 360 yen to one dollar, this would amount to $27,777.77.
[21] *Asahi Nenkan, 1962*, p. 275.

entiate between a bribe and a political contribution. The high cost of subsidizing the party and the adverse publicity resulting from this activity led to the abolition of the conference in 1961. The Liberal-Democratic Party then organized a People's League which raises funds exclusively for LDP candidates. Most of the funds for the support of Socialist candidates come from labor unions.

Each of the great factions in the Liberal-Democratic Party has affiliated with it a fund-raising organization, which usually bears a more or less academic-sounding name. Thus, the Fujiyama faction is supported by the "International Political, Economic, and Cultural Research Association." The faction's funds are spent not only for election campaigns of its members to the Diet but may be generously disbursed during a party convention in order to elect the faction leader as party president.

The Liberal-Democrats are supported by organizations of small business and agriculture as well as by big business. Thus, seven national mass organizations of barbers and cosmeticians, laundrymen and dry cleaners, hotel managers, innkeepers, public bath operators, theater owners, and culinary employees help the party. These groups, of course, expect and often get legislation favorable to them.

The close ties between the zaibatsu and the party politicians in the prewar era tended to discredit political parties and the Diet as organs representing the interests of the masses of the people. The Liberal-Democratic Party is the descendant of both the Seiyūkai Party, which was subsidized by the Mitsui monopoly, and the Minseitō, which was affiliated with the Mitsubishi. Today, the ruling Liberal-Democratic Party is the party of business.

The main source of funds for political activity is big business. Running a poor second are labor unions. Some businesses and business groups help out the Socialist and Social-Democratic Parties as well as the Liberal-Democrats. Sometimes a businessman will contribute to the Communist or Socialist Party. It is as true in Japan as it is in the United States that without money one can get nowhere in politics. Among interest groups in Japan, none wields a political clout comparable to that of big business. It often appears that big business rules Japan through the Liberal-Democratic Party. At any rate, big business, the conservative party, and the bureaucracy function rather smoothly together to govern.

The Predominance of Business

Business is generally recognized as the dominant interest group in Japan; the other interests are not very well organized and it overwhelms all other groups combined. This situation results from the

1945 elimination of the military, which since 1931 had been the dominant group, and from the postwar national focus on productivity. Both the Occupation authorities and the Japanese government emphasized productivity for various reasons: to make Japan less dependent upon the American taxpayer, to reduce social discontent by raising living standards, and to provide logistical support to United Nations forces in the Korean War. Without having to build up their own defense establishment and without having to fight futile wars to defend a colonial empire, the Japanese could concentrate on economic expansion.

Some might argue that comparable economic growth could have been carried out under a socialist rather than a capitalist system. The Japanese generally are not as antipathetic to government involvement in the economy as Americans profess to be. At the end of the war, most railroads and communications systems were already public owned, sweeping economic controls were enforced by the state, and the great holding companies were dissolved. Some expansion of the public sector did occur in the postwar period, although less than in Great Britain, France, and Italy.

Why did Japan ultimately follow the capitalist rather than the socialist line of postwar development? An obvious answer is that both the Occupation and the governments with which it worked favored capitalism over socialism. More important, perhaps, is that the sovereign voters favored the conservative parties, which have consistently held a comfortable majority of the seats in both houses of the Diet. The crucial decision seems to have been made in the 1949 general election when the Liberal Party of the anti-Communist Yoshida won an absolute majority in the lower house, and the conservative Democratic Party won the number two position. The leftist parties together won fewer than one-fifth of the seats. Once it was decided that Japan would remain capitalist, the increase in productivity resulting from the skill, thrift, and hard work of the Japanese benefited the growth of capitalism. The labor union movement, although led by radicals, had to work with the system in order to get wage increases. With the accompanying improvement in the nation's standard of living, there was no popular demand for an experiment with socialism. Capitalism in Japan has many faults, which are constantly exposed in the highbrow journals, and Marxist ideology prevails among intellectuals. However the majority of people have benefited from the postwar productivity and cannot be persuaded of the moral wickedness of capitalism. It may well be that in the future ecological preservation may be given a higher priority relative to productivity, but the fight against pollution is being carried out incrementally, with regulation rather than revolution.

Given the basic importance of the economy to society in the industrial age, it is in the nature of things that the managers of the economy have a powerful voice in the affairs of state. In Japan, of course, the economic managers are the capitalists, and they work closely with the Liberal-Democratic Party and the governmental bureaucracy.

Suggested Reading

Abegglen, James C. *The Japanese Factory: Aspects of Its Social Organization.* Glencoe, Ill.: Free Press, 1958.

Allen, G. C. *Japan's Economic Expansion.* London: Oxford University Press, 1965.

Ayusawa Iwao. *Organized Labor in Japan.* Tokyo: Foreign Affairs Association of Japan, 1962.

Battistini, Lawrence H. *The Postwar Student Struggle in Japan.* Tokyo: Tuttle, 1956.

Colbert, Evelyn S. *The Left Wing in Japanese Politics.* New York: Institute of Pacific Relations, 1952.

Cole, Allan B. *Japanese Society and Politics: The Impact of Social Stratification and Mobility on Politics.* Boston, Mass.: Boston University, 1956.

Cole, Allan B. *Political Tendencies of Japanese in Small Enterprises.* New York: Institute of Pacific Relations, 1959.

Dator, James Allen. *Soka Gakkai, Builders of the Third Civilization: American and Japanese Members.* Seattle: University of Washington Press, 1969.

Dimock, Marshall E. *The Japanese Technocracy: Management and Government in Japan.* New York: Walker, 1968.

Dorsey, Stuart, ed. *Zengakuren: Japan's Revolutionary Students.* Berkeley, Calif.: Ishi Press, 1970.

Earhart, H. Byron, *Japanese Religion: Unity and Diversity.* Belmont, Calif.: Dickenson, 1969.

Farley, Miriam S. *Aspects of Japan's Labor Problems.* New York: John Day, 1950.

Fujiwara Hirotatsu. *I Denounce Soka Gakkai.* Tokyo: Nishinhodo Co., 1970.

Ishida, Takeshi. *Japanese Society.* New York: Knopf, 1971.

Japan: A Businessman's Guide. New York: American Heritage Press, 1970.

Kahn, Herman. *The Emerging Japanese Superstate: Challenge and Response.* Englewood Cliffs, N.J.: Prentice-Hall, 1970.

Levine, Solomon B. *Industrial Relations in Postwar Japan.* Urbana: University of Illinois Press, 1958.

Lockwood, William W. *The Economic Development of Japan: Growth and Structural Change.* Expanded edition. Princeton, N.J.: Princeton University Press, 1968.

Mitchell, Richard Hanks. *The Korean Minority in Japan.* Berkeley: University of California Press, 1967.

Morris, Ivan. *Nationalism and the Right Wing in Japan: A Study of Post-War Trends.* London: Oxford University Press, 1960.

Offner, C. B., and H. Van Straelen. *Modern Japanese Religions: With Special Emphasis upon Their Doctrines of Healing.* New York: Twayne, 1963.

Okochi Kazuo. *Labor in Japan.* Tokyo: Government Printing Bureau, 1958.

Packard, George R., III. *Protest in Tokyo: The Security Treaty Crisis of 1960.* Princeton, N.J.: Princeton University Press, 1966.

Riesman, David, and Evelyn Thompson Riesman. *Conversations in Japan: Modernization, Politics, and Culture.* New York: Basic Books, 1967.

Silberman, Bernard S., ed. *Japanese Character and Culture: Selected Readings.* Tucson: University of Arizona Press, 1962.

Thomsen, Harry. *The New Religions of Japan.* Tokyo: Tuttle, 1963.

Uyehara, Cecil H. *Leftwing Social Movements in Japan: An Annotated Bibliography.* Tokyo: Tuttle, 1959.

White, James W. *The Sokagakkai and Mass Society.* Stanford, Calif.: Stanford University Press, 1970.

Yanaga, Chitoshi. *Big Business in Japanese Politics.* New Haven, Conn.: Yale University Press, 1968.

4

Political Parties

Parties in Modern Polities

That political parties may be found in all modern states, whether democratic or totalitarian, suggests that the parties perform essential functions in contemporary political systems. Almost universally, political parties, with varying degrees of effectiveness, recruit candidates for public office, aggregate demands to form political programs, and inform the public of issues. In two-party or multiparty states, the parties present the voters with competing slates of candidates and platforms from which the voters may choose their public officials and governmental policies. In one-party systems, the voters have little or no choice.

Political parties play such an important role in modern democracies that the vitality of party politics is often regarded as an indicator of the vitality of democracy itself. If political parties did not exist to provide voters with meaningful choices, representative democracy might conceivably be impossible. By eliminating an overabundance of candidates and consolidating a great number of often conflicting demands, the parties provide candidates and programs which can command broad support among the citizenry. If each voter in a large state had to choose among a great number of candidates unidentified as to party, he would find it difficult or impossible to elect officials who could cooperate effectively in the various branches of the government to enact and enforce a coherent program. In modern states, because the public demands that the government act effectively to solve crucial problems, politicians normally have found it expedient to organize into identifiable groups (political parties) which can provide the cooperation in the legislative and executive branches necessary to enact and enforce a program. In modern polities, the original impetus to form a party may come from the executive branch, which wants to ensure the

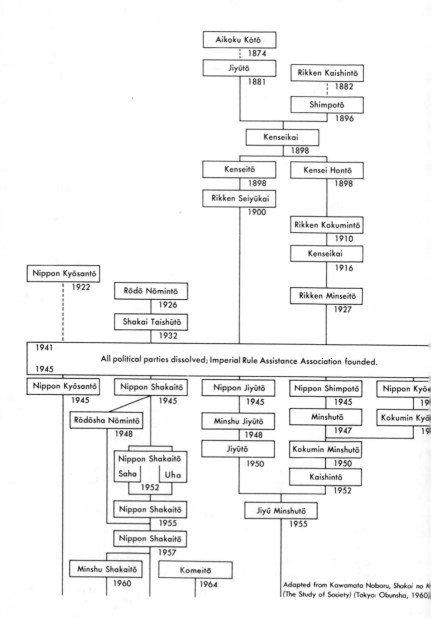

Figure 2

THE EVOLUTION OF JAPANESE POLITICAL PARTIES

Adapted from Kawamata Noboru, *Shakai no K* (The Study of Society) (Tokyo: Obunsha, 1960).

election of a congenial majority in the legislature, or from opposition politicians, who want to win a majority in parliament and seize control of the executive branch.

In the parliamentary-cabinet system of democracy, of which Japan is an example, political parties ideally provide both the ministers in the cabinet and a stable, coherent majority in the parliament to support the cabinet's legislative program. When, for any reason, the parliamentary majority ceases to support the cabinet, the latter resigns or a new parliamentary election is held so that the program and personnel of the cabinet enjoy the support of a stable majority in the parliament.

In Chapter 1, we traced the beginnings of political parties in Japan from their organization in the late nineteenth century through their rise to political dominance in the 1920s, to their decline and demise in the 1930s and early '40s. This history indicates that, at least so far as Japan is concerned, democracy has been strongest when the parties were strong and weakest when the parties were weak.

The political party system is sometimes regarded as a subsystem of the political system which performs essential roles in modern polities, often serving as links between interest groups on the one hand and the authoritative decision-making organs of the government on the other. Thus the structures and functions of political parties are central concerns of the student of government.

The Liberal Party (1945–1955)

The conservative political parties which emerged in 1945 were essentially resuscitations of the prewar political parties which had been dissolved in 1940 at the time of the formation of the Imperial Rule Assistance Association by Prince Konoye. Members of the prewar Seiyūkai, for the most part, formed the Jiyūtō (Liberal Party), while the prewar Minseitō members joined the Shimpotō (Progressive Party). The leadership of both of these parties was drastically affected by the purges of 1946 and 1947 and by the depurge which began in 1949.

The founder of the Liberal Party, Hatoyama Ichirō, originally hoped to bring into a single conservative party all antimilitary, constitutionally liberal elements in the Diet, especially those who were fellow members of the Dōkō Kai, an anti-Tōjō group in the Diet between November, 1941, and May, 1942. The Dōkō Kai had been made up of Seiyūkai, Minseitō, and Shakai Taishūtō (Social Mass Party) people. Only former Seiyūkai members, however, joined Hatoyama's postwar Liberal Party; the rest chose to form parties of their own. When the second postwar Diet opened in November, 1945, the Liberal

Party included forty-six members in the House of Representatives and held second place among political parties. Following the January, 1946, purge directive, the numerical strength of the party in the lower house briefly dropped to eighteen.[1]

The Liberals advocated the popular election of prefectural governors, free trade, and the preservation of the Emperor system. The rival Progressive Party, led by Prime Minister Shidehara, suffered even more from the purge than did the Liberals, and as a result of the April, 1946, election the Liberals emerged as the plurality party in the House of Representatives. On the eve of being appointed Prime Minister to head a coalition government, Hatoyama was purged by direct order of General MacArthur. Hatoyama yielded the presidency of the party to Yoshida Shigeru reportedly on the understanding that when Hatoyama was depurged Yoshida would give up the presidency.

Yoshida Shigeru

Throughout most of its existence, the party was dominated by Mr. Yoshida, who headed the Cabinet from May, 1946, to May, 1947, and four successive Cabinets from October, 1948, to December, 1954. Yoshida was born in Tokyo in 1878, graduated from Tokyo Imperial University, and in 1906 entered the diplomatic service. He became Ambassador to Italy in 1930 and served as Ambassador to Great Britain from 1936 to 1939. His marriage to a daughter of Count Makino Nobuaki, Foreign Minister and Lord Privy Seal, was an additional boon to his career. During the Pacific War, Yoshida was briefly arrested for advocating that Japan make an early peace. He served as Foreign Minister in the Shidehara Cabinet and was Prime Minister both at the time of the promulgation of the new Constitution and on the occasion of the signing of the San Francisco Peace Treaty.

His bureaucratic background and autocratic temper made him scornful of the politicians in the Diet, and he ruled his Cabinets with an iron hand. His diplomatic experience and staunch conservatism enabled him to work harmoniously with the American occupiers. He governed Japan during the extremely difficult period of postwar depression and enforced the harsh and unpopular deflationary policies dictated by the Occupation. He was the butt of relentless criticism by the press and by labor leaders, but could usually ride out crises on the basis of the Liberal strength in the Diet. Yoshida induced a substantial number of able bureaucrats to enter the Liberal Party and run for the

[1] Kenneth E. Colton, "Pre-War Political Influences in Post-War Conservative Parties," *The American Political Science Review,* Vol. XLII, No. 5 (October, 1948), 945.

Diet. This tactic was quite successful, and the Liberal Diet members soon came to include many of Yoshida's bureaucratic protégés. He took full advantage of the Prime Minister's constitutional authority to select and remove Cabinet members and appointed more Cabinet ministers (a total of 118) than any other Prime Minister in Japanese history.

In the general elections of January, 1949, the Liberal Party (then known as the Democratic-Liberal Party) became the first party after World War II to win an absolute majority of the seats in the House of Representatives. It won a majority again in the 1952 election. Following his depurge in 1951, Hatoyama insisted that Yoshida step down from the party presidency. When Yoshida stubbornly clung to his position in spite of his reported promise to Hatoyama, the latter formed an opposition faction within the party. At the time of the 1953 election the "Hatoyama Liberal Party" won thirty-five seats at the expense of the Liberals, who lost their aboslute majority. As a result of corruption involving his immediate associates, the Hatoyama issue, and the rising nationalist feeling, the "pro-American" Yoshida began to lose the support of the business community and of substantial sections of his party. His fifth Cabinet resigned on December 7, 1954, and the leadership of the Liberals passed to the party's former vice president, Ogata Taketora, who died shortly. Yoshida continued to be influential in the councils of the Liberal-Democratic Party and remained a force to be reckoned with in Japanese politics until his death in 1967.

The Democratic (Progressive) Party (1945–1955)

When it was first organized in November, 1945, the Progressive Party claimed to include about 288 Diet members. The vast majority of these, however, had been connected with the quasi-totalitarian Great Japan Political Society (Dai Nippon Seiji Kai), the 1945 successor to the Imperial Rule Assistance Political Society. As a consequence, the 1946 purge deprived the party of all but thirty-two of its Diet members. Most of the members of parliament who remained after the purge had belonged to the prewar Minseitō.[2]

Shidehara Kijuro

Shidehara Kijūrō had been Foreign Minister in the 1920s and early 1930s and had distinguished himself for his "conciliatory" policy towards China. He was presumed to be acceptable to the victorious

[2] *Ibid.,* 943–945.

Allies and was appointed Prime Minister in October, 1945. He was the leader of the Progressive Party at the time of the election of 1946. The Progressives were junior partners in the first Yoshida Cabinet. In 1947, Ashida Hitoshi left the Liberals to join the Progressives in forming an ostensibly new party, the Democratic Party (Minshutō). The Democrats advocated "reformed capitalism" and ideologically stood somewhere between the Liberals and Socialists. The Democrats participated in the coalition Cabinet of the Socialist Prime Minister Katayama in 1947, and in the following year, Ashida headed a Cabinet which included Socialists as well as Democrats. In the meantime, during the controversy over coal nationalization in 1947, Shidehara and some friends left the Democratic Party to form the conservative Dōshi Club. In 1948, the Dōshi Club coalesced with Yoshida's Liberals to form the Democratic-Liberal Party.

Ashida Hitoshi

Ashida Hitoshi was a graduate of Tokyo Imperial University who entered the foreign service in 1912. He was councillor in the Turkish and Belgian Embassies in 1929 and 1930 and retired from the diplomatic service in 1932. In the same year he was elected to the House of Representatives, where he served until his death in 1959. He was president and editor of the *Japan Times,* an English-language daily newspaper, and his well-known liberal views qualified him to serve as Welfare Minister in the Shidehara Cabinet and Foreign Minister in the Katayama Government. He became president of the Democratic Party in 1947 and was Prime Minister in 1948. A series of scandals rocked the Ashida government, and it resigned in October, 1948, after a troubled existence of only seven months.

Inukai Ken, the son of the assassinated Prime Minister Inukai Tsuyoshi, succeeded Ashida to the presidency of the party. Following the Democratic-Liberal Party landslide in 1949, the Democrats split over the question of whether to participate in the third Yoshida Cabinet or to go into the opposition. The coalitionist faction joined Yoshida's Democratic-Liberals. In 1950, the remaining Democrats coalesced with the People's Cooperative Party to form the National Democratic Party (Kokumin Minshutō), under the presidency of Tomabeji Gizō.

In 1952, the party took the name Reform Party (Kaishintō), and Shigemitsu Mamoru, who had recently been released from Sugamo Prison, where he had served a sentence as a war criminal, became the president of the party. He had been Foreign Minister in the wartime

Cabinets of Tōjō and Koiso and had signed the 1945 Instrument of Surrender. The party was again internally divided on the question of cooperation with the Yoshida Cabinet.

Hatoyama Ichirō

In November, 1954, the Reform Party was reorganized to include the Liberal Hatoyama Ichirō and his faction and numerous depurgees. Hatoyama was elected president and Shigemitsu vice president. The reorganized party took the name of Japan Democratic Party (Nihon Minshutō). The Japan Democrats were now even more conservative than the Liberals and wished to demonstrate their independence from America. They declared that their purposes were to "clean up the nation's political life; to achieve complete independence and correct the various reforms inaugurated under the Occupation; to carry out an autonomous people's diplomacy to reduce international tension and to help rehabilitate Asia; to stabilize the people's livelihood through overall planning and to strengthen racial unity and enhance morality."[3]

The resignation of Yoshida's fifth Cabinet in December, 1954, made necessary the designation by the Diet of a new Prime Minister. Since no party had a majority, an interparty understanding was needed to elect a Prime Minister. The Left Wing and Right Wing Socialists gave their votes to Hatoyama on the understanding that he would dissolve the Diet and call for new elections after taking office. The first Hatoyama Cabinet, therefore, was a caretaker Cabinet, lasting only three months. The Democrats won a plurality in the February, 1955, elections.

The Liberal-Democratic Party

The Conservative Merger

The electoral decline of the Liberal Party in 1953, Prime Minister Yoshida's inability to cope with intraparty factional strife, turmoil in the Diet in 1954, and the steady rise of Socialist strength in the Diet convinced the leaders of the business world of the need for political stability and effective leadership. They came to the conclusion that the merger of the Liberal and Democratic Parties was necessary to meet the emerging Socialist threat to capitalism. The bitter struggles between and within the two rival conservative parties were seen as a wasteful

[3] Hugh Borton et al., *Japan Between East and West* (New York: Harper, 1957), p. 17.

diversion of energy which was needed to meet the Socialist challenge. The funds used by the conservatives to carry on their internecine struggles had for the most part been supplied by business, which was becoming tired of seeing its contributions wasted in this fashion. The leaders of the four leading business associations, i.e., the Keidanren, the Dōyūkai, the Japan Chamber of Commerce and Industry, and the Nikkeiren, maintained intimate contacts with conservative politicians and issued public statements demanding more reason and stability in Japan's political life.[4]

After the Socialist Party reunified in October, 1955, the two conservative parties, under pressure from the financial community, finally combined in November, 1955, to become the Liberal-Democratic Party (LDP, or Jiyū-Minshutō, frequently abbreviated to Jimintō).[5] For the first time since the war, the two-party system prevailed in Japan. The new Liberal-Democratic Party had a comfortable majority in the Diet and was evidently in a position to enact its legislative proposals. Since its formation, it has been the governing party.

The Liberal-Democratic Party has been as ridden with factionalism as were the two parties from which it was formed. Therefore, it has not always been able to show a united front against the opposition. In December, 1956, Hatoyama resigned because of ill health, and Ishibashi Tanzan, a former purgee who had been Finance Minister in the first Yoshida Government, was elected party president and designated Prime Minister. After only two months as Prime Minister, he also retired because of illness. Kishi Nobusuke, who had been serving as "Acting Prime Minister" and Foreign Minister, was designated Prime Minister in February, 1957, and chosen party president the following month.

Kishi Nobusuke

Satō Nobusuke was born in Yamaguchi Prefecture in southwestern Japan in 1896. One of a family of ten children, he was adopted by an uncle who could support his education; his name was changed to that of his uncle, Kishi, whose daughter he later married. After a brilliant record at Tokyo Imperial University, Kishi Nobusuke entered the Ministry of Agriculture and Commerce. As an advocate of greater controls over the economy, he was a leader of the "new bureaucrat"

---

[4] These highly influential organizations are described in Chapter 3.

[5] For the details, see Chitoshi Yanaga, *Big Business in Japanese Politics* (New Haven, Conn.: Yale University Press, 1968), pp. 121–128. English-language newspapers in Japan very often use the term "Tories" to designate the Liberal-Democrats. Of course, the Japanese conservative party has a very different tradition from the Conservative Party of Great Britain.

faction. In 1932, he was appointed Vice Minister of Industry in the Manchukuo Government, where he fostered cooperation between the Japanese military and the zaibatsu. In 1941, he became Minister of Commerce and Industry in the Cabinet of Tōjō Hideki and was a signer of the declaration of war against the United States. At the end of the war he was arrested as a war crimes suspect by the Allied authorities, but the Tokyo war crimes trial ended before Kishi was brought before the court. Kishi was released from Sugamo prison in December, 1948, but was not removed from the list of purgees until April, 1952, when Japan regained her independence.

Satō Eisaku was a leader in Yoshida's Liberal Party when his brother Kishi was released from prison and helped Nobusuke to enter the party in 1953. However, Kishi was expelled from the Liberal Party because of his anti-Yoshida intrigues. He helped to organize first the Japan Democratic Party and then the Liberal-Democratic Party. Owing largely to the sudden death of Ogata and the illnesses of Hatoyama and Ishibashi, Kishi became Prime Minister in 1957. Shortly after the Girard incident, in which an American GI killed a Japanese woman, he visited President Eisenhower and addressed a joint session of Congress. Although he was not able to obtain the return of the Ryukyu and Bonin Islands to Japan, he persuaded the Americans to withdraw their ground forces from Japan.

Kishi's capacity for fund raising and backstage maneuvering accounted for much of his success in politics. To the political left and to much of the center he became a symbol of all that was worst in Japanese political life: a "war criminal" and a self-seeking politician more solicitous of the well-being of the capitalists who financed him than of the common people. He was one of the most widely disliked Prime Ministers in Japanese history and a scapegoat for popular frustrations. Americans, however, were prone to regard him as a repentant convert to democracy and a dependable advocate of the anti-Communist alliance. During his administration, notwithstanding the existence of gross economic inequalities, Japan became more prosperous and attained a higher average standard of living than ever before in her history. Kishi was forced to resign in 1960 as a result of Socialist opposition and mass demonstrations on the one hand and the ambitions of rival faction leaders in his own party on the other.

Ikeda Hayato

A principal political rival of Kishi, Ikeda Hayato, was born in 1899 in Hiroshima Prefecture, the youngest son of a sake-brewer. He graduated from Kyoto Imperial University and distinguished himself as a tax expert in the Finance Ministry. He was one of the bureaucrats recruited by Yoshida to run for the Diet in 1949. He won a seat and became Finance Minister in Yoshida's third Cabinet. There he enforced the stringently deflationary Dodge Plan and a policy of close economic cooperation with the United States. He was one of the six Japanese who signed the Japanese Peace Treaty in San Francisco in 1951. In addition he served as Minister of International Trade and Industry in the fourth Yoshida Cabinet, Minister of Finance in the Ishibashi Cabinet and first Kishi Cabinet, Minister without portfolio in the second Kishi Cabinet, and Minister of International Trade and Industry in the second Kishi Cabinet (reconstructed). He was notorious for his bureaucratic cold-heartedness and lack of tact and, in 1952, was forced to resign his ministerial post as a result of a vote of no confidence provoked by an undiplomatic remark.

Ikeda had close and cordial ties with financial circles. In 1960, he was elected to succeed Kishi as party president with the support of Yoshida Shigeru and Satō Eisaku over the strong opposition of the vice president, Ōno Bamboku, and the executive board chairman, Ishii Mitsujirō. Five days later, the Diet designated him as Prime Minister. As Prime Minister, Ikeda was distinguished by his "low posture," which contrasted with Kishi's "high posture"; he avoided Kishi's uncompromising tactics in dealing with the opposition.

Ikeda advocated the welfare state and a strong economy based on private enterprise, which was necessary to finance the welfare state. His policy was to double the national income within ten years. When ill health forced Ikeda to resign after only four years in office, the goal of doubling the national income had been largely fulfilled.

Satō Eisaku

On November 9, 1964, the ailing Ikeda announced his resignation and the nomination by party leaders of Satō Eisaku as the sole candidate to succeed him as party president. Satō became Prime Minister on the same day and was elected LDP president by acclamation on December 1.

Satō, like his elder brother Kishi Nobusuke, studied at Tokyo Imperial University. In 1924, he entered the Transportation Ministry, where he rose to the position of Vice Minister. Unlike Kishi, he was neither indicted as a war criminal nor purged from public office at the end of the war. He became Chief Cabinet Secretary in Yoshida's second Cabinet in 1948. He retired from the bureaucracy, joined the Liberal Party, and in 1949 he was elected to the House of Representatives from Yamaguchi Prefecture. He immediately became Secretary

General of the Liberal Party, and in 1951 he became Minister of Electric Communications[6] in Yoshida's third Cabinet. In 1952, he became Minister of Construction and concurrently Minister of State in charge of the Hokkaido Development Agency in Yoshida's fourth Cabinet. In 1953, Satō, then Liberal Party Secretary-General, was the central figure in the "shipbuilding scandal" which rocked the political world. Many Diet members and government officials were arrested in connection with the handling of political contributions. The order for Satō's arrest was blocked by the Minister of Justice on direct instructions of the Prime Minister. Yoshida resigned the following year, and Satō went into eclipse. Satō re-emerged in 1958 as Finance Minister in his brother Kishi's second Cabinet, and served as Minister in charge of the Hokkaido Development Agency and the Atomic Energy Agency in Ikeda's third Cabinet. He became Prime Minister in 1964 and, by the summer of 1970, had served as LDP president longer than any of his four predecessors and as Prime Minister of Japan longer than anyone since Yoshida, his erstwhile sponsor. His capable handling of the problem of turmoil in the universities, the automatic continuation of the United States–Japan Security Treaty and his arrangement with Nixon for the reversion of Okinawa helped to account for his unprecedented election to a fourth term as party president in October, 1970. In 1971, Satō's prestige was rudely shaken when President Nixon, without first consulting the Japanese government, announced his plan to visit Communist China and later imposed a 10 percent surcharge on imports.

LDP Organization

In the United States, party membership, whether Republican or Democratic, is simply a matter of individual choice: there is no formal requirement to become or to remain a "member" of the party. A principal privilege of party affiliation is to participate in the selection of delegates to the state and/or national party conventions and in the selection of party nominees for public offices. In Japan, party membership is more formal; one is expected at least to pay dues, although some members may be behind with their payments. In Japan, the members of a party are not to be confused with those who vote for the party's candidates. Thus with about 561,622 members,[7] the LDP attracted about 22,381,000 votes in the 1969 lower house election.

[6] This Ministry existed only from June 1, 1949, to July 31, 1952.

[7] As of August 31, 1969, *Asahi Nenkan, 1970,* p. 277. The LDP had 744,914 members on November 30, 1970 (*Asahi Nenkan, 1971,* p. 284).

In Japan, no governmentally enacted law prescribes the organization of political parties. The formal organization of the LDP is outlined in the party regulations which were enacted by the party itself. There is a prefectural federation in each of the forty-six prefectures, with headquarters in the prefectural capitals. Each federation has a chief, secretary general, executive council, policy affairs research council, organization committee, and other organs which correspond fairly closely to organs in the national headquarters in Tokyo. Throughout the country, making up the prefectural federations, are about 500 party branches.

The most important LDP official is the president. Because the Liberal-Democrats have consistently controlled a majority of the seats in both houses of the Diet since the party's inception, they have sufficient votes to elect (the Constitution says "designate") their president as Prime Minister of Japan.[8] The foregone conclusion that the LDP president will almost inevitably become Prime Minister arouses intense public interest in the struggle for the LDP presidency.

The LDP president's term of office is two years, but, as in the cases of Ishibashi and Ikeda, ill health may make resignation necessary before the completion of a full term. An LDP member normally must have been elected to the Diet quite a few times to acquire the seniority necessary for serious consideration as party president, so that the presidents are apt to be rather old men, and their health may become a problem.

The president is elected at a party conference. There is no formal procedure for nominating candidates, but it is generally known which faction leaders are running and which are supporting someone else. The electors are the LDP members of the lower and upper houses and forty-six delegates, each representing a prefectural federation. Voting is by secret ballot, and if no one wins a majority on the first ballot, there is a run-off election between the two leaders on the first ballot. The vote of an elector is normally determined by how his faction has decided its members will vote, but the secret ballot allows some electors to stray from the path of factional loyalty. Candidates generously spend money to sway the electors, and the faction leader with the most money is therefore a leading contender for party presidency. Although the incumbent LDP president, who is concurrently Prime Minister, obviously has a great advantage over his rivals, the intraparty factional rivalries are often such that the re-election of the incumbent president is not always a sure thing.

No single faction has ever controlled enough votes to elect its leader, and it has been necessary that a coalition of factions somehow be

---

[8] For the legal procedure for selecting the Prime Minister, see Chapter 6.

formed to support a single candidate. Sometimes, two candidates may agree to deliver their votes on the second ballot to whichever of the two gets the more votes on the first ballot. The election is an extremely tense affair, and rumors of intrigue, deals, and betrayals are usually rife.[9] In late 1964, when it became necessary to select a new president because of Ikeda's illness, it seemed most undesirable to aggravate the interfactional bitterness which had been exacerbated by the presidential election of the preceding July. Party leaders therefore agreed to nominate a president through private consultations. Satō Eisaku was their choice, which was immediately confirmed by a vote of LDP Diet members and later by acclamation at a party conference.

In 1966, Satō was elected president for a second term and in 1968 for a third term according to normal procedure by the party conferences. In the 1968 election, the results were as follows:

Satō Eisaku	249
Miki Takeo	107
Maeo Shigesaburo	95
Fujiyama Ai-ichiro	1
Invalid	2
Total	454

In October, 1970, Satō was re-elected to an unprecedented fourth term as LDP president. Satō received 353 votes, while Miki, his only opponent, won 111.

Besides the president, the leading officials of the party are the secretary general, the chairman of the executive council, the chairman of the policy research council, and the vice president (a post sometimes left vacant). The party president usually appoints these men just before he (in his capacity as Prime Minister) chooses the members of his Cabinet. In this manner, the party officers together with the Chief Cabinet Secretary are able to advise the Prime Minister on appointments to the Cabinet.

The secretary general must be especially hard-working and influential since he must normally be aware of everything of any importance happening in the party, being largely in control of the party bureaucracy. With the finance accounts bureau chief and the chairman of the finance committee, the secretary general controls party finances, collecting funds and disbursing them largely as they please to defray the campaign expenses of worthy party members.[10] The secretary general appoints the twenty parliamentary vice ministers and the chairman of

[9] For graphic accounts of recent presidential elections, see Nathaniel Thayer, *How the Conservatives Rule Japan* (Princeton, N.J.: Princeton University Press, 1969), pp. 148–179.

[10] *Ibid.*, p. 277

the standing and special committees of the lower house.[11] Obviously, the experience and contacts gained as secretary general are useful to an ambitious politician in reaching the party presidency and with it the prime ministership.

It has been mentioned that the chairman of the policy research council is one of the most important officers of the party. This council is made up of fifteen divisions consisting entirely of LDP Diet members. Party regulations require that every LDP Dietman serve in one of the divisions. The chairman and vice chairmen of the divisions are chosen by the secretary general of the party in consultation with the chairman of the policy affairs research council. The divisions correspond roughly to the ministries in the government and also to the standing committees of the upper and lower houses of the Diet. They are: cabinet, regional administration, defense, justice, foreign affairs, finance, education, social welfare, labor, forestry and agriculture, marine products, commerce and industry, transportation, communications, and construction. Many of the divisions have ad hoc subcommittees to deal with particular problems. In addition, many special committees and investigative commissions exist outside of the divisions. Evidently the proliferation of committees is a response to pressures by interest groups. In Japan, as elsewhere, the demand for action is often met by the establishment of a committee.

Public policy in Japan is largely first formulated within the divisions and committees of the LDP policy research council. The divisions maintain contacts with the ministries, which draft appropriate bills. In the Diet standing committees and Diet plenary sessions, the division members advocate and support the policies which they had initiated in their divisions. It is said that the divisions and committees in the policy research council are of greater importance than the Diet committees because the former are the main scene of interest demands and policy making.[12] The executive council is the formal decision-making body of the LDP. It usually confirms the decisions of the leading party executives and committees.

The many officers and organs of the LDP, only some of which have been described above, impose a strict discipline on the LDP members of the Diet. Once the party organization has determined its policies, the LDP members are expected to vote almost automatically for the bills which implement these policies. With a monopoly of the posts in the Cabinet and with stable majorities in both houses of the Diet, the Liberal-Democratic Party rules Japan.

[11] *Ibid.,* p. 279.
[12] Frank Langdon, *Politics in Japan* (Boston, Mass.: Little, Brown, 1967), p. 134.

Factions in the LDP

The Liberal-Democratic Party, as we have seen, is dominated by the LDP Diet members and the central party organs located in Tokyo. Its many branches throughout the country, however, are not in themselves sufficiently large and well funded to get out the votes necessary to win majorities in the two houses of the Diet. Individual LDP candidates must rely on their own personal supporters and on their factions in order to succeed politically. Since 1960, the supporter organizations (kōenkai) of individual candidates have grown considerably in number, size, and importance. A candidate with a strong kōenkai to raise funds and campaign for him is correspondingly less dependent on the party. At the same time, money and effort that might otherwise be channeled into the local party organization are expended on the kōenkai. Similarly, the funds which are raised by factions leave less money to go to the party.

The history and functioning of the Liberal-Democratic Party show it to be an amalgam of factions. Some of the LDP factions preceded the formation of the LDP in 1955, and occasionally when a faction leader dies, the faction remains intact to be inherited by one of his followers, as was the case of the Ikeda faction, later the Maeo faction. To win a Diet seat, a politician needs the endorsement of his party, and he needs money. Since party endorsements are determined at the party headquarters by conferences among faction leaders, the politician must normally adhere to one or another faction. Having been endorsed, he needs money to campaign. Since the party rarely can supply even one-third of what he needs, he looks to his faction leader for financial assistance, since the faction leaders are distinguished from their fellows by their unusual ability to collect contributions. In order to get a ministership in the Cabinet, the support of a faction is essential. And finally in order to become party president and Prime Minister, a candidate needs the votes of not one but several factions. Thus factions perform absolutely essential functions at various stages of the electoral process, so that politicians must remain loyal to them and work through them.

As we have seen, factions vote as blocs in party presidential elections. The factions supporting the party president are referred to as mainstream factions, those opposing the president are known as anti-mainstream factions. Other distinctions are sometimes made, depending upon the power interrelationships within the LDP. Every time there is an election for the upper or lower house, the relative strengths of the factions change. These changes in factional strength are usually reflected in changes in the composition of the Cabinet. Some faction leaders are more talented than others in attracting new blood into their factions. Nakasone Yasuhiro, a man to watch in the next few years, has been particularly effective in this regard.

The 1969 election brought about the following changes in factional strengths in the lower house:[13]

	Before 1969 Election	After 1969 Election
Satō	50	61
Maeo	41	44
Miki	37	39
Nakasone	25	35
Fukuda	26	29
Kawashima	17	19

Because members of rival LDP factions often compete for votes in the same electoral districts, the factions often work at cross purposes with each other, resulting in the waste of money and effort. However, no single faction is either rich enough or influential enough to sponsor candidates in more than a fraction of all of the lower house electoral districts. The relation between a faction leader and his followers resembles the relation of oyabun and kobun (boss and henchmen) depicted in samurai movies, where the feudal loyalties owed to the overlord are exalted. Ever since the LDP was founded, factions have been excoriated as corrupt and undemocratic by journalists and reformers, and their abolition is frequently called for. But until more effective means of party financing and leadership recruitment have been devised, the factions will probably remain.

The Program and Prospects of the LDP

Because the LDP has governed Japan ever since 1955 and probably will continue to do so for at least a few more years, the LDP program is the program of the government. Many of the government's policies are discussed elsewhere in this book, and we shall merely mention here some of the themes which the LDP has stressed in the recent past.

---

[13] *Japan Times,* December 29, 1969. LDP faction strengths at the time of the formation of the third Satō Cabinet in January, 1970, were as follows: Satō, 63; Maeo, 43; Miki, 39; Fukuda, 37; Nakasone, 35; Kawashima (now Shiina), 19; Sonoda, 13; Ishii, 13; Funada, 11; Murakami, 10; Fujiyama, 6; Ishida, 4; formerly affiliated with Matsumura, 3 (*Asahi Nenkan, 1971,* pp. 284–286). The Maeo faction later became the Ohira faction.

In 1969, the LDP promised to end the extreme disruption and violence on university campuses, which it blamed on radical leftists. Their platform advocated such policies as the following: The reform of the university system and educational system should be considered, but student violence should not be tolerated; while university officials should be expected to curb campus unrest, violence should be ended, and if necessary the police might be called onto the campus; law and order should be maintained; the Security Treaty with the United States, the basis of peace and of Japan's security, should be continued in effect; Japan's self-defense should be consolidated; the participation of Okinawans in national politics should be rapidly realized; a system of allowances for children should be inaugurated; taxes should be greatly reduced, centering on a cut in the taxes of salaried men; the reversion of the northern territories (the Kurile Islands, etc.) should be pressed for.

The LDP platform should perhaps be evaluated differently from the platforms of other political parties. Being the party currently in power and being the only party with any prospect of forming a government in the near future, the LDP is expected to implement the policies it advocates and cannot politically afford to advance policies in an electoral campaign which it cannot possibly carry out later. Unlike the LDP, none of the opposition parties stands the remotest chance of forming a one-party government in the next five years, and these parties may therefore promise everything to everyone without being held responsible for delivering on their utopian promises.

The public may thus discount the opposition platforms as so much ideological baggage, irrelevant to the immediate problems of the day. At the same time, if an interest group really wants the government to take positive action, it appreciates the need to do business with the LDP.

The future of the Liberal-Democratic Party is dimmed by the gradual decline of its percentage of the popular vote. Although the absolute number of LDP votes between 1955 and 1970 in lower house elections has remained constant between 22.3 million and 23.4 million, the Kōmeitō and Communists have been gaining electoral strength. In 1967 and 1969 the LDP votes were less than a majority (48.8 percent and 47.6 percent, respectively). For the time being, the electoral system converts the LDP electoral plurality into majorities in the two houses of the Diet, and the conservatives are aware that the time may come when, in order to form a government, they may have to enter into a coalition. The declining Socialist Party is ideologically incompatible with the conservatives, and the most likely partners in an LDP-led coalition would be the Kōmeitō and the Democratic-Socialists. All three parties are unequivocally anti-Communist and have often collaborated in the Diet and in local politics. The LDP leaders, although indebted to big business for campaign funds, are well aware that their political future depends on their responsiveness to public opinion.

The Socialist Party

The Socialist Party (Shakaitō) was organized in November, 1945, from remnants of the prewar Laborers and Farmers Party, the Farmers Party, and the Socialist Mass Party. None of these parties had ever enjoyed substantial electoral success before the war, partly because of government suppression of their activities, especially after the passage of the 1925 Peace Preservation Law. Prominent organizers of the postwar Socialist Party were Kagawa Toyohiko, the Christian socialist leader, Abe Isoo, the founder of the Japan Socialist Party in 1901, and Takano Iwasaburō, of the former Socialist Mass Party. Almost every shade of utopian, Fabian, and Marxian socialism was represented in the membership. At the time of its formation, the Socialist Party claimed seventeen members in the Diet, but most of them were purged in 1946. In the election for the lower house held in the same year, the Socialists won nearly 18 percent of the votes and ninety-two seats. The Socialists welcomed the liberal SCAP-draft Constitution and voted for it in the Diet in 1946.

From the beginning, the postwar Socialists have rejected Communist efforts to form a united front, but in late 1946 and early 1947, they joined in mass rallies calling for the resignation of the Yoshida Cabinet, which was becoming increasingly unpopular as the result of its failure to solve the economic crisis. In the 1947 electoral campaign, the Socialists advocated state control of the coal, iron, steel, and fertilizer industries, preparatory to state ownership. Although the Yoshida Administration succeeded in passing an electoral law unfavorable to the parties of the left, the Socialists managed to win a plurality of 143 seats in the House of Representatives. Over a month was required to form a Cabinet, originally intended to be a four-party coalition (Socialists, Liberals, Democrats, and People's Cooperatives), but at the last minute the Liberals backed out.

Katayama Tetsu

Katayama Tetsu, Chairman of the Socialist Party, headed the coalition Cabinet. Katayama was a Christian labor lawyer, college lecturer, and author of books on law; he had been elected several times to the

Diet in the 1930s. He was not an aggressive and dynamic leader, but his broad tolerance and unquestioned honesty were necessary to hold the widely divergent factions in the party together. As a concession to other parties in the coalition, left-wing Socialists were excluded from the Cabinet. The Prime Minister had the difficult, and as it ultimately proved, impossible job of keeping the left-wing Socialists and the Democrats both happy at the same time. The Socialists proposed the nationalization of the coal industry but had to modify their stand because of the reluctance of the other coalition parties. After much wrangling in the Diet and within the coalition parties, a mild Temporary Coal-Mining Bill was passed.

A great controversy broke out over the dismissal of the Socialist Minister of Agriculture and Forestry, Hirano Rikizō, whose subsequent purge was widely believed to be politically motivated. The Cabinet appeared unable to meet the economic problems which it faced, and when the left-wing Socialists opposed the financial policies of the Katayama Administration, the only Socialist-led Government in Japan's history came to an end. Left-wing as well as right-wing Socialists participated in the short-lived Ashida Government, but the Socialist Party was compromised by the implication of some of its leaders in the financial scandals which came to light at that time.

The 1949 election was disastrous for the Socialists, whose strength in the House of Representatives dropped from 143 to forty-eight. The issue of the peace settlement split the party into a right wing, under the leadership of Asanuma Inejirō, and a left wing, led by Suzuki Mosaburō. The right-wing Socialists supported the San Francisco Peace Treaty but opposed the Security Treaty with the United States, while the left wing, which advocated a peace with the Soviet Union and Communist China as well as with the non-Communist nations, opposed both pacts.

Socialist Reunification

In October, 1955, the Socialists reunited into a single party with Suzuki as chairman of the central executive committee and Asanuma as secretary general. In the four years following its reunification, the Japan Socialist Party (JSP) gained strength in the electorate and in the Diet, becoming the opposition in what seemed to be a "two-party system." (The Communist Party had almost no seats.) In the 1958 election the Socialists won 166 seats, their most ever. Some observers speculated that the Socialists, who seemed to appeal more effectively than the conservatives to youth, might in a few years bring an end to the conservative dominance and form a Cabinet, if need be by forming some kind of coalition. However, in 1960, a small right-wing faction led by Nishio Suehiro seceded to form the Democratic Socialist Party (DSP). Factional disputes continued to rage over questions of ideology and party offices through the 1960s. Often party conferences were thrown into complete turmoil. The rise of the Kōmeitō in the late 1960s appears to have cut deeply into Socialist strength. In the 1967 general election, the Democratic-Socialists and Kōmeitō won twenty-five and thirty seats respectively, suggesting that the two-party system was giving way to a multiparty system. In the 1969 general election, the three minor opposition parties (Kōmeitō, DSP, and JCP) won a total of ninety-two seats, while the Socialists won only ninety. The Socialists no longer held a majority of the opposition seats, and with no indication that they could halt their decline, their position as leader of the opposition was gravely weakened. The Kōmeitō became the party to watch. The trend to multipartyism appeared now to be hurting the Socialists a great deal more than it was hurting the LDP.

Factionalism prevents the Socialist Party from presenting a clear, constructive program to the voter. Under the present electoral system, the Socialists do not have enough confidence to nominate candidates for even half of the seats in the lower house. Thus it has not been mathematically possible for the Socialists to win a majority in the House of Representatives.

The main support for the Socialists comes from the Sōhyō labor confederation, white collar employees, civil servants, and intellectuals. The Socialists appeal very little to farmers, who fear that the radical ideology might result in the collectivization of agriculture. Much of the party's support is in the nature of protest against the economic hardships which many people in Japan suffer, notwithstanding the postwar recovery. The Socialists make a strong appeal for the peace vote in Japan by advocating the termination of the security treaty with the United States and the "normalization of relations with China," i.e., the recognition of Communist China. Also, moderates sometimes vote Socialist to register their opposition to the "reactionary" proposals of the conservatives, such as rearmament, centralization of control over the police and education, and constitutional revision. So long as the conservatives are prevented from winning a two-thirds majority in either house of the Diet, the amendment of the Constitution can be prevented.

Personal and ideological factions have been a constant threat to the unity of the party. Ideologically, the Socialists include dyed-in-the-wool orthodox Marxists who advocate the revolutionary overthrow of capitalism as well as revisionists, radical and moderate labor leaders, humanitarians, neutralists, and assorted do-gooders. The question of relations with the Communist Party is often troublesome, the left-wing Socialists being more prone to united front activities than the right. Being too heavily dependent on the radical Sōhyō labor confederation for support, the Socialists often pursue policies which alienate other elements of the population.

In the 1960s much internal dispute concerned "structural reform" advocated by the personable Eda Saburo with the support of younger elements in the party. Structural reform was never clearly defined but seemed to imply that a take-over of the government by the Socialists was not a prerequisite to ameliorating the lot of the people; rather, the Socialists would seek to force concessions favorable to the people from the conservative government. The structural reformers also insisted on broadening the appeal of the party to attract the middle classes in addition to organized labor. Sasaki Kōzō, a principal left-wing leader and ideologist, has constantly attacked structural reform as revisionism and a betrayal of sound Marxist principles. Eda, who is a popular television personality, has from time to time served as secretary-general of the party.

After 1965, when the JCP began to break away from the Chinese Communists, leftist leaders in the JSP began to demonstrate strong Maoist sympathies. Some were even accused of profiting from the trade of pro-Peking firms. The Maoist leaning of the leftist leaders scandalized many members of the party as well as many other Japanese as the excesses of the proletarian cultural revolution became known in Japan. The Socialist Youth League engaged in extremely violent behavior on campuses and streets from 1967 to 1970. The failure of the JSP to restrain their youth corps was said to be a principal reason for the party's poor showing in the Tokyo Metropolitan Assembly election in 1969, when they lost their number one place to the Kōmeitō, and did badly in the lower house election in the same year.

The Japan Socialist Party is much more radical than socialist parties in European countries. Whereas the Socialist International is committed to opposition to Communist expansion and the support of NATO, the Japanese Socialists advocate a policy of neutrality and have declared their friendship with the Russian and Chinese Communists and opposition to "American imperialism."

The JSP frequently sends delegations to conferences with Communist leaders in foreign countries. For example, in 1969 and 1970 official JSP delegations visited Rumania, East Germany, North Korea, and the U.S.S.R. Especially after the Japanese Communists broke with Moscow in 1964 and then with Peking in 1966, Japanese Socialists as well as Communists have been representing Japan in the councils of world communism. The Japanese Socialists are committed to "peaceful revolution" to overthrow capitalism and establish socialism but have not unequivocally renounced the use of extraparliamentary methods to achieve their goals.

The JSP platform in 1970 provided that the fundamental task of the party in the present stage of capitalist development is to realize a socialist society by carrying out a peaceful revolution through the democratic and peaceful reformation of capitalism. The revolution is to be carried out by acquiring an absolute majority in the Diet, using democratic procedures without relying on violence or arms. The Socialist Party would obtain political power on the basis of support by democratic institutions and the organizations of workers, farmers, and the general citizen strata, stabilize its authority, and convert the capitalist society into a socialist one.

The Socialist Party would assume the task of restoring the complete independence of Japan. It would achieve complete economic independence in peace, restore territorial sovereignty, dissolve the United States–Japan Security Treaty and Administrative Agreement, revise unequal treaties, and regain diplomatic autonomy. As to the character of the party, it would be a class-mass political party, a unified body of working strata comprising the majority of farmers, fishermen, middle and small merchants and industrialists, intellectuals, and others, but centering on the working class.

The Socialist Party, throughout this stage of realizing socialism in Japan and afterward, would rise to power without abandoning democracy; the freedoms of speech, assembly, association, religion, and conscience; completely secret, equal, and free elections, etc. These democratic freedoms would be protected above all by socialism. The Socialists would welcome the free criticism of the people and the existence and criticism of opposition parties; the return and transfer of power would be determined by the free will of the people.[14]

The program described above was virtually identical with what it had been ten years previously. The political and diplomatic situation in Japan, however, had changed substantially, as in the greater prosperity of the country, the rise of the Kōmeitō, the Vietnam war, Nixon's Guam doctrine, and the imminence of the reversion of Okinawa to Japan. Talk of establishing a Socialist government and establishing a socialist society had a hollow and irrelevant ring in the early 1970s in the light of the Socialist setbacks in 1967 and 1969. Socialist proposals for the elimination of pollution, university unrest,

[14] As summarized in *Asahi Nenkan, 1971*, p. 287.

and other problems perforce have a utopian character so long as the party has no prospect of attaining political power nationally.

Socialist Party Organization

The political parties of the left (JSP, DSP, and JCP) are similarly organized on the top level. Each has a national convention (taikai) made up of delegates of local party units and of affiliated organizations. The convention elects a central executive committee, a chairman of the central executive committee, and a secretary-general. The convention normally adopts a party platform. The central executive committee handles the affairs of the party between conventions and supervises the secretariat. The secretariat is assisted by a number of committees and bureaus, each of which is normally headed by a member of the central executive committee. The national party headquarters is in Tokyo. Here the party officials, bureaucrats, and journalists (the parties sponsor newspapers and magazines) carry on their activities in close proximity to the Diet. The competition for top party posts is intense, and sometimes, in order to avoid internecine warfare, it is necessary to leave certain top party posts vacant or to set up some kind of regency for an extended period.

The Socialist Party has been defective in local organization. In large measure organized labor makes up for this deficiency. In the 1958 election, 73 percent of the Socialist candidates sponsored by Sōhyō were elected, 68 percent of the Socialist candidates sponsored by Zenrō, the other leading labor federation, were elected, and 84 percent of the Socialists jointly sponsored were elected. At the same time, Socialist candidates not sponsored by organized labor did very poorly.[15] The Japanese Socialist Party is widely regarded as a mere appendage of the Sōhyō. Nevertheless, the Socialist Party has sometimes been successful in recruiting members and getting votes from farmers and small businessmen. For example, in the 1971 upper house election, the Socialists apparently won the support of many farmers who had been angered by the government's reducing the price of rice. The prefectural organizations appear to be relatively indifferent to the doctrinal disputes which seem important on the national level.

At the end of 1970, the party had only about 34,000 members, about 15,000 fewer than it had ten years before. In the 1969 lower house election its candidates drew 10,074,000, or 21.5 percent, of the

[15] Robert A. Scalapino and Junnosuke Masumi, *Parties and Politics in Contemporary Japan* (Berkeley and Los Angeles: University of California Press, 1962), p. 98.

votes cast and won only ninety seats as compared with 140 seats two years before. The Socialists may have halted their losing streak in the June, 1971, upper house election when they increased their seats in that chamber from sixty-one to sixty-six.

The Democratic-Socialist Party

The reunification of the Socialist Party in 1955 by no means eliminated the ideological and personal feuds that had constantly plagued the Socialist movement even in the prewar era. In the 1959 House of Councillors election, the Socialists received a million fewer votes than they had won in the 1956 election. Many party members became greatly disenchanted with the principles and policies sponsored by the leadership. The Socialist International, which included most of the Socialist parties of the world, had been discarding the Marxian doctrine of basing the Socialist Party on a single class and had assumed an increasingly strong anti-Communist attitude. The Japan Socialist Party, on the other hand, was quite out of step with the trends of the world Socialist movement. It advocated a policy of neutrality and appeared to support anti-Americanism and pro-communism. Furthermore, it seemed too willing to resort to unparliamentary tactics. The failure of the Socialist Party to win popular support outside of organized labor was apparently making it impossible to win majorities in the two houses of the Diet.

In October, 1959, a group within the Japan Socialist Party led by Nishio Suehiro, who had been Vice Prime Minister in the Ashida Government, issued a statement that "there is an urgent desire in Japan for a democratic socialist party which, while abiding by parliamentarianism, will fight both extreme leftists and rightists, and promote the general welfare of all sections of the working people, without special favor or partiality to labor unions." The members of the "Socialist Reconstruction League" led by Nishio formally seceded from the Socialist Party to organize a "genuine" Socialist Party.

The Democratic-Socialist Party (Minshatō) was formally founded at a meeting in Tokyo in January, 1960. The nucleus of the party was made up of about fifty erstwhile Socialist members of the Diet. The moderate Zenrō labor confederation threw its support to the new party. Nishio Suehiro was elected chairman of the executive committee and former Prime Minister Katayama became supreme adviser. The party leaders proclaimed their opposition to capitalism and totalitarianism of both left and right and their determination to emancipate all members of society from oppression and exploitation and to establish a society which would guarantee respect for the individual and the free development of the human character. The new party would be a people's party rather than a class party as advocated by the left wing of the Socialist Party and the Sōhyō leaders.

The Democratic-Socialists opposed the 1960 United States–Japan Security Treaty on the ground that it would strengthen the military alliance between the two countries. However, during the course of the antitreaty struggle, the Democratic-Socialists, consistent with their policy of defending parliamentary government, refused to resort to boycott and violence to oppose the treaty as did the Socialists. The Democratic-Socialists were therefore widely accused of being half-hearted and insincere in their opposition to the Security Pact and of playing into the hands of the conservatives.

At the first meeting of the Democratic-Socialist Party in January, 1960, Nishio charged that the Socialist Party suffered from the illusion that a Marxist revolution was possible in Japan. At the same time, he said, the conservative Liberal-Democratic Party had degenerated into the political agent of big business. The goal of the new party was to give political expression to the aspirations of a vast segment of the nation including impoverished farmers, fishermen, and small businessmen whose voices had not been heeded by either the Liberal-Democrats or the Socialists.

The Democratic-Socialists recognized that the society in which they lived was capitalistic, Nishio said. They did not propose to overthrow it overnight but would try to change it gradually by piling up patiently one small reform upon another, one improvement upon another. Nishio proposed the practice of political tolerance: totalitarianism, either left or right, stifled opposition. The Democratic-Socialists intended to achieve socialism through democratic methods; the essence of democracy was the belief in the value of dissent and of efforts of persuasion.[16]

In the campaign for the 1960 election, the Democratic-Socialists stressed their devotion to orderly parliamentary government in contrast to the unparliamentary tactics of the Liberal-Democrats and the Socialists.[17] They advocated an economic program that would make all Japanese into members of the middle class. However, the 1960 election for House Representatives was a disaster for the Democratic-Socialists. Although they won 8.8 percent of the votes, they won only 3.6 percent of the seats. The party representation in the lower house dropped from forty members to a mere seventeen, and even former Prime Minister Katayama went down in defeat. In 1961, the Demo-

[16] *Japan Times,* January 25, 1960.
[17] The author is indebted to Mr. Nishio for the privilege of discussing with him in 1960 the program of the Democratic-Socialist Party.

cratic-Socialists cooperated with the Liberal-Democrats in the formulation of the Antiviolence Bill, thus alienating themselves from much of the left. Nevertheless, when the bill was brought up in the House of Councillors, certain leading Liberal-Democrats allowed it to be blocked by the Socialists, much to the chagrin of the Democratic-Socialists, whose political future was closely tied to the measure. The Democratic-Socialists lost five of their sixteen seats in the 1962 House of Councillors election, and their prospects seemed very bleak.

The Democratic-Socialists have managed to build up very slowly their electoral strength from about 2.5 million votes in 1960 to 3.6 million in 1969. As a result of the 1969 election, the party had thirty-one seats in the lower house, and after the 1971 election it had thirteen seats in the upper house. Its membership of 50,000 is about equal to that of the JSP. Its main support comes from the moderate Dōmei (former Zenrō) labor union confederation and socialist intellectuals who find the apparently pro-Communist stance of the JSP unacceptable. Although it advocates socialism and the gradual abolition of Japan's alliance with the United States, on some important issues, most notably the 1965 Japan–South Korea treaty, it has collaborated with the Liberal-Democrats in the Diet. It also cosponsors with the LDP candidates for some local chief executive posts in opposition to the Communists and Socialists. This collaboration has, in the view of some observers, reduced the DSP to the status of a satellite of the LDP. When the Kōmeitō won forty-seven seats in the House of Representatives in 1969, it took from the DSP the position of number three party in the lower house. The Kōmeitō thus appears to be superseding the DSP as the middle-of-the-road party and potential partner for coalition with the LDP in the future.

The Kōmeitō

The Kōmeitō (Clean Government Party) is unique among Japanese political parties because it is sponsored by a religious organization, the Sōka Gakkai. The Sōka Gakkai, described in the preceding chapter, is the extremely influential layman's affiliate of the Nichiren Shōshū (sect) of Buddhism. At its inception, the Kōmeitō attracted virtually all of its votes from among the members of the Sōka Gakkai, but since 1967, it seems to be gathering votes from non-Gakkai people as well. The foreign observer is tempted to compare the Kōmeitō with the Christian democratic parties in Western Europe, which are informally connected with the Roman Catholic Church. The European Catholic Parties, however, have much longer histories, more established traditions, and more practical experience in politics; furthermore, they project a much clearer image. Their members have frequently headed governments. The Kōmeitō, on the other hand, has not yet obtained a plurality of seats in the national Parliament, much less occupied a position in the Cabinet, so that we can only conjecture what that party would do if it ever seized political power.

The Sōka Gakkai first entered politics in 1955, when its Culture Department sponsored candidates in local elections and 98 percent of its candidates won seats. In 1956, it sponsored six candidates for the upper house, three of whom won seats. Three years later, 272 of its 304 candidates in local elections won seats, and in the House of Councillors election, all six of its candidates were elected. In voting in the national constituency of the upper house, 8.5 percent of all the ballots were cast for Sōka Gakkai candidates. Thus the Gakkai had surpassed the Communists' popular appeal. In 1961, the Culture Department was raised to the status of a bureau, and a new Political Department was created within that bureau. Later the same year, the Kōmei Seiji Remmei, or Kōseiren (League for Fair Politics), was established as a political organization formally separate from the Sōka Gakkai.[18] In the 1962 upper house election the Kōseiren won seven seats in the national constituency and two in the prefectural constituencies and surpassed the Democratic-Socialists to become the number three party in the upper house.

The national constituency of the upper house provided an ideal opportunity for the Sōka Gakkai. Every three years, fifty nation-at-large seats were at stake, and each voter cast his ballot for one candidate, making it possible even for a small minority element to elect at least one or two candidates. In the 1950s and early 1960s, the Gakkai abstained from lower house elections, where there was much less chance for a small group to win seats. The Kōseiren claimed to be above the corruption and dishonesty of partisan politics and to represent the interests of all of the people rather than of self-seeking politicians and of the labor unions and capitalists represented by the Socialists and Liberal-Democrats. The Kōseiren leader said that they were not interested in putting up candidates for the undignified lower house (where incidentally, the electoral system seemed unfavorable to the Sōka Gakkai).

In 1964, the Gakkai issued a statement entitled "Demands of the Times and of the People," calling for the creation of a new political party. The people's distrust of politicians, the egoism and ideological bankruptcy of youth, the political corruption, the abstention of Gakkai

---

[18] James W. White, *The Sōkagakkai and Mass Society* (Stanford, Calif.: Stanford University Press, 1970), pp. 133–134.

members from lower house elections (where there were no Gakkai-sponsored candidates), and the wishes of the Gakkai's Youth Division were all cited as reasons for founding a new party.[19] Thus in November, 1964, the Kōseiren was dissolved and the Kōmeitō was established. The Kōmeitō would be a full-fledged political party, putting up candidates for the lower as well as upper houses of the Diet.

In 1967, the Kōmeitō won twenty-five seats in the House of Representatives and in 1969 it nearly doubled its representation to forty-seven, outstripping the Democratic-Socialists to become the third largest party in the House of Representatives. In Tokyo politics, the Kōmeitō has become a major force. In the 1963 Tokyo gubernatorial race, the Gakkai backed the successful conservative candidate who was also supported by the much more influential LDP. Possibly to counter criticism that the party was reactionary like the LDP and to clarify its image as a true middle-of-the-road party, the Kōmeitō in 1967 sponsored its own candidate for the governorship. In the three-way race with the Kōmeitō candidate and the LDP-sponsored candidate, the candidate supported by the Socialists and Communists won. Although its candidate lost badly, as had been expected, the Kōmeitō's participation had perhaps affected the outcome of the election: if it had not sponsored a candidate and Gakkai members had been free to choose between the conservative and progressive candidates, the outcome of the election might have been different.

In the 1970 gubernatorial election in Kyoto, the Kōmeitō joined the LDP and DSP to sponsor a candidate to oppose the incumbent supported by the Communists and Socialists. The Kōmeitō thus compromised its independent image, but it insisted that in national politics it was in opposition to the LDP. The Kōmeitō and Communist parties had just distinguished themselves in the 1969 lower house election as the two growing parties and were seen to be in direct confrontation in the Kyoto election. The victory of the progressive incumbent was especially embarrassing to the Kōmeitō.

As of November, 1970, the Kōmeitō had 106,000 party members. It is not necessary to be a member of the Sōka Gakkai to join the Kōmeitō. In late 1971 it had forty-seven seats in the lower house and twenty-three in the upper.

The central concern of critics of the Kōmeitō is the question of whether or not the party would, if it got the power to do so, establish Nichiren Shōshū as the officially favored religion of the Japanese state. During the 1930s and World War II, the government had enforced a kind of state of religion, focused on the purported divinity of a Japa-

[19] *Ibid.*, pp. 136–137.

nese race and the Emperor, and there is adequate precedent for the establishment of a state religion. The Sōka Gakkai leaders and followers are intense, often fanatical believers and consider the propagation of their faith their highest duty in life; they might be sorely tempted to use the authority of the government to favor their kind of Buddhism over all other sects in Japan, Christian and Shinto as well as Buddhist. However, some of their leaders were imprisoned for their religious professions during the war, and the Sōka Gakkai declares its support for the new Constitution, which provides that the Emperor is a symbol, not a god, and that the state and religion shall remain separate. Evidently in order to assuage some of the fears, in 1970 all of the leading officers in the Kōmeitō resigned their leadership positions in the Sōka Gakkai, and it was declared that the two organizations were separate. Before it met, the Kōmeitō was expected to formulate in its 1970 Congress an official explanation of its relationship with the Sōka Gakkai, but it failed to do so.

In districts where the Kōmeitō does not sponsor candidates, the support (or lack of it) of the Kōmeitō may be crucial to the success of conservative or Socialist candidates. Politicians are therefore wary of criticizing the Kōmeitō. By threats of boycotts, the Kōmeitō has frightened publishers from printing books and articles critical of the party.

As the party attempts to enlarge its constituency beyond the Sōka Gakkai, it must perforce cast off the image of sectarian narrowness and favoritism, and it has already made steps in this direction. In order to acquire enough political influence to initiate important legislation, it will have to demonstrate wisdom and acumen. If it becomes an effective, pragmatic political party, sensitive to the needs of the great majority of the population and capable of participating in the government without insisting on special privileges for the Nichiren Shōshū, it may represent a positive force for democracy.

The Japan Communist Party

"Peaceful Revolution"

On October 4, 1945, MacArthur ordered the Japanese government to release the Japanese who had been imprisoned for political offenses; among those freed were the veteran Communist leaders Tokuda Kyūichi and Shiga Yoshio. The Communists reorganized the party and immediately made themselves widely unpopular by demanding the trial of the Emperor as a war criminal and the abolition of the Emperor system. In January, 1946, Nosaka Sanzō (Okano Susumu) returned from Yenan, the Chinese Communist capital, where he had been engaged in the Communist indoctrination of Japanese prisoners of war. Nosaka urged that the Party make itself "lovable" and tone down the anti-Emperor agitation. Communists rapidly infiltrated the nascent labor unions. They emphasized peaceful rather than violent revolution, and in the April, 1946, election won five seats in the House of Representatives.

The Communists had hailed the Allied Occupation troops as liberators, and it appeared to many Japanese that General MacArthur, in giving the Communists freedom to speak, organize mass demonstrations, and publish their own newspapers, favored the communization of Japan. But following a demonstration in Tokyo on May 19, 1946, MacArthur and the Emperor both issued warnings against violent demonstrations. The Communists drew up a constitution for the establishment of a Japanese People's Republic and were the only party in the Diet to vote against the draft Constitution supported by General MacArthur. Communists in the labor movement led in organizing a general strike to be carried out on February 1, 1947. The Communists were apparently aiming to overthrow the Yoshida Cabinet and to form a people's front government in which they would participate. Shortly before the deadline, the Supreme Commander for the Allied Powers issued an order to the labor leaders to call off the strike, and when they reluctantly did so, the Communist leadership lost much prestige.

In 1947 and 1948, the failure of the Socialists in the Katayama Cabinet to socialize the economy and solve urgent economic problems and the scandals which besmirched the Ashida coalition discredited the Socialist and Democratic Parties. As the voters turned away from the moderate left and center, Japanese politics were polarized. In the 1949 election, the Liberals under Yoshida won an absolute majority, and the Communists won 10 percent of the votes and thirty-five seats, to become the fourth largest party in the House of Representatives. No doubt an important factor was that the Communist Party appeared to many voters to be the only real opposition party, since the Liberals, Democrats, and Socialists had all been carrying out the policies of the Supreme Commander. A vote for the Communists was a protest vote not only against the bourgeois parties and ineffectual Socialists, it was also a vote against the policies of the Occupation. Occasionally labor disputes, in which Communist agitation figured prominently, resulted in violence. For example, during the railroad strike in 1949, Shimoyama Sadanori, president of the Japanese National Railways, was found lying across the tracks in Tokyo, murdered and with one arm and both legs cut off. There were two instances of derailments in which people were killed. General MacArthur urged Yoshida to outlaw the Communist Party. The Prime Minister, despite his strong anti-Communist attitude, took the view that to outlaw the party on the authority of SCAP would not provide a permanent solution and that proposed legislation banning the party would meet serious obstacles. Yoshida preferred to rely on the voters to repudiate the Communist Party, whose activities made it increasingly unpopular.[20]

Cominform Criticism and Violent Revolution

The legal labor union and parliamentary activity of the Communists seemed to be paying off. Nosaka and other Communist leaders had repeatedly emphasized their faith in the possibility of a "peaceful revolution" to achieve socialism. But in January, 1950, the Japan Communist Party was suddenly shaken by an article in the organ of the Cominform, *For a Lasting Peace: For a People's Democracy,* which attacked Nosaka Sanzō as a servant of American imperialism with a bourgeois attitude.[21] The Cominform accused Nosaka of spreading the false notion that peaceful transition to socialism was possible in Japan during the Occupation. Nosaka's theory, the Cominform charged, had nothing whatever in common with Marxism-Leninism, and was both undemocratic and antisocialist; it served only the imperialist occupiers in Japan and the enemies of independence.[22]

The Cominform criticism seemed to confirm the views of leftist elements in the Japanese Communist Party, such as Shiga Yoshio, who had for some time been warning against "right-wing opportunism." The success of Communist armed revolution in China and Southeast Asia raised serious doubts in the minds of many Japanese Communists as to the efficacy of their soft line. Sharp factional disputes arose within the party, especially between the "internationalists" and the "mainstream faction," but following a purge of dissident elements, the party rallied around its triumvirate—Tokuda, Nosaka, and Shiga, in that order. The Communists embarked on a campaign against "American imperialism" which, they said, was converting Japan into a military base, restoring fascism and the police state in Japan, and subjugating the Japanese economy to the dictates of Wall Street—monopoly capitalism. On May 30, 1950, Communist-inspired demonstrators stoned and mauled American military personnel in Tokyo, and when the Japanese arrested were tried by Allied authorities, the

---

[20] Shigeru Yoshida, *The Yoshida Memoirs: The Story of Japan in Crisis* (Boston, Mass.: Houghton Mifflin, 1962), pp. 234–236.

[21] Murakami Kanji, *Nihon Kyōsantō* (Japan Communist Party) (Tokyo: Hobunsha, 1956), pp. 69–79.

[22] Rodger Swearingen and Paul Langer, *Red Flag in Japan: International Communism in Action 1919–1951* (Cambridge, Mass.: Harvard University Press, 1952), p. 199.

Communist daily *Akahata* (Red Flag) referred to the culprits as "patriots."

On June 6, 1950, the Supreme Commander directed Prime Minister Yoshida to purge from political life the twenty-four members of the central committee of the Japan Communist Party.[23] Seventeen editors of the *Akahata* were also disqualified. Instead of reporting regularly to local authorities as they were required to do under the purge order, some of the central committee members went "underground," i.e., into hiding, and some escaped to the Asiatic continent. MacArthur's action was only one phase of the great "Red Purge." The Japanese government, information media, and industry took informal steps to remove Communists and fellow travelers from their jobs. In 1949, 10,793 were removed from government posts. By October, 1950, 690 persons in broadcasting, news agencies, and newspapers had been dismissed, and 9,514 workers in private industry had lost their jobs, making a total of 20,997 dismissals.[24]

When war broke out in Korea on June 25, 1950, and the *Akahata* and other Japanese Communist publications turned out propaganda favoring the cause of the North Korean Communists, the Japanese Communist papers were banned. The Communists were evidently planning an armed uprising against the "American imperialists" in Japan so that American troops could not be spared to fight in Korea.

The Communists made political capital of the unpopular repressive measures of the Yoshida regime and took a conspicuous part in the demonstrations against the Subversive Activities Prevention Bill. On May 1, 1952, they instigated a riot on the Palace Grounds against the measure, and in the course of the disturbance, blood flowed and American automobiles were set afire.

In the October, 1952, election, the Communists, whose violent tactics had alienated the people and whose leaders had been banned from public life, lost all of the seats that they had held in the House of Representatives.

Peaceful Coexistence and the Sino-Soviet Dispute

In 1955, after the Korean War and the Occupation had ended, the Japanese Communist leaders came out of hiding. The Soviet Union began peace talks with Japan, and Nosaka resumed the "peaceful

[23] Portions of the letter are cited in Hans H. Baerwald, *The Purge of Japanese Leaders under the Occupation* (Berkeley and Los Angeles: University of California Press, 1959), p. 19, and in Courtney Whitney, *MacArthur: His Rendezvous with History* (New York: Knopf, 1956), pp. 309–310.

[24] Baerwald, p. 79n.

revolution" line. Tokuda Kyūichi had died in Peking in 1953, and Nosaka was the undisputed leader of the party. One Communist was elected to the House of Representatives in the 1953 election, two in 1955, one in 1958, and three in 1960. There has always been at least one Communist in the House of Councillors, and following the 1962 election there were four.

The JCP was notably successful in influencing the student and peace movements. During the 1960 protests against the United States–Japan Security Treaty, the mainstream leaders of the Zengakuren national student organization were radicals who had been expelled from the Party in 1958 for left-wing adventurism, while the less violent anti-mainstream leaders were in good standing with the JCP. The rival student factions took somewhat different lines of action during the 1960 riots, reflecting contrasting views on the possibility of peaceful coexistence. Within the JCP itself, ideological storms were brewing, as might be expected in light of the bewildering shifts in party line from peaceful to violent revolution and back again.

When the world Communist movement was initially shaken by the Sino-Soviet dispute about Albania, in 1961, the Japanese Communist leaders naturally feared that the emerging controversy in world communism might exacerbate the divisions already afflicting the JCP. They assumed a neutral attitude and tried to mediate between Moscow and Peking. At the same time, they insisted on the right of each national Communist party to make up its own mind on issues, inferentially supporting a view which, although ostensibly neutral, denied the pre-eminence of the Communist Party of the Soviet Union. The Soviet policy in the Sino-Indian war in 1962 and the partial nuclear test-ban treaty in 1963 intensified the Sino-Soviet dispute, as China accused the USSR of ganging up with the United States against China in an effort to rule the world jointly by maintaining a nuclear monopoly.

In May 1964, when the test-ban treaty was presented for approval to the Japanese House of Representatives, the JCP could no longer avoid being counted on this hot issue. Four of the five Communist Representatives voted against the treaty but Shiga Yoshio voted for it, thus exposing a serious rift in the party. The JCP Central Committee voted to expel both Shiga and Suzuki Ichizō, of the House of Councillors, for actively supporting the treaty in opposition to the party line. Shiga and Suzuki refused to accept the legality of their expulsions and refused to resign their seats in the Diet as the party demanded. They and two other expelled party leaders organized the "Japan Communist Party (Voice of Japan)." They claimed to represent orthodox communism in contradistinction to the Peking-oriented leadership, which they referred to as the "Japan Communist Party (Yoyogi)." (Yoyogi is the section of Tokyo in which the party maintains its headquarters.) The Soviet Union was reported to be supplying the Voice of Japan with funds, and Yoyogi complained that the Soviet Union was interfering in Japan's internal affairs. However, the Voice of Japan was unable to attract a significant following. At the same time, the Soviet Union complained of anti-Soviet activities in the Japan-Soviet Friendship Society. Yoyogi published bitter anti-Soviet diatribes in its daily *Akahata* and other organs, which Peking frequently reprinted.

In 1965, the disastrous defeats suffered by the Peking-oriented Communists in Indonesia and Ghana and the escalation of the Vietnam conflict could not be ignored by the JCP. Early in the following year, Secretary-General Miyamoto Kenji led a JCP mission to North Korea, Communist China, and North Vietnam to unite world communism in order to halt "American imperialism." The North Koreans and North Vietnamese were very cordial to the Japanese mission. The Chinese, however, insisted that a united front with the Soviet Union to resist America was impossible, because the Soviet Union was actually collaborating with the United States. The Chinese insisted that the JCP carry out a violent revolution in Japan and accept the thought of Mao Tse-tung as the supreme authority in Marxism-Leninism. As the Proletarian Cultural Revolution swept through China, relations between the Japanese and Chinese comrades began to cool.

By mid-1966, the JCP adopted a policy of "autonomy and independence." Yoyogi began to denounce "sectarian dogmatism" (an alleged heresy of Peking) with the same fervor it had been denouncing Soviet revisionism. A "Japan Communist Party (Liberation Front)," led by Shida Shigeo denounced the Miyamoto leadership for its "petty bourgeois revisionism," and in reply, the *Akahata* accused the Shida group of "ultra left-wing adventurism and flunkeyism towards the Communist Party of a certain foreign country." Nishizawa Takaji, the son-in-law of the late JCP Secretary-General Tokuda Kyūichi, denounced the Yoyogi line and was expelled in late 1966. He and his wife reviewed a Red Guard rally in Peking as honored guests of Mao Tse-tung. His monthly magazine, *The Study of the Thought of Mao Tse-tung* carried letters from all over Japan critical of the revisionist Miyamoto leadership.

In Peking, Japanese Communist youths, evidently inspired by the Chinese Red Guards, beat up the *Akahata* correspondent and the JCP representative. In 1967, the JCP recalled the two men. Just before they left China they were beaten by Red Guard demonstrators, and they received medical treatment at a stopover in North Korea. The *Akahata* complained bitterly of the "unjust attacks, intervention, and wrecking activities" provoked against the JCP by the "extreme-left, opportunist, big powerism elements in the Chinese Communist Party."

Thus the Cultural Revolution led to a break with Peking. A drift back towards Moscow seemed to be in the making, but the Soviet military occupation of Czechoslovakia in 1968 dampened the JCP's enthusiasm for a reconciliation. In 1970, the posture of the JCP, like that of the North Korean and North Vietnamese Communists, continued to be neutrality and autonomy in the Sino-Soviet dispute. The Japanese Socialists often are on better terms with Peking and Moscow than is the JCP. But the supreme irony is that China and the Soviet Union both seem more friendly toward Japanese capitalists than toward Japanese Communists. The eagerness of the Russians and Chinese to trade with Japanese capitalists and to cultivate conservative Japanese politicians, largely ignoring the ideological fulminations of the JCP against these groups, will probably remain an exasperation for the Japanese comrades for years to come. In addition, the Sino-Soviet dispute and Cultural Revolution have irreparably shattered the monolithic unity of international communism, and it seems unlikely that the JCP, having savored and benefited from independence from foreign dictation, will soon again subject itself to alien domination.

Since 1961, the program of the party has declared that the revolution confronting Japan is a new people's democratic revolution against two enemies: American imperialism and Japanese monopoly capitalism. The central tasks of the party are to oppose the warlike, reactionary, and racist policies of these enemies and to form a democratic united front, on the basis of which a people's democratic government would be established. This government, a democratic dictatorship of the people, centering on the workers and farmers, would unite with the forces of world peace, democracy, and socialism, fulfill the tasks of independence and democracy, block the revival of political and economic control by monopoly capitalism, abolish monarchy by basically reforming reactionary state functions, create a people's republic, and establish a people's democratic state system with the Diet as the highest organ of the state. At the stage of monopoly capitalism, the task of the revolution in Japan is to prepare the way for the transition to socialist change, thus hastening the development of a socialist revolution aimed at the complete abolition of the capitalist system.[25]

Thus the Japanese Communists are committed to united front tactics and a two-stage revolution with the idea of ultimately communizing Japan through participation in a transitional regime which they would dominate. This line was followed in the establishment of "people's democracies" in Eastern Europe and the People's Republic of China.[26]

---

[25] *Asahi Nenkan, 1971,* p. 291.
[26] Cf. Mao Tse-tung, *On New Democracy* (Peking: Foreign Language Press, 1954).

Whether or not the JCP plans to resort to violence in order to achieve its successive goals is a crucial question. In 1955, the party renounced left-wing adventurism and has since avoided advocating violence. However, in practice, the mass demonstrations led by Communists and Socialists, particularly the Security Treaty riots in 1960, have often resulted in clashes with the police. The JCP, like the Socialists, are willing to use extraparliamentary tactics to obtain political goals. They emphasize the importance of the freedoms of speech and assembly and advocate revolutionary goals, but when violence breaks out they blame the police or left-wing "adventurists." In the widespread university disorders in 1968 and 1969, the Communist-connected student leaders were less violent than Socialist, Trotskyite, and Maoist elements, and occasionally were able to mediate between the ultraradicals on the one hand and moderates and school administrators on the other. Thus the Communists, like the Japanese military in the 1930s, can pose as advocates of law and order while extreme militants professing a similar ideology engage in violent revolution. In the 1969 lower house election following leftist turmoil on campuses all over Japan, the Socialists suffered a massive defeat partly because of their inability to control the violent Socialist Youth League, while the Communists, who were able to maintain discipline in their Democratic Youth League, increased their seats from five to fourteen.

The JCP has constantly proclaimed its devotion to democratic freedoms ever since World War II, but in countries ruled by Communists such freedoms have been extinguished. The Japanese public are very much attached to their constitutional freedoms and are understandably concerned that a Communist take-over would end freedom in Japan. In 1969, Kurahara Koreto, speaking for the Central Committee, asserted that even when the Communist Party assumes political authority it will permit anti-Communist parties to exist and to enjoy the freedoms of speech, press, and assembly provided that these opposition parties do not advocate illegal counterrevolutionary measures. However, once the Communists were in power, presumably they would define illegality, and in light of the record of world communism, few informed people could be taken in by Communist professions that they detest violence and love freedom. They advocate double standards: it is peaceful for Communists to use force unlawfully to seize power, but a government which lawfully uses force to stop them is guilty of violence; once in power, Communists are free to do whatever they wish, but anti-Communists are permitted only the freedom to obey. Totalitarianism has had little appeal in Japan since 1945. Insofar as the Communists have enjoyed any political success, it has been because they have capitalized on urgent concrete issues such as the controversial alliance with America and the Okinawa question. However, these issues can be invoked with equal success by other opposition parties, and they are issues that the conservative government is often in a position to defuse or to co-opt.

Party Organization

The All-Japan Communist Party Congress formally constitutes the supreme authority within the party. Since 1958, it has been the policy to convene the Congress every two years. Delegates are elected by party members through their local organizations. The Congress formulates the party platform, discusses governing regulations, and lays down the principles of political action. In view of its size and infrequency of its meetings, the Congress is unable to initiate policy. The principle of "democratic centralism" applies, i.e., after free discussion, policies are determined by majority vote, but control is from the top down and everyone is required to carry out and support party policies.

The Congress elects the members and alternates of the central committee. The central committee in 1966 consisted of sixty-six regular members and forty-two alternate members—a total of 106. As of 1971 Nosaka Sanzo was its chairman. It meets at least once every three months. Its directorate consists of eleven regular members and eight alternates. This inner circle of old-timers runs the party with an iron hand. The eighteen-member secretariat of the central committee is headed by the secretary-general (Miyamoto Kenji as of 1971), who is regarded as the most powerful individual in the party.

The numerous party publications include materials in foreign languages. The principal of these is the *Akahata* (Red Flag), which in 1970 published 400,000 copies daily and 1,450,000 copies on Sunday. One of the main duties of the party members is to sell this newspaper, which not only propagates the party view among the public but brings in substantial revenue to the party. The other principal party publications are the monthly theoretical journal, *Vanguard* (*Zen-ei*) and *Materials on World Politics* (*Sekai Seiji Shiryō*). Members of the party are required to contribute 1 percent of their monthly salary as dues, and the Communist Party is second only to the LDP in the funds at its disposal for political activity. During the early Occupation, when medicines were in short supply, Communists sold santonin, an antituberculin drug, apparently smuggled from Russia, in order to raise money. Communists have reportedly peddled heroin and other narcotic drugs smuggled from Communist China, and the Russian circus and ballet, during their tours in Japan, are said to have contributed their receipts to the JCP.

The party claimed about 300,000 members in 1970, and in recent years they have been organized in about 13,000 cells, 239 district committees, and forty-six prefectural committees. In the 1969 lower house election, the JCP won 6.8 percent of the votes (as compared with 4.8 percent in 1967) and fourteen seats (as compared with five seats in 1967). The Communists were jubilant when they won 12 percent of the votes cast in the prefectural constituencies in the 1971 upper house election. In late 1971, the party occupied fourteen seats in the House of Representatives and ten seats in the House of Councillors, making it the number five party in both houses.

The disparity between the percentage of votes received and percentage of seats won is greater for the JCP than for any other party, and it appears that the JCP suffers more than the rest from the nature of the electoral system. However, unlike the Kōmeitō, the JCP sponsors many candidates whom it does not expect to win, so that Communist-inclined voters are sometimes induced to throw away their votes on hopeless Communist candidates. The JCP does best in the national constituency of the upper house, where its proportion of the seats most closely approximates its proportion of popular votes. It does most poorly in the prefectural constituencies of the upper house; in 1971, with twelve percent of the vote it won only one of the 76 contested seats.

Communist views are widely disseminated in Japan and are supported by the other parties of the left, which may be influenced by Communist positions. Communists are very active in the peace and student movements and seem to exercise influence substantially in excess of that suggested by their small representation in the Diet. The party has made an impressive comeback since the bleak days of the mid-fifties when it was seeking to cast off the violent image which it had acquired following the Cominform criticism in 1950. The secessions of rightist and leftist elements in the 1960s have evidently not greatly hurt the party. It remains to be seen whether the JCP can ever again win thirty-five seats in the House of Representatives as it did in 1949 or whether it can grow much beyond its present parliamentary strength in the face of the rise of the Kōmeitō.

Japan's Political Party System: An Evaluation

With the December 1969 election, Japanese politics entered a new era. The two-major-party system had begun with the reunification of the Socialist Party and the amalgamation of the two conservative parties into the Liberal-Democratic Party in 1955. The Democratic Socialists and the Kōmeitō had not yet come into existence, and the Communists had been thoroughly discredited by their commitment to violence. In the late 1950s the LDP electoral strength began to erode and Socialist strength grew so that for a while it appeared possible that the Socialists might, within a decade or so, become the governing party. But in 1960, some right-wing Socialists seceded to form the DSP, and the Sōka Gakkai (and later its Kōmeitō) became prominent in politics. The JCP slowly began to recoup its losses. Both the JSP and the LDP began to lose electoral strength, and with the 1967 election, the trend towards multipartyism became noticeable. This trend continued in the subsequent elections. In the 1969 general election, the Socialists lost their majority position among the opposition parties. The sudden increase of Kōmeitō and Communist strength suggested that in the future the leadership might pass to the Kōmeitō. In the meantime, the opposition remained fragmented among four ideologically incompatible parties, while the LDP ruled the country largely unchecked. Prime Minister Satō's foreign and domestic policies, which had fostered economic growth and were accomplishing the reversion of Okinawa, had been vindicated by a plurality of the electorate. The LDP seemed pretty well entrenched in power, and within that party, Satō had been strengthened. Satō was elected for a fourth term as his party's president in late 1970 and would likely retain the prime ministership until 1972. Possibly the one-and-a-half party system, in which the conservative party was the permanent government and the Socialist Party the permanent opposition, had been replaced, not by a multiparty system but by a single-party-dominant system in which one party permanently held power while the opposition was in disarray.

The Japanese party system differs in a number of important respects from the party system in the United States. First, since the Japanese parties function in the framework of the parliamentary-cabinet form of democracy, they concentrate their energy on the election of members of parliament and are not involved in nominating presidential candidates. Second, the Japanese parties do not have strong grass roots. They are thought of primarily as organizations of politicians rather than as organizations of ordinary citizens. Third, internal personal and ideological factionalism has been a constant threat to the unity and even to the continued existence of the political parties. Fourth, whereas the American parties become active on a national basis only once every four years for a presidential election, Japanese parties are perennially busy preparing either for a lower house election, which usually occurs every two or three years, or for an upper house election, which occurs regularly every third year. Fifth, the Japanese political

Table 1

House of Representatives Election Results

	April 10, 1946	April 25, 1947	January 23, 1949	October 1, 1952	April 19, 1953	February 27, 1955
Liberal-Democratic						
Progressive (Democratic)	94	121	69	85	76	185
Liberal (Democratic-Liberal)	140	131	264	240	199	112
Hatoyama Liberal					35	
Cooperative (People's Cooperative)	14	29	14			
Socialist	92	143	48			
Right-Wing Socialist				57	66	67
Left-Wing Socialist				54	72	89
Democratic-Socialist						
Labor-Farmer			7	4	5	4
Communist	5	4	35	0	1	2
Kōmeitō						
Minor Parties	38	25	17	7	1	2
Independent	81	13	12	19	11	6
Total seats	464	466	466	466	466	467

	May 22, 1958	November 20, 1960	November 21, 1963	January 1, 1967	December 27, 1969
Liberal-Democratic	287	296	283	277	288
Progressive (Democratic)					
Liberal (Democratic-Liberal)					
Hatoyama Liberal					
Cooperative (People's Cooperative)					
Socialist	166	145	144	140	90
Right-Wing Socialist					
Left-Wing Socialist					
Democratic-Socialist		17	23	30	31
Labor-Farmer					
Communist	1	3	5	5	14
Kōmeitō				25	47
Minor Parties	1	1			
Independent	12	5	12	9	16
Total seats	467	467	467	486	486

Table 2

House of Councillors Election Results

(Figures in parentheses refer to the prefectural constituencies. Figures not in parentheses refer to the national constituency.)

Date	Total	Democratic Party	Liberal Party	Kokumin Kyōdō Party	Socialist Party	Democratic-Socialist Party
April 20, 1947	100 (150)	6 (22)	8 (30)	3 (6)	17 (30)	
June 4, 1950	56 (76)	1ᵃ (8)ᵃ	18 (34)		15 (21)	
April 24, 1953	53 (75)	3ᵇ (5)ᵇ	16 (30)		11 (17)	
		Liberal-Democratic Party				
July 8, 1956	52 (75)	19 (42)			21 (28)	
June 2, 1959	52 (75)	22 (49)			17 (21)	
July 1, 1962	58 (78)	21 (48)			15 (22)	3 (1)
July 4, 1965	52 (75)	25 (46)			12 (24)	2 (1)
July 7, 1968	51 (75)	21 (48)			12 (16)	4 (3)
June 27, 1971	50 (7_)	21 (4_)			11	4

Date	Laborers' and Farmers' Party	Communist Party	Ryokufukai	Miscellaneous	Independent
April 20, 1947		3 (1)		6 (7)	57 (54)
June 4, 1950	1 (1)	2	6 (3)	1 (2)	12 (7)
April 24, 1953			8 (8)	(1)	15 (14)
July 8, 1956		1 (1)	5	1	5 (4)
June 2, 1959		1	4 (2)	1	7 (3)
July 1, 1962		2 (1)	Dōshikai 2	Kōmeitō 7 (2)	8 (4)
July 4, 1965		2 (1)		9 (2)	2 (1)
July 7, 1968		3 (1)		9 (4)	2 (3)
June 27, 1971		5 (1)		8 (2)	1 (1)

a Progressive Party (Shimpotō)
b Progressive Party (Kaishintō)

Note: After the 1971 election, the total number of seats in the House of Councillors held by each party was (pre-election strengths shown in parenthesis): Liberal-Democrats, 135 (136); Socialist, 66 (61); Kōmeitō, 23 (24); Democratic Socialist, 13 (9); Communist, 10 (7); and independent, 5 (8).

Table 3

Results of House of Councillors Elections in 1968 and 1971*

	July 7, 1968			June 27, 1971			[Seats held by each party after 1971 election]
	votes	% of votes	seats	votes	% of votes	seats	
Liberal-Democratic	20,120,088 (19,405,545)	46.7% (44.9%)	21 (48)	17,673,706 (17,915,347)	44.6% (44.0%)	21 (42)	[135]
Japan Socialist	8,542,204 (12,617,680)	19.8% (29.2%)	12 (16)	8,432,465 (12,597,643)	21.3% (31.0%)	11 (28)	[66]
Kōmeitō	6,656,771 (2,632,528)	15.4% (6.1%)	9 (4)	5,572,577 (1,351,855)	14.1% (3.4%)	8 (2)	[23]
Democratic-Socialist	2,578,580 (3,010,089)	6.0% (6.9%)	4 (3)	2,424,222 (1,919,643)	6.1% (4.7%)	4 (2)	[13]
Communist	2,146,873 (3,577,179)	5.0% (8.3%)	3 (1)	3,179,129 (4,878,569)	8.0% (12.0%)	5 (1)	[10]
Various	157,500 (106,587)	0.4% (0.2%)	0 (0)	47,990 (77,376)	0.1% (0.2%)	0 (0)	[0]
Independents	2,872,279 (1,910,371)	6.7% (4.4%)	2 (3)	2,313,990 (1,916,490)	5.8% (4.7%)	1 (1)	[5]
Totals	43,074,297 (43,259,979)		51 (75)	39,644,079 (40,696,923)		50 (76)	[252]

* Figures in parentheses refer to the prefectural constituencies. Figures not in parentheses refer to the national constituency. Figures in brackets refer to seats representing *both* national and prefectural constituencies.

parties are not organized on a federal and decentralized basis, as is the case in the United States, and the governorship of a political subdivision may not directly lead to the office of national chief executive. Sixth, the democratic principle of rotation in office has not operated effectively because the Socialists have never had the parliamentary majority necessary to form a one-party Socialist Cabinet. Seventh, the opposition parties tend to take impractical and doctrinaire, if not irresponsible, stands on many issues since they are not accustomed to governing and have no immediate prospect of assuming such a responsibility. Eighth, the Japanese parties are more sharply divided along ideological lines than are the American parties. Ideological issues project themselves into virtually every political conflict, and every issue is apt to be interpreted in terms of its implications for social stability or class struggle. The conservative fear of revolution and the radical fear of a revival of fascism and militarism are extremely vivid, and color attitudes towards educational reform, rearmament, political demonstrations, labor struggles, constitutional revision, foreign relations, and parliamentary procedure. There appears to be little common ideological ground between right and left, and there are no "bipartisan" policies.

A popular attitude towards politicians is that they are corrupt, self-seeking, and uninterested in the welfare of the people. The notion that political parties can be effective vehicles for the expression of the will of the people has not taken strong root. The failure of the politicians to gain the confidence of the people in the 1920s opened the way for militarism and fascism in the 1930s. The rise of the Kōmeitō is stimulating the older parties to come up with more effective programs. At the same time, Japan's postwar prosperity seems to have helped people to resign themselves philosophically to the well-publicized faults of the political parties.

Suggested Reading

Beckmann, George M., and Genji Okubo. *The Japanese Communist Party, 1922–1945.* Stanford, Calif.: Stanford University Press, 1969.

Curtis, Gerald. "The Kōenkai and the Liberal Democratic Party," in *The Japan Interpreter,* Vol. VI, No. 2 (Summer, 1970), 201–218.

Curtis, Gerald. *Election Campaigning: Japanese Style.* New York: Columbia University Press, 1971.

Fujiwara Hirotatsu. *I Denounce Soka Gakkai.* Tokyo: Nisshin Hodo Co., 1970.

Fukui, Haruhiro. *Party in Power: The Japanese Liberal-Democrats and Policy Making.* Berkeley: University of California Press, 1970.

Heidenheimer, Arnold J., and Frank C. Langdon. *Business Associations and the Financing of Political Parties: A Comparative Study of the Evolution of Practices in Germany, Norway, and Japan.* The Hague: Martinus Nijhoff, 1968.

Kublin, Hyman. *Asian Revolutionary: The Life of Sen Katayama.* Princeton, N.J.: Princeton University Press, 1965.

Kurzman, Dan. *Kishi and Japan: The Search for the Sun.* New York: Oblensky, 1960.

Palmer, Arvin. *Buddhist Politics: Japan's Clean Government Party.* The Hague: Martinus Nijhoff, 1970.

Scalapino, Robert A. *Democracy and the Party Movement in Prewar Japan: The Failure of the First Attempt.* Berkeley: University of California Press, 1953.

Scalapino, Robert A. *The Japanese Communist Movement, 1920–1966.* Berkeley: University of California Press, 1967.

Scalapino, Robert A., and Junnosuke Masumi. *Parties and Politics in Contemporary Japan.* Berkeley: University of California Press, 1962.

Stockwin, J. A. A. *The Japanese Socialist Party and Neutralism: A Study of a Political Party and Its Foreign Policy.* London: Cambridge University Press, 1969.

Swearingen, Rodger, and Paul Langer. *Red Flag in Japan: International Communism in Action, 1919–1951.* Cambridge, Mass.: Harvard University Press, 1952.

Thayer, Nathaniel. *How the Conservatives Rule Japan.* Princeton, N.J.: Princeton University Press, 1969.

Totten, George O., III. *The Social Democratic Movement in Prewar Japan.* New Haven, Conn.: Yale University Press, 1966.

Totten, George O., Allan B. Cole, and Cecil H. Uyehara. *Socialist Parties in Postwar Japan.* New Haven, Conn.: Yale University Press, 1966.

Yoshida, Shigeru. *The Yoshida Memoirs: The Story of Japan in Crisis,* trans. Ken-ichi Yoshida. Boston, Mass.: Houghton Mifflin, 1962.

* 5 *

The Legislature
and the Courts

Making and Interpreting Laws

The demands of the populace are, in industrialized societies, largely articulated and aggregated by interest groups and political parties. The conversion of these demands into authoritative, or legally binding, decisions is accomplished by the formal organs of government which have the constitutional authority to issue and enforce such decisions. These governmental structures and how the parties work through them are the topics of the next few chapters. In Japan, as we shall see, the influence on the governmental decision-making structures exercised by the Liberal-Democratic Party, which represents business, overwhelms that exercised by the other parties. The other parties sometimes seek to modify the rules of the game in order to counteract the predominance of the conservatives.

Electoral Systems and Party Strategies

The Lower House

Japan is a unitary state, and the qualifications for voting and the electoral system are determined by the national government rather than, as in the United States, by the governments of regional subdivisions. The principal electoral laws for the House of Representatives have been those of 1889,[1] 1900, 1919, 1925, 1945, and 1947.[2] In

[1] "Law of the Election of the Members of the House of Representatives," in Itō Hirobumi, *Commentaries on the Constitution of the Empire of Japan* (Tōkyō: Insetsu [*sic*] Kyoku, 1889), pp. 195–246.

[2] "The Law for the Election of Members of the House of Representatives," in Government Section, Supreme Commander for the Allied Powers,

1950, a Public Offices Election Law, subsequently amended at intervals, laid down provisions for elections of members of both houses of the Diet and of prefectural and local officials.

In 1890 in the first election for the newly established House of Representatives, only 1.1 percent (450,852) of the total population of Japan (39,902,000) was allowed to vote. A voter had to be a male, at least twenty-five years of age, who paid more than fifteen yen direct national tax for more than one year, or paid an income tax for more than three years. In 1902 the tax qualification was lightened, with the result that the electorate was doubled in number. The tax requirement was reduced to three yen direct national tax and the residence period was reduced to six months in 1919, so that in the following year there were slightly over 3,000,000 qualified voters in a total population of about 56,000,000. The early twenties witnessed a hard-fought struggle for "universal suffrage" (i.e., suffrage for adult males), and in 1925, the Diet passed a Universal Suffrage Act, which conferred the right to vote on all males over twenty-five. Nearly 10,000,000 of the 12,500,-000 qualified voters cast their vote in the 1928 election, the first in which universal manhood suffrage applied. The struggle for universal suffrage and its final realization greatly stimulated the rise to power of democratic political parties in the 1920s. Although women still did not have the right to vote, it appeared that this right would be granted soon. Unfortunately, the Peace Preservation Law and the weak position of the Diet with respect to the military oligarchy which ruled Japan in the 1930s more than counterbalanced the democratic features of the electoral system.

In October, 1945, General MacArthur directed the Japanese government to provide for female suffrage in the forthcoming general election. The Diet revised the electoral law to give the vote to women and reduce the voting age from twenty-five to twenty; and in April, 1946, women voted for the first time in Japanese history. Article 44 of the 1947 Constitution provides that "The qualifications of . . . electors shall be fixed by law. However, there shall be no discrimination because of race, creed, sex, social status, family origin, education, property or income." This democratic provision applies to both houses of the Diet.

In the 1890 election, the country was divided into small districts, each sending one, or in some cases two, members to the House of

Political Reorientation of Japan: September 1945 to September 1949, 2 vols. (Washington, D.C.: Government Printing Office, n.d. [1949?]), Vol. II, 822–845. (These volumes will subsequently be referred to as *Political Reorientation.*)

Representatives. The system has been changed from time to time, but that in use since 1925, excluding the 1946 election, has been the "medium-district system."

Shortly before the 1967 election, the number of electoral districts was increased from 117 to 123, each sending from three to five members to the House of Representatives, except the district of Amami Guntō, which would elect only one Representative. The number of seats in the lower house was increased from 467 to 486. In 1970, Okinawa, still under American occupation, was assigned five seats in the lower house, bringing the total membership to 491.

The electoral districts are made by dividing up the forty-six prefectures in such a way that the districts do not cross prefectural boundaries. Each voter casts his ballot for only one candidate. The candidates receiving the highest numbers of votes win. Thus, for example, in the Shizuoka Prefecture third district, which is entitled to four seats in the House of Representatives, the four candidates receiving the highest number of votes win the four seats. In this system, a party which commands only a minority of the votes in the district may win one or more seats. The Japanese system is a form of "limited voting," i.e., the individual elector is permitted only to vote for fewer candidates than the total number of seats to be filled for his electoral district.

In the Japanese system, candidates of the same party often find themselves competing against one another for votes. Kishi Nobusuke and his brother Satō Eisaku have both repeatedly competed for Liberal-Democratic votes in the second district in Yamaguchi prefecture. Notwithstanding this disadvantage, both have been repeatedly elected. A member of the Socialist Party might receive many more votes than he needs to win and deprive a fellow Socialist of necessary votes. However, if the Socialist voters divide their votes among too many Socialist candidates, the Socialists might win few or no seats. It is therefore necessary for each political party to ensure that it puts up the optimum number of candidates in each district. Party leaders try not to put up too many candidates, which would scatter the vote excessively, or too few candidates, which would waste votes.

There are no primary elections or nominating conventions in Japan. A person becomes a candidate for either house of the National Diet simply by notifying the chairman of the local election board and filing a deposit of 100,000 yen ($277.00). The money is not returned unless the candidate polls one-fifth of the valid votes cast divided by the number of seats to be filled from the district. Independent candidates as a rule have little chance to be elected, so that it is usually necessary to be officially sponsored by a political party and to run as a party candidate. Party nominations are made by an election committee in the central headquarters of the party.

For strategic reasons, party officials do not wish to sponsor too many candidates, but there are usually more aspirants than a party wishes to nominate. Consequently, there is often a fierce struggle among rival faction leaders within a party over the limited number of nominations to be allotted to each faction. Sometimes parties nominate more candidates than prudent, given the electoral system and the party's relative popularity, because of the pressure for nominations. When a party sponsors more candidates in an election than it sponsored in a preceding election, it boasts of this fact as evidence of its confidence in its electoral success.

In the 1969 election, the Liberal-Democrats sponsored 328 candidates; the Socialists, 183; the Democratic-Socialists, 68; the Communists, 123 (one candidate in each district); and the Kōmeitō, 76. From these figures, it is evident that it would be impossible for any single party to win all of the 486 seats, since none put up that many candidates. Likewise, the only party which could possibly win a majority (244) of the seats would be the Liberal-Democratic.

Thus, even before the election it was clear to the voters that the Liberal-Democrats were the only party capable of winning a majority of seats and establishing a one-party cabinet. A vote for any other party would be a vote for a coalition cabinet made up of an unpredictable combination of men and parties. Such a coalition cabinet would likely be unstable and short-lived, like the Katayama and Ashida Cabinets of 1948. Voters wishing a strong, stable government—and such voters seem to be in the plurality—will therefore vote Liberal-Democratic.

The electoral system in Japan operates more favorably for some political parties than it does for others. Parties do not receive seats proportionately to their popular votes. In the 1969 lower house election, the percentage of votes and the percentage of seats for each party were as follows:

Party	Percentage of Votes	Percentage of Seats
Liberal-Democrats	47.6	59.3
Socialists	21.4	18.5
Kōmeitō	10.9	9.7
Democratic-Socialists	7.7	6.4
Communists	6.8	2.9
Independents	5.3	3.3

Each political party, given its own peculiarities and the exigencies of the situation, has its distinctive electoral strategy. The Communists always run one candidate in each district, even though the chances of winning in most instances are practically nil. The Communists have sufficient funds to do this, and the purpose of campaigning is as much to propagate Communist ideas as it is to win seats. The Kōmeitō follows the opposite strategy: it sponsors a candidate only when his victory is almost assured. (The Kōmeitō, of course, expects all Sōka Gakkai voters to vote for their candidates.) Kōmeitō sponsorship is therefore a valuable political asset. The electoral system greatly favors the two major parties over the three minor parties. In the 1957 and 1969 elections, the Liberal-Democrats failed to receive a majority of the popular votes but won a comfortable majority of the seats in the lower house. The political opposition therefore questions the right of the parliamentary majority to decide issues without gaining the concurrence of the minority.

In Japan as elsewhere, politicians like to tinker with the electoral system to make it work most advantageously for them. The majority party or majority coalition may want to change the rules of the game in its favor, and the opposition strongly objects. In 1956, Liberal-Democratic Prime Minister Hatoyama submitted a bill to the Diet providing for the small district system. He alleged that the medium-district system prevented the proper development of the two-party system since there was the possibility that a third or fourth party might be formed, making coalition cabinets necessary. Besides, he held that elections under the present system cost too much.

The opposition charged that the Prime Minister's real motive in advocating small districts was to decrease Socialist strength, which had to gather its votes from relatively large districts. The small district system would have an additional advantage for the Liberal-Democrats because it might reduce factional struggles within the party for nomination and for election. It was also widely understood that a change in the electoral system might work sufficiently to the advantage of the Liberal-Democrats so that they would win the two-thirds majority in the lower house necessary to amend the Constitution. The Hatoyama electoral bill ("Hatomander"), however, was rejected because of opposition not only from the Socialists but also from the antimainstream factions in the Liberal-Democratic Party, which feared that the electoral reform would strengthen the mainstream factions of the party.

After the 1967 election, conservatives were concerned lest further slippage in their popular vote, which had just fallen to less than a majority, would, after a future election, result in the loss of the Liberal-Democratic control of the Diet. Some advocated an electoral reform which would prevent what they regarded as a disaster.

While the Liberal-Democrats tend to advocate the single-member district system, the Socialists have advocated large districts with proportional representation. Such a reform would probably help all of the opposition parties. However, following the 1960 election, in which the Socialists won more seats in proportion to their popular votes than did any other party, the Socialists became less dogmatic in their advocacy of proportional representation. In Japan, as in many other countries, electoral reform has lagged behind urbanization. The apportionment of seats among urban and rural areas was accomplished when the proportion of the population living in the country was much larger than it is today, so that rural interests are over-represented to the disadvantage of city dwellers. In Japan, this favors the conservative (Liberal-Democratic) party, which may use its parliamentary majority to block significant reform. In the light of the record, it may be assumed that considerations of political expediency rather than abstract theory will continue to determine the nature of the electoral system.

The Upper House

At the time of the drafting of the new Constitution, MacArthur's Headquarters strongly felt that the House of Peers should be abolished. Furthermore, there was strong objection to any form of functional or corporate upper house (i.e., an upper house representing vocational or economic groups).[3] The Americans held that no upper chamber corresponding to the United States Senate was necessary in Japan, because Japan was not a federation of states each of which required representation in the national legislature.[4] Japanese officials proposed that a House of Councillors be established to consist of members elected for the various districts or professions and members appointed by the Cabinet upon resolution of a committee consisting of members of both Houses. An upper house, the Japanese felt, was necessary as a check against hasty, ill-considered measures supported by a majority party in the lower house.[5]

A compromise between the Japanese and American points of view emerged with the establishment of a House of Councillors, the members of which would, according to the Constitution, be elected for six years, election for half of the members taking place every three years.

[3] *Ibid.,* Vol. I, 103.

[4] Matsumoto Jōji, "Nihonkoku Kempō no Sōan ni tsuite" (Concerning the Drafts of the Constitution of Japan), *Kempō Chōsakai, Kenshi Sōdai Nijūhachi Go* (Materials on the Constitution, General No. 28), (October, 1958), pp. 11–12.

[5] *Ibid.,* p. 12.

The precise composition of the House of Councillors was left vague by the Constitution. However, like the lower chamber, it would consist of elected members, "representative of all of the people" and there could be "no discrimination because of . . . social status, family origin, education, property or income." Although the electoral system would be determined by ordinary law, it would seem difficult, in the light of the Constitution, to make the House of Councillors a vocational, corporate, or aristocratic chamber.

The House of Councillors consists of a total of 252 members, of whom 152 represent prefectural constituencies, and 100 represent the national constituency, i.e., are elected by the nation at large. (In 1970, the representation of Okinawa was provided for by adding two seats to the hitherto 150 seats representing prefectural constituencies, bringing the total membership of the upper house to 252.) Since the terms are staggered, every three years seventy-six members are elected in the prefectural constituencies (including Okinawa), and fifty members elected in the national constituency. Each of the forty-seven prefectures (including Okinawa) is entitled to from two to eight seats in the House of Councillors, the more populous prefectures having more seats than the less populous. In House of Councillors elections, each voter selects one candidate in the prefectural constituency and one candidate in the national constituency. As in the case of the lower house elections, the candidates receiving the most votes win.

The purpose of the large electoral districts was to ensure that the political composition of the House of Councillors would be dissimilar from that of the House of Representatives. It was hoped that the large prefectural and national constituencies would provide an opportunity for persons of wide reputation to win political office without having to become involved in the rough-and-tumble of partisan politics and that councillors, who are required to be at least thirty years of age, as contrasted with the representatives who need be only twenty-five, would be superior in dignity, experience, and impartiality to the representatives. After over twenty years of operation, however, the House of Councillors is not greatly different from the House of Representatives in terms of either age or politics. The relative strengths of the parties are about identical in the two chambers.

The possibility to gerrymander is as great with the House of Councillors districts as with the lower house districts. Conservatives sometimes allege that the national constituency should be abolished since most of the candidates in the national constituency are completely unknown to the voters and interest in the election is minimal. On the other hand, the Socialists have advocated that all of the seats of the House of Councillors be based on the national constituency, each party receiving a number of seats proportional to its votes. When people vote according to personalities of the candidates they are apt to vote conservative; when they vote according to party platform, the Socialist party stands more chance than it would otherwise.

There has been no reapportionment of the seats among the prefectural constituencies since 1947. Since then, the population of the cities has grown much faster than that of the rural areas, so that the urbanized prefectures are grossly underrepresented compared with the rural prefectures. This system has worked to the advantage of the Liberal-Democratic Party, which normally does well in rural areas. In 1971, in rural Kōchi prefecture (which was entitled to elect one councillor), the Liberal-Democratic candidate was able to win the seat with only 128,591 votes, but in Tokyo prefecture (which could elect four councillors), one Socialist candidate received 640,893 votes but failed to be elected. For Tokyo, there was one seat to be filled in the upper house for every 2,000,000 voters, while the Tottori prefecture, there was one seat to be filled for only 395,000 voters. The small parties as a rule do badly in the rural prefectural constituencies. In 1971, the Communists won twelve percent of all of the votes cast in the prefectural constituencies, but won only one of the 76 seats at stake. They complain bitterly of the inequities of the electoral system. The Kōmeitō and Democratic-Socialists do not even propose candidates in some of the prefectural constituencies. Since 1965, the malapportionment of seats in both houses of the Diet has enabled the Liberal-Democrats consistently to win majorities of the seats in both houses without receiving majorities of the popular vote. Thus critics of the government's policies have argued that the legislative branch lacks a democratic mandate. Although electoral reform (which might include lowering the voting age to eighteen) is much discussed, given the present balance of political forces, it seems rather unlikely that either the Liberal-Democrats or the Socialists will change the electoral systems for the two houses of the Diet in the foreseeable future.

The Organization of the Diet

The terms of the members of the lower house are fixed by the Constitution at four years, subject to being shortened as the result of a dissolution. Since World War II the members of the House of Representatives have never served out full four-year terms. The term of office of councillors is six years, with the terms of half of the members expiring every three years. The House of Councillors may not be dissolved.

Each house elects a speaker and a vice speaker. Ideally the speaker is politically neutral, but neutrality is a virtually impossible achievement since the speaker is bound to make himself *persona non grata* to one party or another when he makes decisions respecting the frequent partisan obstructive tactics.

The Liberal-Democrats always have the majority needed to elect their choice for both speaker and vice speaker. The Socialists, as the leading opposition party, insist that by right they should get their choice as vice speaker. The struggle over these and other matters relating to the organization of the lower house provides occasions for delay and obstruction for the opposition when it wishes to block the passage of impending legislation. The governing party, faced with threatened or actual boycotts by the opposition at the very beginning of the parliamentary session, may have to make some concessions to the opposition just to get the latter to attend the Diet. A delay in the opening of the lower house is more or less usual, while the chairmen or secretaries-general of the political parties make the deals necessary for the "normalization" of the Diet proceedings. The failure of the government to make reasonable concessions or the failure of the opposition to accept reasonable terms may result in a longer than usual delay of the opening, and the press and public opinion will then blame one party or the other, often both, for sabotaging parliamentary democracy.

In highly stable political systems, it seems simple to distinguish between procedural and substantive matters. In postwar Japan, however, the two are inextricably intertwined. Faced with government majorities in both houses of the Diet, about the only means to defeat government bills available to the opposition parties is to impede the legislative process itself. There are many points in this process at which obstruction may be accomplished, beginning with the election of the officials of the lower chamber.

As in the United States, each house is organized into committees to consider proposed legislation. The first houses under the new Constitution each had twenty-one standing committees (Jōnin Iinkai), but the number was subsequently reduced to sixteen. There are in each House standing committees on (1) Cabinet, (2) Local Administration, (3) Judicial Affairs, (4) Foreign Affairs, (5) Finance, (6) Education, (7) Welfare and Labor, (8) Agriculture, Forestry and Fisheries, (9) Commerce and Industry, (10) Transport, (11) Communications, (12) Construction, (13) Budget, (14) Accounts, (15) Steering, and (16) Discipline. Most of these committees correspond to ministries in the executive branch.

Special committees study particular problems, and the names of these committees reveal the topics that are of special concern in Japan today. In 1970, there were special committees in both houses for fire countermeasures, election law revision, science and technology, pollution control, commodity prices, Okinawa and the northern territories, and traffic safety. In addition, the House of Representatives had a special committee on coal policy.

The number of members in each committee ranges from twenty to fifty in the lower chamber and from ten to forty-five in the upper. Committee chairmen are appointed on the basis of partisan political considerations. The seniority system, which prevails in the United States Congress, is not used. Since 1958, the chairmanships in the lower house standing committees have been monopolized by the majority Liberal-Democratic Party, but chairmanships of the other Diet committees are divided among the Socialists, Democratic-Socialists, and Kōmeitō, as well as Liberal-Democrats. Memberships in each committee are allocated to parties on the basis of party strength in the house.

The Diet committees hold public hearings, make investigating trips, including travel abroad, have the power of subpoena, and may use the services of the National Diet Library. Probably the most important committee is the Budget Committee of the House of Representatives. Here the discussion is wide ranging and well covered by the press, and some of the most important statements of government policy are made. The opposition likes to trap government spokesmen into embarrassing slips of the tongue which later require clarification or toning down.

The standing committees have been criticized as too inclined to support the legislative proposals of the government. However, it is difficult to see how the committee members could act in a completely independent fashion without breaking party discipline and possibly forcing the resignation of the cabinet. The coalition Cabinet of the Socialist Prime Minister Katayama Tetsu was forced to resign in 1948 partly because of the defeat which it suffered in the Budget Committee led by the committee chairman, a Socialist, who disagreed with the Government's fiscal policies. The government party members of a committee, out of loyalty to their party, are more or less duty bound to see to it that their party platform is legislated into reality, and the government party is not embarrassed. The opposition members of a committee often resort to filibusters, boycotts, and occasionally to riots in order to prevent committee approval of a government bill. It is notable that in Great Britain, where the parliamentary-cabinet system operates most smoothly and efficiently, standing committees are tame institutions and on the whole support the government. The principal functions of the committee system in Japan are (1) to educate the public, since committee meetings are usually open and well publicized by the press, and (2) to provide an arena for criticism and obstruction by the opposition.

Making Laws

The Diet, according to the Constitution, is "the sole lawmaking organ of the State."[6] Its function thus resembles that of the Congress of the United States, in which are vested all legislative powers granted by the United States Constitution. However, the legislative power of a parliament in a parliamentary system such as the Japanese is very different from that in a presidential system such as the American. In the parliamentary system, if the legislature rejects a measure deemed vital by the executive, a political crisis arises which may result in either the resignation of the cabinet or the dissolution of the parliament with new elections or both. Thus, in the parliamentary form of democracy, the legislative process is fraught with greater political significance than in a presidential democracy, and bills are not considered on their merits alone but in terms of the politically crucial relation between the legislature and the executive. In the parliamentary system, a principal function of the legislature is to supervise the executive.

If the parliament frequently disregards the wish of the cabinet concerning important measures, and if the cabinet cannot dissolve the parliament, ministerial instability, such as characterized the French Third and Fourth Republics, will result. On the other hand, if the cabinet normally enjoys the support of a comfortable majority, i.e., if the cabinet and the majority in the parliament are of the same political party or harmonious coalition of parties, there is apt to be no serious difference of views on legislation, and the parliament tends to be a "rubber stamp" for bills presented by the cabinet. The result is a so-called "cabinet dictatorship," such as is sometimes said to exist in Great Britain. When this situation arises in Japan it is apt to be labeled by the opposition as the "tyranny of the majority."

In Japan, voting in the House of Representatives runs strictly along party lines.[7] The government party (or parties) normally vote for government bills, the opposition party (or parties) vote normally against them.

Bills introduced by individual Diet members often require budgetary outlays not provided for in the budget, thus endangering the govern-

---

[6] Constitution, Article 41.

[7] Nobutaka Ike, *Japanese Politics: An Introductory Survey* (New York: Knopf, 1957), p. 184.

ment's fiscal policy. It has been found necessary to develop some procedure whereby the government party and cabinet may curb the introduction of pork-barrel legislation catering to special interest groups and particular localities. Consequently, under the third Hatoyama Cabinet, the political affairs research committee of the Liberal-Democratic Party and the Cabinet undertook to clear individual members' bills.[8] The policy organs of the ruling Liberal-Democratic Party are today a crucial factor in the legislative process.

How are laws made? Bills (hōan or hōritsu-an) may be introduced by the Prime Minister, representing the Cabinet, or, infrequently, by a member of either house. The speaker of the house to which the bill is introduced as a rule refers the bill to the appropriate standing or a special committee of the house. When a bill is considered urgent, committee examination may be omitted by decision of the steering committee. After study and approval by a committee, the bill is submitted to a plenary session of the house for deliberation and a vote. In the event of a tie, the speaker casts the deciding vote. After approval by one house, the bill is sent to the speaker of the other, where it must again be submitted to deliberation in committee and plenary sessions. When passed by both houses the bill becomes law.

If the House of Councillors rejects a measure passed by the representatives or fails to take action on the measure within sixty days (time in recess excepted), the House of Representatives may override the veto of the House of Councillors by a two-thirds majority. In the event of a difference of view between the House of Representatives and the House of Councillors, the former may call for a meeting of a joint committee of both houses to deliberate on the measure.[9]

The procedure for the enactment of the budget and for the approval of treaties is different from that for other legislation. The budget or treaty must first be submitted to and approved by the House of Representatives. The representatives' decision is that of the Diet (1) when the House of Councillors makes a decision different from that of the representatives and when no agreement can be reached even through a joint committee of two houses, or (2) when the House of Councillors fails to take action within thirty days (period of recess excluded) after

---

[8] Hattie Kawahara Colton, "The National Diet After Independence," *The Annals of the American Academy of Political and Social Science*, Vol. CCCVIII (November, 1956), 25–26. See also Dr. Colton's article, "The Working of the Japanese Diet," *Pacific Affairs*, Vol. XXVIII (December, 1955), 363–372, reprinted in Lyman Jay Gould and E. William Steele, eds., *People, Power and Politics: An Introductory Reader* (New York: Random House, 1960), pp. 374–384.

[9] Constitution, Article 59.

the receipt of the budget or treaty passed by the representatives.[10] A dramatic application of this provision occurred in 1960, when the United States–Japan Security Pact, after approval by the House of Representatives, was not deliberated upon in the House of Councillors because of the decision of the latter to deliberate without the Socialists, who were boycotting the house. Three hundred thousand demonstrators surrounded the Diet building awaiting the "automatic approval" (shizen shōnin) of the pact, which would occur at midnight, June 18, thirty days after the Liberal-Democrats in the House of Representatives had approved the pact in the absence of the Socialist members. The parades, the speeches, the shouts, and the placards of the multitude were of no avail against the inexorable ticking of the clock.

Bills which apply to only a single local entity must be approved by a majority vote of the people of the entity before becoming law.[11]

The Diet may initiate amendments to the Constitution when two-thirds of all of the members of each house vote in favor of the proposed amendment. The proposal must then be ratified by a majority vote of the people in order to become part of the Constitution.[12] Thus far, the 1947 Constitution has not been amended because none of the much publicized proposals for constitutional change has been supported by a sufficient majority in either house.

The lower house seems to have primacy over the upper in view of the former's power to override the veto of the latter and to make the final decision on treaties, the budget, and the designating of the Prime Minister. But in certain unusual circumstances the House of Councillors may play a more decisive role. When the House of Representatives is dissolved, the House of Councillors is closed at the same time. In case of a national emergency, the Cabinet may convoke the House of Councillors in emergency session to take provisional measures which become null and void unless agreed to by the House of Representatives within ten days after the opening of the next session of the Diet.[13] This provision of the Constitution was invoked in 1952 and again in 1953.[14]

Under the old Constitution, the sanction of the Emperor was necessary before a bill could become law. Under the present Constitution, the assent of the Emperor is unnecessary, and the Emperor has no

[10] Constitution, Articles 60, 61.
[11] Constitution, Article 95.
[12] Constitution, Article 96.
[13] Constitution, Article 54.
[14] *Asahi Nenkan, 1970,* Supplement, p. 73.

power to veto the bill. Instead, the Constitution simply states that the Emperor promulgates laws.[15]

Obstructionism

With the polarization of Japanese politics into two ideological camps, conservative and reformist, the parliamentary process in Japan has deteriorated to the point that it sometimes appears that democratic government itself is in danger. Certain measures proposed by the conservative majority have been so unacceptable to the Socialist minority that the latter feels that extralegal methods may justifiably be used to obstruct the objectionable bills, many of which would reverse the democratic reforms of the Occupation. The conservative-sponsored electoral bills (1947, 1956), the Subversive Activities Prevention Bill (1952), the Police Bill (1954), the Police Duties Revision Bill (1958), the United States–Japan Security Pact (1960), and the Antiviolence Bill (1961) were held by the Socialist opposition to be in clear violation of the spirit and letter of the democratic Constitution. The passage of these measures by the Government using its majority in the Diet, would, it was held, endanger the existence of democracy itself.

Since the coming into being of the two-party system in 1955, there has been a gross imbalance of political forces in the Diet, the Liberal-Democrats holding nearly two-thirds of the seats, the Socialists and their allies holding slightly over one-third in each house. The Liberal-Democrats dominate the executive, legislative, and judicial branches of the government. In order to prevent the "tyranny of the majority," the majority must use obstructionist tactics.

In the United States Senate, a minority may obstruct the will of the majority with a filibuster which prevents a vote from being taken on the measure which the minority opposes. Other devices for the protection of minorities are the presidential veto, judicial review of legislation, and states' rights, all of which place limits on the power of the majority in the national legislature. In Japan, there is no executive veto, practically speaking, since the bills laid before the Diet have been either sponsored or approved by the cabinet. The Supreme Court is distrusted as partisan. States' rights are nonexistent since the political system is unitary rather than federal.

The Socialists make frequent use of the filibuster both in committees and in plenary session to prevent votes from being taken before the expiration of parliamentary sessions and to defeat motions to extend the session. Another device is the suwarikomi, or "sit-down" (literally,

[15] Constitution, Article 7.

sit and fill up). On a number of occasions, Socialist members of the lower house, aided by their secretaries, have blocked the corridors of the Diet to prevent the Speaker of the House of Representatives from calling the meeting to order. In 1954, 1960, and 1961, the Speaker called in police to physically remove the Socialists who were preventing him from convening the House of Representatives. The suwarikomi is also used by demonstrators around the Diet building and in labor and other disputes. The advantage for the sit-downers is that they may obstruct the orderly process of law without incurring the onus of initiating violence. It is the police who are blamed for starting trouble when they try to remove sit-downers.

The parliamentary opposition may, as a last resort, riot within the august chambers of the Diet to prevent a vote from being taken. In 1961, when the Speaker called for a vote on the Antiviolence Bill, the tumult was so great that neither he nor the members voting could be heard. He nevertheless announced on the microphone that the bill was passed and sent it to the House of Councillors. There the Liberal-Democrats were reluctant to provoke Socialist violence, and the Socialists were willing to compromise. It was agreed to suspend discussion of the controversial measure until the next session of the Diet. The bill was never passed, as the government considered other legislation more urgent and did not want to invite trouble by resuming deliberation on such a controversial measure.

Another obstructive device is the boycott. An opposition boycott cannot of itself prevent the formation of a quorum, which is one-third of the membership in each House. However, by nonattendance, the Socialists can make the majority party appear to be behaving "undemocratically" if the latter votes on a measure in the absence of the opposition. The Socialists have on frequent occasions boycotted committee meetings and plenary sessions of both houses. An extreme form of the boycott was suggested in 1960 by the threat of the Socialist members to resign their seats in the Diet if the Government refused to do the bidding of the Socialists.

A bicameral system provides more scope for obstruction than a single-chamber system. If the opposition cannot defeat a measure in one house, it can try again in the other.

The mobilization of great mass demonstrations around the Diet protesting a government bill creates the impression that the "people" are against the proposal, especially if the newspapers support the demonstrators, which is sometimes the case. Political strikes, usually led by the Sōhyō labor federation, are also an important political weapon of the Socialists. In some instances, the strikes or demonstrations are illegal or are violent, but usually they are not. Sometimes extremists, either Communists or rightists, attempt to make political capital by instigating or provoking violence; public opinion, however, tends to react negatively against excessive violence. When bloodshed does occasionally occur, the left accuses rightists of provocation (often a true charge) or the police of "brutality." The Government blames the violence on Communist agitators and declares its determination not to give in to mob rule. Both sides in the political crisis are usually bitter and self-righteous. The struggle is basically ideological and frequently the participants, all of whom are zealous to "protect democracy" and "parliamentary government" as they interpret the terms, lose sight of the immediate issues. The conservatives are normally unable to organize mass demonstrations. Instead, they are embarrassed by the notorious activities of small rightist terrorist organizations, which promote assassination and start fights with peaceful leftist demonstrators. Attempts by the government to limit demonstrations are of course labeled by the opposition as attacks on basic democratic freedoms and are met with more demonstrations. However, in order to mount demonstrations and strikes sufficient to bring about the defeat of a given bill, the issue must be one that gets the support of the press and seizes the imagination of the populace. Such issues are fairly few in number but arise about once every four or five years.

The obstructive and extraparliamentary tactics of the left over the parliamentary majority have been notably successful in several instances. Prime Minister Hatoyama's Electoral Reform Bill of 1956 was defeated. In 1958, Prime Minister Kishi withdrew the Police Duties Revision Bill but did not resign as was demanded. In 1960 Kishi promised to resign, and later did, but managed to obtain approval of a controversial treaty in spite of mass demonstrations and repeated political strikes. In 1961, the Antiviolence Bill was shelved by the Ikeda Government. In the light of the effectiveness of their extralegal obstructive tactics, it seems unlikely that the Socialist Party and Sōhyō labor federation will willingly give them up, notwithstanding the pious injunctions of government officials and well-meaning foreign critics.

The Role of the Diet

The Japanese Diet is the oldest parliament in Asia, in continuous existence since 1890. But, as indicated in Chapter 1, the role of the Diet in policy-making before the end of World War II was much restricted. The executive branch represented the bureaucratic and military oligarchy and normally was not responsible to the parliament.

About the most that the Diet could do was to defeat government bills. The Diet did not have the power to convene on its own initiative, to disapprove of treaties, to declare war, or to initiate constitutional amendments. The Diet could pass, reduce, or reject the government-prepared budget but could not increase it. If the parliament rejected the budget, the budget of the previous year could be put into effect by the Government. The members of the lower house had lower court rank than many government officials, and their pay was about half that of vice ministers. The speaker of the House of Representatives was not elected by the representatives but rather was chosen by the Emperor from three members nominated by the House. The Government, if it wished, could prorogue the Diet, i.e., suspend a session for up to fifteen days. Between 1930 and 1935, the House of Representatives sought desperately to amend the Law of the Houses of 1889[16] to enhance the independence, power, and prestige of the Diet. Three times the lower house passed a reform bill, and three times the measure was rejected by the House of Peers, which made common cause with the oligarchic executive to prevent democratization.

In the postwar Constitution the Diet was not only designated the "sole law-making organ of the State" but was declared to be "the highest organ of state power." The Japanese parliament would be "sovereign" like its British counterpart. It was given the powers normally possessed by legislatures in Anglo-Saxon democracies and was organized along the lines of the Congress of the United States. The British type of parliamentary-cabinet system occupied an important place in the thinking of the Japanese and American reformers of the political system. There are, however, a number of important differences between the Japanese and British systems. In Japan the upper chamber of the legislature is not virtually powerless like the House of Lords. In Japan there is an elaborate system of potentially powerful committees unlike those in Britain.

It is possible that the Americans had an only partial understanding of cabinet government as it has actually operated in Great Britain in the twentieth century. "The omnipotence of the House of Commons, the absolute responsibility of the ministers to parliament—these ideas are so mystical that they can be explained only in terms of nostalgia for the nineteenth century."[17]

---

[16] English text in Ito, pp. 172–194, and *Political Reorientation,* Vol. II, 597–602.

[17] Don K. Price and Harold J. Laski, "A Debate on the Parliamentary and Presidential Systems," Roy C. Macridis and Bernard E. Brown, eds., *Comparative Politics: Notes and Readings* (Homewood, Ill.: Dorsey Press, 1961), p. 374.

In 1955 when the two-party system replaced the multiparty system in Japan, any subordinance of the Cabinet to the Diet began to disappear. The Diet became an electoral college registering the will of the people for government by one political party or another. A vote of no confidence in the Cabinet became unlikely because party loyalty inhibited the majority from voting its own Government out of office. In Japan, therefore, the legislature does not govern. The Liberal-Democratic Party governs. Liberal-Democrats in the Cabinet propose legislation, and Liberal-Democrats in the Diet pass it. The checks are the antimainstream factions within the Liberal-Democratic Party, the opposition parties, the press, public opinion, and organized labor. This is not to say that the system is a one-party dictatorship. The sovereign electorate has the right to vote the Liberal-Democrats out of office and vote the Socialists in.

The turmoil of Japanese parliamentary life is in part the result of conflicting conceptions of the proper rules of the Cabinet and the Diet in the political process and of the relation of majority rule to minority rights. Clear precedents and rules have not been established so that excessive time and energy are spent on procedural disputes, which are sometimes solved only by brawling or introducing the police or abdicating to street demonstrators. However, even if the rules were clear, the legitimacy of "bourgeois" parliamentary democracy is not universally accepted, so that extraparliamentary tactics are frequently resorted to in order to "protect democracy" or to achieve ideological ends.

The Legal System

Since the 1890s, Japan has employed the Continental system of codified law as contrasted with the Anglo-Saxon system of common, or judge-made, law. The codes were drawn up after German and French models largely in order to hasten the end of extraterritoriality (exemption from Japanese law) enjoyed by foreigners in Japan. Extraterritoriality was a keenly felt limitation on Japanese sovereignty and a most unpopular feature of Japan's "unequal treaties" with Western states. The codes were similar to those of Europe in form and content, but where the family system was concerned, they embodied traditional Japanese Confucian ethics. During the Occupation, the Diet enacted sweeping revisions in the codes to bring them into conformity with the democratic provisions of the new Constitution.

The Diet, which is "the highest organ of state power," is "the sole law-making organ of the state," and the prefectural assemblies cannot enact law codes peculiar to their own jurisdictions as can state legislatures in the United States. The laws passed since 1945 are written in the grammar of the colloquial language rather than in the stilted classical language of prewar law. The term, roppō, literally six laws, refers to the total body of Japanese law, including among other things the Constitution, the criminal code, the civil code, the commercial code, the code of criminal procedure, and the code of civil procedure. The roppō zensho, or compendium of laws, printed in fine print in a single 1500- or 2500-page volume, may be conveniently purchased at bookstores. Thus, the text of the law is readily available for any interested person to consult, and the law is not the exclusive province of judges and lawyers.

It is not feasible to discuss here all of the major changes in the Japanese legal system required by the new Constitution. Many are discussed elsewhere in this book. To the Japanese, the reforms relating to the family system have been of great importance, affecting their most intimate personal relationships. The postwar Constitution requires that "all of the people shall be respected as individuals" (Article 13), and that "all of the people are equal under the law and there shall be no discrimination in political, economic or social relations because of race, creed, sex, social status, or family origin" (Article 14). "Marriage shall be based on the mutual consent of both sexes, and it shall be maintained through mutual cooperation with the equal rights of husband and wife as a basis. With regard to choice of spouse, property rights, inheritance, choice of domicile, divorce and other matters pertaining to marriage and the family, laws shall be enacted from the standpoint of individual dignity and the essential equality of sexes" (Article 24). These constitutional provisions struck at the legal basis of the Japanese family system, which had developed in the course of Japan's long feudal history and had been sanctioned by Confucianist teaching. The new Constitution in effect declared that the individual, not the family, was the basis of society, that women would enjoy the same rights as men, including an equal right to divorce, and that marriage was based on the consent of the partners rather than the decision of parents. The special rights of the eldest son (primogeniture) as well as the inequality of husband and wife were denied by the constitutional requirement of equality of individuals. The revised Civil Code, including domestic law, spelled out in detail the concrete significance of the newly introduced principles of the individualism and equality. These changes were much welcomed by youths and intellectuals in the early years of the Occupation and have since captured the imagination of most of the public.

Of course, there still remain vestiges of the Confucian familism in the text of the Civil Code, in the everyday practices of the people, and in the decisions of the courts, and these remnants provide fertile grounds for legal and ideological controversy. For example, if a son is found guilty of murdering his father, the law provides that his punishment is greater than it would be for someone other than the son who had committed the murder. This provision enshrines the Confucian virtue of filial piety by making patricide a graver crime than ordinary murder. The Japanese Supreme Court, in a famous split decision, upheld the constitutionality of this peculiar legal principle, which the majority of the court regarded as a "beautiful custom."[18]

Japanese conservatives often blame the rise of immorality and juvenile delinquency, the disrespect for authority, the lack of deference towards parents and elders, and the breakdown of families on the alien principles of individualism and equality in the new Constitution and Civil Code. However, most of the sweeping changes in family life in Japan since World War II are attributable not to changes in the law but to changes in the economy and demography. The majority of Japanese now live in cities, often in crowded apartments, rather than in farm villages. The peasant farm was the economic base of the Confucian male-dominated family, which included the married son and the subservient daughter-in-law. Today, young married couples often live their own lives in city apartments, miles from parents and in-laws. No matter how nostalgic parents or children may be for the Confucian ideals, those ideals are not as relevant to the industrial economy as they were to the agricultural economy. Women can be more independent today, because they can find good jobs in the city. Old people try to make do on social security rather than live out their declining years on a farm which their eldest son manages. Children leave home to go to work or to college rather than remain indefinitely on the family farm.

Law in modern society may serve either of two functions. It may reform the social order: in this sense it is a progressive force. Or it may preserve the social order: in this sense it is a conservative force. Many critics of the new Japanese legal system held that it did violence to Japanese social traditions and could therefore not endure. Today it appears that much of the old legal system could not in any event have survived the industrialization and urbanization which have revolutionized Japanese family life. Japan, like the United States, is now moving

[18] The Fukuoka patricide decision of 1950, translated by Kurt Steiner in John M. Maki, ed., *Court and Constitution in Japan: Selected Supreme Court Decisions, 1948–60* (Seattle: University of Washington Press, 1964), pp. 129–156.

into the age of the information explosion and computer technology. An increasingly large proportion of the population will be engaged in the tertiary sector of the economy (i.e., services), as compared with the secondary (production) sector and primary (extractive) sector. The modernization of the educational and transportation systems and the preservation of a livable environment will likely be the major problems for solution by legal changes in the decades immediately ahead.

The Judicial System

Under the Meiji Constitution, the Minister of Justice exercised administrative supervision over the courts, and the government appointed and dismissed judges, so that the judicial branch was not independent from the executive. During the Occupation the judicial system was thoroughly reformed.[19] The Court of Administrative Litigation, which had been inspired by the European example for trying of cases in administrative law, was abolished, and such cases are now handled by the regular courts. There is no system of state courts paralleling the national courts, as in the United States, since Japan is a unitary state. All courts are organs of the national rather than the local governments.

The relation of the courts to the rest of the government was altered to ensure the rule of law and the independence of the judicial branch. In postwar Japan, as in the United States, the Constitution is the "supreme law of the land."[20] Japan's Supreme Court is "the court of the last resort with power to determine the constitutionality of any law, order, regulation, or official act."[21] The power of judicial review is explicitly granted the Japanese Supreme Court by the new Constitution; the Court does not derive this power merely from its own interpretation of the Constitution, as occurred in the United States. As in the United States, the Supreme Court rules on constitutionality only when there is a question whether the law or order concerned should be applied in an actual lawsuit. The Supreme Court, with the exception of certain laws passed to implement Occupation directives, has never held any law unconstitutional but has upheld many as constitutional.

Probably the Sunakawa affair aroused more public excitement than any other case before the Supreme Court. The arrest of demonstrators

---

[19] Court Organization Law of April 16, 1947, in *Political Reorientation,* Vol. II, 885–893.

[20] Constitution, Article 98.

[21] Constitution, Article 81.

who opposed the enlargement of the American air base at Sunakawa (Tachikawa) near Tokyo resulted in the sensational decision of the Tokyo District Court that the 1951 United States–Japan Security Treaty was invalid because the stationing of American military forces in Japan violated Article 9, the disarmament clause, of the Constitution. If this decision had been allowed to stand, American military forces would have had to leave the country and the proposed new United States–Japan Security Treaty would probably have been invalidated along with the 1951 treaty. The constitutionality of Japan's own Self-Defense Forces also seemed to be involved. Thus, a great deal hung on the Supreme Court's decision, which quashed the lower court's judgment and upheld the Security Treaty.

The famous decision in the Sunakawa case (1959) is notable for its apparent partial definition of the scope of judicial review. The Supreme Court held that the 1951 United States–Japan Security Treaty, the constitutionality of which was being questioned, related to the very existence of Japan as a sovereign power, "and any legal determination as to whether the content of the treaty is constitutional or not is in many respects inseparably related to the high degree of political consideration or discretionary power on the part of the Cabinet which concluded the treaty and on the part of the Diet which approved it. Consequently, as a rule, there is a certain element of incompatibility in the process of determination of its constitutionality by a court of law which has as its mission the exercise of the purely judicial function. Accordingly, unless the said treaty is obviously unconstitutional and void, it falls outside the purview of the power of judicial review granted to the court." Thus, it appears that the Court will seldom, if ever, pass on the constitutionality of treaties.[22]

Japan's hierarchy of courts includes, from top to bottom, one Supreme Court, eight High Courts, forty-nine District Courts (with 235 branches), and 570 Summary Courts. There are also forty-nine Family Courts (with 235 branches).

The Chief Judge of the Supreme Court is designated by the Cabinet and appointed by the Emperor.[23] Imperial appointment supposedly endows the Chief Judge with prestige comparable to that of the Prime Minister. The fourteen other judges are appointed by the Cabinet subject to popular review. At the first House of Representatives election following the appointment and every ten years thereafter, the voters review the appointment. If they disapprove, the judge is dis-

---

[22] For text of the Supreme Court decision on the Sunakawa case, see John M. Maki, ed., pp. 298–361, or Theodore McNelly, *Sources in Modern East Asian History and Politics* (New York: Appleton-Century-Crofts, 1967), pp. 195–200.

[23] Constitution, Article 6.

missed.[24] Actually, no more than 11.05 percent of the votes have ever been cast against any judge, so that no judge has ever been voted out of office. The system of popular review could conceivably result in drawing the Court into the rough and tumble of partisan politics, but so far it has not.

The judges of the inferior courts are appointed by the Cabinet from a list of persons nominated by the Supreme Court. All judges of inferior courts serve for ten years with the privilege of reappointment. Judges may not be removed unless judicially declared mentally or physically incompetent to perform their official duties.[25] All judges retire at an age specified by law. Judges may be impeached by a Court of Impeachment made up of members of both houses of the Diet.[26]

The Supreme Court is vested with a sweeping rule-making power under which it determines the rules of procedure and of practice, and of matters relating to attorneys, the internal discipline of the courts and the administration of judicial affairs. The Supreme Court may delegate some of its rule-making authority to lower courts. Public procurators (prosecutors) are subject to the rule-making power of the Supreme Court.[27] The present Constitution does not provide for a jury system.

Corresponding to each court at every level are public procurators who represent the state in criminal cases. Thus, there are a Supreme Public Procurator's Office, High Public Procurator's Offices, District Public Procurator's Offices, and Local Public Procurator's Offices. The procurators are civil servants under the supervision and control of the Minister of Justice.

The status-of-forces agreement between the United States and Japan gives Japan the authority to try American soldiers for offenses committed while not on official duty. This agreement, which was applied in the Girard case, is important to the preservation of Japanese sovereignty and national prestige.

As in the United States, trials sometimes are delayed or prolonged excessively because of technical legal problems or an overload of work for the courts. Cases involving persons implicated in civil disturbances are especially apt to be drawn out. This is particularly unfortunate, because these cases are often fraught with great significance in the turbulence of Japanese politics. A notorious instance concerned 219 defendants accused of rioting on May Day, 1952. Nearly a thousand witnesses testified, and after the prosecution and defense rested their cases, the court worked for four years on its verdict. The Tokyo

[24] Constitution, Article 79.
[25] Constitution, Articles 78–80.
[26] Constitution, Article 64.
[27] Constitution, Article 77.

District Court finally issued its decision on January, 1970, over seventeen years after the riot. During the long proceedings, sixteen of the defendants died. One hundred ten were found not guilty and ninety-three were found guilty but were given suspended sentences or were assessed slight fines. In November, 1969, the Nagoya District Court found eighty-three persons guilty of rioting in July, 1952, seventeen years before. Justice delayed is justice denied, and in Japan, as elsewhere, speedier trials are being demanded.

Suggested Reading

Baerwald, Hans H. "Nikkan Kokkai: The Japan-Korea Treaty Diet," in Lucian W. Pye, ed., *Cases in Comparative Politics: Asia.* Boston, Mass.: Little, Brown, 1970, pp. 19–57.

Belli, Melvin M., and Danny R. Jones. *Belli Looks at Life and Law in Japan.* Indianapolis, Ind.: Bobbs-Merrill, 1960.

EHS Law Bulletin Series: Japanese Laws in English Version. Tokyo: Eibun-Hōrei-Sha, 10 vols., various years.

George, James, Jr. "Law in Modern Japan," in Hall, John Whitney, and Richard K. Beardsley, *Twelve Doors to Japan.* New York: McGraw-Hill, 1965.

Gokijō, Kakiwa. "The Judicial System of Japan," *The Annals of the American Academy of Political and Social Science,* Vol. CCCVIII (November, 1956), 28–39.

Henderson, Dan Fenno, ed. *The Constitution of Japan: Its First Twenty Years, 1947–67.* Seattle: University of Washington Press, 1968.

Hozumi Nobushige. *Ancestor Worship and Japanese Law,* 4th rev. ed. Tokyo: Maruzen, 1938.

Koshi, George. *The Japanese Legal Advisor: Crimes and Punishments.* Rutland, Vt.: Charles E. Tuttle, 1970.

Maki, John M., ed. *Court and Constitution in Japan: Selected Supreme Court Decisions, 1948–60.* Seattle: University of Washington Press, 1964.

Ministry of Justice. *The Constitution of Japan and Criminal Statutes.* Tokyo: Government Printing Bureau, 1958.

Ministry of Justice. *Criminal Justice in Japan.* Tokyo: Government Printing Bureau, 1958.

Schubert, Glendon, and David J. Danelski, eds. *Comparative Judicial Behavior: Cross-Cultural Studies of Political Decision-Making in the East and West.* New York: Oxford University Press, 1969.

Von Mehren, Arthur Taylor, ed. *Law in Japan: The Legal Order in a Changing Society.* Cambridge, Mass.: Harvard University Press, 1963.

6

The Executive

The Parliamentary-Cabinet System

The two principal types of democratic government are the congressional-presidential (or presidential) system and the parliamentary-cabinet (or parliamentary) system. The distinction between the two systems lies in the relationship between the legislature and the executive.

In the parliamentary-cabinet system, such as that in England and Japan, the prime minister and cabinet depend for their appointment and continuance in office on the approval of a majority in the lower house of the legislature. When the prime minister loses the support of the lower house, he is expected either to resign or to request the head of state to dissolve the lower house in the hope that the newly-elected legislature will support him. If the new house proves unwilling to back the prime minister, the latter resigns and the chief of state appoints a new prime minister acceptable to parliament.

The most notable advantage of the parliamentary system over the presidential system (such as that in the United States) is that long-standing deadlocks between the legislature and executive are prevented; the two branches cannot indefinitely veto each other's programs. In some countries, a notable disadvantage of the parliamentary system is that no one proposed for the prime ministership is able to obtain the support of a stable majority, because no party or coalition of parties controls a majority in the legislature. As a result, it might take weeks to find a prime minister, or a prime minister is able to serve in office only for a very brief and troubled period, so that the government is unable to carry out strong consistent policies. In a democracy the executive must be responsible, i.e., subject to removal by the parliament or the people; however, the executive must be given enough authority and be permitted to remain in office long enough to be able to govern. In Japan since 1955, the parliament has not passed votes of no confidence, because the consistently Liberal-Democratic Prime Minister has been supported by a well-nigh permanent Liberal-Democratic majority in the lower house. Only if he becomes seriously ill or when important factions within his party desert him must a Prime Minister resign. Because of party discipline, the legislators in the ruling party always vote for the Cabinet's programs, so that in effect the Cabinet tends to dominate the parliament rather than vice versa. The responsibility and effectiveness of the executive in Japan will be one of the topics discussed in this chapter.

Another problem in the parliamentary-cabinet system relates to the image and role of the head of state, who may be either a hereditary monarch or a directly or indirectly elected president. Although the powers of the head of state in the ideal parliamentary system are in principle to be exercised by him only on the advice of the prime minister, representing parliament, in actual practice his powers may be used without reference to the will of the legislature. The prime minister may make use of the head of state's emergency or decree powers when parliament is uncooperative. Or, when it is difficult to determine who in parliament can command majority support, the head of state's discretion in the selection of a prime minister may be considerable. Sometimes a charismatic head of state may interpret his own personal powers very broadly. Obviously if the head of state, be he a monarch or an elected president, acts without reference to the will of the legislature, the parliamentary system may give way to something else. In the case of postwar Japan, the Emperor may act only on the advice of the Cabinet, and he has no powers that may be usurped or exercised by irresponsible oligarchs or by the military, as occurred before the war.

The Functions and Organization of the Cabinet

While the Emperor is the symbol of the state under the new Constitution, the Prime Minister is the head of the government. Since World War II the roles of the Prime Minister and Cabinet have grown vastly more important than they formerly were. The Meiji Constitution made only one or two references to Ministers of State (Daijin), and the words cabinet (Naikaku) and prime minister (Sōri Daijin) do not appear in the document. But the 1946 Constitution devotes all of Chapter V to the organization and powers of the Cabinet. The Privy Council, the Elder Statesmen, the Imperial Household Ministry, the Lord Keeper of the Privy Seal, and the Imperial High Command no longer exist as rivals or superiors of the Cabinet within the executive branch.

From the beginning of the Occupation, General MacArthur's staff regarded the Prime Minister as the chief executive and channeled their orders through him, thus enhancing his authority. When the Office of

Figure 3
Satō Eisaku

Prime Minister Satō as depicted in a popular weekly magazine after his conference with President Nixon in November, 1969. Here his given name precedes the family name, American style, and the letters USA are emphasized, indicating Mr. Satō's pro-American bias.
(Yokoo Tadanori, in *Asahi Journal* 2 [November 30, 1969]. P. 99.)

the Lord Keeper of the Privy Seal was abolished in November, 1945, the Prime Minister took custody of the Imperial Seal and control of official access to the Emperor. Under the new Constitution, the Emperor acts only on the advice of the Prime Minister and his Cabinet; the Prime Minister is the effective chief executive and is responsible only to the Diet and to his party.

The Cabinet was first brought into existence in 1885, in anticipation of the enactment of the Imperial (Meiji) Constitution four years later. Under the Meiji Constitution the determination of the "organization of the different branches of the administration" was the prerogative of the Emperor, and in 1889 an Imperial Rescript described the organization and functions of the Cabinet.[1] The Emperor no longer exercises this power, and today the Diet, the "highest organ of state power," determines the main outline of cabinet organization by law.[2]

The Formal Functions of the Cabinet

Under the old regime executive power belonged to the Emperor, and the Ministers of State simply advised the Emperor and exercised powers delegated to them by His Majesty. But Article 65 of the 1947 Constitution provides that "Executive power shall be vested in the Cabinet" so that the Cabinet exercises executive authority in its own right. The Cabinet, in addition to other general administrative functions, is required by Chapter V of the Constitution to (1) administer the law faithfully and conduct affairs of state, (2) manage foreign affairs, (3) conclude treaties with Diet approval, (4) administer the civil service according to standards established by law, (5) prepare the budget and present it to the Diet, (6) enact Cabinet orders (seirei) to execute the provisions of the Constitution and the law, and (7) decide on general amnesty, special amnesty, commutation of punishment, reprieve and restoration of rights. All laws and Cabinet orders must be signed by the competent minister of state and countersigned by the Prime Minister.

In addition to the above powers, the Constitution requires the Cabi-

---

[1] Text in Supreme Commander for the Allied Powers, Government Section, *Political Reorientation of Japan: September 1945 to September 1948*, 2 vols. (Washington, D.C.: Government Printing Office, n.d. [1949?]), Vol. II, 596 (these volumes will subsequently be cited as *Political Reorientation*), in W. W. McLaren, "Japanese Government Documents," *Transactions of the Asiatic Society of Japan*, Vol. XLII, Part 1, 1914, 232–233, and in Harold S. Quigley, *Japanese Government and Politics: An Introductory Survey* (New York: Century, 1932), pp. 359–360.

[2] E.g., Cabinet Law, *Political Reorientation*, Vol. II, 851.

net to exercise important functions connected with other organs of the government. The Cabinet (1) advises the Emperor on "acts in matters of state," (2) designates the Chief Judge of the Supreme Court, (3) appoints all judges of the Supreme Court (except the Chief Judge) and all judges of inferior courts, (4) determines the convocation of extraordinary sessions of the Diet, (5) convenes the House of Councillors in emergency session, (6) expends monies from the reserve fund, (7) submits final accounts of expenditures and revenues of the State, (8) reports regularly to the Diet and the people on the state of national finances, and (9) proposes bills, budgets, and other measures to the Diet.

In practice, a principal function of the Cabinet is *legislative,* since the Cabinet initiates virtually all of the bills which are enacted by the Diet.

The Cabinet performs its functions at cabinet meetings presided over by the Prime Minister. Since Meiji times, regular cabinet meetings (teirei kakugi) are held every Tuesday and Friday morning. In addition, if necessary, special meetings (rinji kakugi) are held. By long established custom, decisions are made by unanimous agreement, and the substance of cabinet discussions are supposed to be kept secret.

The Organization of the Cabinet

The Cabinet has grown substantially in the nearly ninety years of its existence. The first Cabinet of Prince Ito, in 1885, contained only ten men: the Prime Minister and the Ministers for Foreign Affairs, Home Affairs, Finance, Army, Navy, Justice, Education, Agriculture and Commerce, and Communications. Under the new Constitution, the number of Cabinet Ministers is determined by the Diet.

In late 1971, under the Prime Minister, twelve Ministers headed Ministries, and seven Ministers without portfolio were known as State Ministers. The twelve Ministries were Justice, Foreign Affairs, Finance, Education, Health and Welfare, Agriculture and Forestry, International Trade and Industry, Transportation, Posts and Telecommunications, Labor, Construction, and Home Affairs (Autonomy). The Minister of Home Affairs served concurrently as Director-General of the Hokkaido Development Agency. The seven State Ministers were: the Chief Cabinet Secretary, the Chairman of the National Public Safety Commission (concurrently Director General of the Administrative Management Agency), the Director General of the Prime Minister's Office, the Director General of the Science and Technology Agency (concurrently Chairman of the Atomic Energy Commission), the Director General of the Defense Agency, the Director General of the Economic Planning Agency, and the Director General of the Environment Agency. (The last-mentioned post was created in 1971.)

Normally, at about the same time that the Cabinet is selected, the major posts in the Liberal-Democratic Party are filled, and although these officials are not technically part of the Cabinet, newspapers usually list their names along with those of the Cabinet Ministers. These four LDP offices are the Vice President, Secretary General, Chairman of the Executive Board, and Chairman of the Policy Board.

The auxiliary organs of the Cabinet are the Cabinet Secretariat and the Legislative Bureau. Their organization and that of the other necessary offices in the Cabinet are determined by law. The Cabinet Secretariat (Naikaku Kambō) is formally charged with "preparing the agenda of Cabinet meetings and other miscellaneous affairs of the Cabinet."[3] The Director of the Cabinet Secretariat, or Chief Cabinet Secretary, is responsible for the proper functioning of the Cabinet Secretariat. He is a principal political adviser to the Prime Minister especially during the formation of a Government, and he often makes announcements to the press on behalf of the Prime Minister and the Cabinet. He is at all times well informed on questions under discussion in the Cabinet, since the Secretariat prepares the cabinet agenda.

The Legislative Bureau (Hōseikyoku) is "in charge of examining and drafting cabinet bills and cabinet orders, as well as examining drafts of treaties, and other legal matters."[4] All draft laws and cabinet orders proposed by the Ministries must be submitted to the Legislative Bureau to be formally drafted. The substance of a bill is the responsibility of the Ministry, while its legal aspects are taken care of by the Bureau. The high legal competence of the Bureau ensures that cabinet bills will command respect from a technical point of view and has contributed greatly to the strength of the executive branch in its dealings with the legislative.

The National Personnel Authority (Jinji-in), concerned with administering the civil service, is a nonpolitical extraministerial agency created by act of the Diet and administratively placed under the Cabinet. The Board of Audit (Kaikei Kensa-in) is independent of the Cabinet. In accordance with Article 90 of the Constitution, it audits the final accounts of the expenditures and revenues of the State.

---

[3] Cabinet Law, Article 12.
[4] *Ibid.*

The Prime Minister

Formal Powers

Under the Meiji Constitution, the Prime Minister was not mentioned; but in Article 66 of the new Constitution he is declared to be the "head" of the Cabinet, and his position has been conspicuously strengthened. He has the power to appoint and to dismiss other ministers without consulting the Diet. He exercises control and supervision over the various branches of the administration and represents the Cabinet in submitting bills and reporting on general and foreign affairs to the Diet. All laws and cabinet orders must not only be signed by the competent minister but countersigned by the Prime Minister. He presides at cabinet meetings. Following discussion of the Cabinet, he decides jurisdictional disputes among cabinet ministers and may suspend the official act or order of any administrative office pending action by the Cabinet. The supremacy of the Prime Minister in the Cabinet is further emphasized by the constitutional requirement that the entire Cabinet must resign if the post of Prime Minister falls vacant.

Election

Under Article 10 of the Meiji Constitution, the Emperor was empowered to appoint and dismiss all civil and military officers, including the Ministers of State. Before World War II, the Prime Minister was chosen by the Emperor on the advice of the genro. After the death of Prince Saionji Kimmochi, the last of the genro, in 1940, the Lord Keeper of the Privy Seal, after consultation with the Imperial Household Minister and the former prime ministers (jūshin) advised the Emperor on the choice. Until 1918, the genro selected Prime Ministers from among the clan oligarchs (frequently themselves genro). After the accession of Hara Takashi, the first commoner to serve as Prime Minister, in 1918 and during the 1920s Cabinet heads were usually, but not always, chosen from party leaders in the Diet. From 1932 to 1945, none of the Prime Ministers was a party leader, and all except three were either generals or admirals.

Under the new Constitution, the Diet, rather than the Emperor, elects the Prime Minister. Before proceeding to other business, the Diet must designate the Prime Minister from among its members by a resolution. If the House of Representatives and House of Councillors disagree and if no agreement can be reached in a joint committee of both houses, or if the House of Councillors fails to make designation within ten days after the House of Representatives has made designation, the decision of the House of Representatives is the decision of the Diet.[5] The Emperor "appoints" the person designated by the Diet.[6]

Although the constitutional procedure is quite clear, before 1955 the selection of a first minister was sometimes an involved process. Before the election of the Prime Minister was held in the Diet, there was a great deal of maneuvering within and among the political parties. If no party had a majority in the House of Representatives, some kind of interparty agreement was necessary in order to choose a Prime Minister. For example, when the Socialist Party headed by Katayama Tetsu won a plurality of seats in the 1947 election, all of the parties except the Communist agreed to form a four-party coalition headed by Katayama. As a result of this understanding, Katayama was almost unanimously elected to the prime ministership. The Liberals then withdrew from the coalition agreement, and it took an entire week for Katayama to form a Government.

When the Katayama Cabinet resigned in 1948, the coalition parties planned to form a new Government under Ashida Hitoshi. The Liberals, under Yoshida, urged that the principle of normal constitutional government required that when the Government resigns it should allow the opposition to form a Government rather than reorganize the coalition Cabinet. In this instance, the Liberals said, the Diet should designate Yoshida as Prime Minister. On February 21, 1948, the House of Representatives elected Ashida and the House of Councillors elected Yoshida to the prime ministership. As provided by the Constitution, a joint committee of both houses met but was unable to come to an agreement. The decision of the Representatives therefore became the decision of the Diet, and Ashida became Prime Minister.

For several years after the 1949 election, the Liberal Party held a comfortable majority in both houses and experienced no difficulty in electing and re-electing Yoshida as Prime Minister. In 1954 when the fifth Yoshida Cabinet resigned, no single party had a majority in the lower house, and it was again necessary to make some interparty agreement on the prime ministership. Hatoyama Ichirō, president of the Democratic Party, promised the Left and Right Socialist members of the lower house that he would dissolve the Diet after becoming Prime Minister if they would vote for him. Hatoyama was then elected with the combined votes of his own party and the Socialists.

[5] Constitution, Article 68.
[6] Constitution, Article 6.

Since the advent of the two-party system in 1955, each party nominates its own leader for the prime ministership and then votes along party lines, so that the outcome of the election is a foregone conclusion. Since Hatoyama's resignation in 1966, much more attention has been centered on the maneuvering among factions in the Liberal-Democratic Party to name a party president, who would certainly be designated the Prime Minister, than on the formal election of the Prime Minister in the Diet. The term of office of the president of the Liberal-Democratic Party is two years, so that there is sometimes a possibility that a Prime Minister may lose his post because he fails to be re-elected party president.

SCAP and the Prime Minister

During the Occupation, General MacArthur's attitude towards Cabinet ministers was usually crucial to their appointment and tenure in office. Thus, when the October 4, 1945, "Bill of Rights" directive called for drastic reforms and the resignation of the Home Minister, the Higashikuni Cabinet resigned en bloc. The appointment of Shidehara as Prime Minister was first cleared with General MacArthur, and the approval of SCAP Headquarters was obtained for the nomination of each minister in Shidehara's Cabinet.[7] When Shidehara resigned following the 1946 election, it appeared that the president of the Liberal Party, which had a plurality in the lower house, would succeed him. However, at this crucial juncture, the Liberal Party leader, Hatoyama Ichirō, was suddenly and unexpectedly purged by direct order of General MacArthur, and the way was open for Foreign Minister Yoshida to become president of the Liberal Party and Prime Minister.

In February, 1947, General MacArthur showed his lack of confidence in Prime Minister Yoshida by directing that a general election be held as soon as possible. As a result of the election, the Liberal Party of Yoshida lost its plurality in the lower house and Katayama succeeded to the prime ministership. After regaining the post of chief executive in 1948, Yoshida managed to retain the office until December, 1954. There is no question that the friendly attitude of General MacArthur was a principal factor accounting for Yoshida's long tenure in office.

[7] Shigaru Yoshida, *The Yoshida Memoirs* (Boston, Mass.: Houghton Mifflin, 1962), p. 82.

Roads to the Prime Ministership

Before being elected Prime Minister, a man normally serves a stint as an ordinary Cabinet minister. But some ministerial posts are more likely than others to lead to the prime ministership. The best stepping-stones to the prime ministry have been the Ministries of Foreign Affairs and of Finance. Eight prime ministers had previously served as Foreign Ministers: Ōkuma, Saionji, Katō Takaaki, Shidehara, Hirota, Yoshida, Ashida, and Kishi. Seven had formerly served as Ministers of Finance: Matsukata, Wakatsuki, Takahashi, Hamaguchi, Ishibashi, Ikeda, and Satō. Two had formerly served as Home Ministers, two as Education Ministers, and two as Communications Ministers. Under the present Constitution, only civilians may serve in the Cabinet, but before 1946, sixteen prime ministers were career military men: ten from the Army and six from the Navy.

Between 1955 and 1972, one had to be a Liberal-Democrat in order to become Prime Minister.

Forming a Government

Following his election as Prime Minister, the new chief executive must appoint the members of his Cabinet, at least half of whom must be drawn from the Diet according to the new Constitution. Since Yoshida's time, all the ministers are normally selected from the Diet. Because the Government must have the support of the Diet in order to have its proposals enacted into law, the political composition of the executive body is of primary importance.

Postwar Governments

Governments in postwar Japan have been based on political parties and have been either coalition or one-party Cabinets. Coalition Cabinets are made up of members of two or more political parties which together have a majority in the lower house. When no single party has a majority, a Cabinet must depend on the support of more than one party for the passage of its bills, and a minority party may find it expedient to form a coalition rather than a single-party Cabinet. After World War II no single party was able to win a majority in the Diet until 1949, and coalition Governments were the rule. The first Yoshida Cabinet was a coalition of Liberals and Progressives headed by a Liberal. The succeeding Katayama Cabinet was a three-party coalition of Socialists, Democrats, and People's Cooperatives, headed by a Socialist. Its successor, the Ashida Government, was a coalition of the same three parties headed by a Democrat (Progressive). The third Yoshida Cabinet could have been a single-party Government because Yoshida's Democratic-Liberals had a comfortable majority in the House of Representatives, but Democrats were brought into the Government reportedly as the result of a suggestion by SCAP Headquarters.

There have been no coalition Cabinets since the third Yoshida Government because the two-party system inaugurated in 1955 has provided comfortable majorities in the Diet for Liberal-Democratic governments. It is conceivable that in a future election neither of the major parties (Liberal-Democratic and Socialist) would win a majority, in which case the minor parties would hold the balance of power in the lower house and make bids for places in a coalition Cabinet or extract other political concessions in exchange for their support.

In Japan, factions within parties are very powerful, and the competition for Cabinet posts is intense. As a consequence, a one-party Cabinet is in the nature of a coalition of factions of the ruling party. Each faction is made up of Diet members whose leader supports their nominations to candidacy, supplies them with funds, and sometimes finds Cabinet posts for them. The principal objectives of factions are the acquisition of money and political office, the supply of which is inadequate to satisfy everyone. It frequently takes several days for a Prime Minister to appoint a Cabinet, since it is necessary to avoid ruffling unduly the factions whose support he will need in his relations with the Diet. The competition for the title of Daijin (Minister) and Seimu Jikan (Parliamentary Vice Minister) is intense, for nearly every politician is more or less afflicted with daijinbyō (minister sickness). The only women ever appointed to the Cabinet were Mrs. Nakayama Masa, Welfare Minister in Ikeda's first Government, and Miss Kondo Tsuruyo, State Minister and Director of Science and Technology Agency and Atomic Energy Commission in Ikeda's second Cabinet as reconstructed in July, 1962. Presumably women may serve in future Cabinets now that the precedent has been set, but traditional sentiment and factional politics will no doubt make female ministers rare.

The role of the Throne in the formation of a Cabinet is, under the new Constitution, purely formal. The Emperor, as has been noted, appoints the Prime Minister designated by the Diet, and he attests the appointment of the other Cabinet ministers, who are appointed by the Prime Minister.

As soon as the new Cabinet is formed, a picture is taken of the Cabinet ministers in formal attire, standing in front of the official residence of the Prime Minister. Newspaper columnists often claim to discern expressions of delight or pain on the faces of the new ministers, suggesting their evaluation of the composition of the new Cabinet. Usually some faction leaders and their followers are gravely offended by their nonrepresentation or underrepresentation in the Government. Journalists speculate on whether the formation of the new Cabinet will ensure the re-election of the Prime Minister, or his choice, as LDP president. The question of who will be the *next* Prime Minister becomes the immediate topic of endless premature speculation. Tales of factional and intrafactional intrigue, personal rivalries, unkept promises, and wounded egos proliferate. The impression is created that the Prime Minister, Japan's most powerful political figure, owes his position to his superior ability as an artful manipulator of his fellow politicians and a fund raiser, skilled in wheeling and dealing. The democratic input into the choice of the Prime Minister and his Cabinet seems minimal. Some observers have urged that a popularly elected president would be much better than a Prime Minister chosen by undemocratic means. Nakasone Yasuhiro, a rising young (young by Japanese standards) politician has urged such a reform. A shift to the presidential system, however, seems most unlikely. It would require a constitutional amendment which commands no significant support among the public, which seems apathetic about this issue.

Cabinet Changes

The turnover of ministerships in Japan is very high, because Cabinets since the war have changed or been reformed on the average of once a year. A single individual may become Prime Minister repeatedly, but every time he forms a new Government he is apt to find new men for most of the seats. Furthermore, during the lifetime of a single Cabinet, there are often substantial changes in personnel. The Prime Minister appoints and dismisses Cabinet members without the formal approval of the Diet. Prime Ministers have made liberal use of their power to dismiss ministers arbitrarily in order to strengthen their own political position and that of the Cabinet as a whole. Yoshida was famous, especially during his relatively long-lived third Government, for the "mass production" (masu puro) of ministers. Kishi, Ikeda, and Satō made wholesale changes in the personnel of their Cabinets in such a way that the "reconstructed" Cabinets were virtually new ones. These reshuffles reflected changes in factional relations within the ruling Liberal-Democratic Party. Legally, a reconstructed Cabinet cannot be considered a new Cabinet because the Prime Minister con-

tinues in office without undergoing the formalities of election by the
the Diet and appointment by the Emperor.

Responsible Government

The Cabinet is "collectively responsible to the Diet."[8] Article 69 of
the Constitution provides that when the House of Representatives passes
a resolution of no confidence in the Cabinet or rejects a confidence
resolution, "the Cabinet shall resign en masse, unless the House of
Representatives is dissolved within ten days." According to Article 7,
the Emperor, with the advice and approval of the Cabinet, dissolves
the House of Representatives. Thus, when the lower house votes no
confidence in the Government, the Government must either resign or
advise a dissolution.

The Resignation of the Cabinet

Under the new Constitution, the lower chamber has never been able
to bring about the fall of a Cabinet with a resolution of no confidence,
but the threat of one was sufficient in 1954. The principal cause of
Cabinet resignations since 1947 has been the constitutional requirement (Article 70) that "the Cabinet shall resign en masse" upon the
first convocation of the Diet after a general election of members of the
lower house. Contrary to British custom, even though the Government
party wins the election, the Cabinet must resign. The victorious party,
of course, may re-elect its leader as Prime Minister.

The Constitution also requires the cabinet to resign when the post of
Prime Minister falls vacant. Hatoyama's third Cabinet, the Ishibashi
Cabinet, and Ikeda's third Cabinet resigned when the ill health of the
Prime Minister made it infeasible for him to remain in office. The
coalition Governments of Katayama and Ashida fell because of dis-
sension both within and among the parties making up the coalition.

Kishi's second Cabinet resigned when the strikes and demonstrations
which were mounted against it became too overwhelming, and some of
Kishi's rivals in his own party deserted him.

Extraparliamentary Factors

In Japan, two important extraparliamentary devices have been used
to hasten the fall of Cabinets. These are popular demonstrations and
terrorism. Street demonstrations against the Portsmouth Treaty in

[8] Article 66, Constitution of Japan.

1905 and the rice riots of 1918 precipitated the falls of the first Katsura Cabinet and the Terauchi Cabinet respectively. Since World War II, demonstrations and a threatened general strike directed against the first Yoshida Government apparently influenced MacArthur in calling for a general election, which resulted in a change of Cabinet. The resignation of the second Kishi Cabinet was partly a consequence of strikes and demonstrations.

Assassination became so conspicuous a political technique in Japan in the 1930s that one knowledgeable foreign observer wrote a description of the political system under the title, *Government by Assassination*.[9] Six prewar prime ministers lost their lives at the hands of terrorists during or after their terms of office: Itō (d. 1909), Hara (d. 1921), Hamaguchi (d. 1931), Inukai (d. 1932), Saitō (d. 1936), and Takahashi (d. 1936). Attempts were made on the lives of others, including Okada, Saionji, and Suzuki. Governments which fell as the result of the assassination of the Prime Minister or members of his Cabinet were those of Hara, Hamaguchi, Inukai, and Okada. The motive and effect of assassinations in the 1930s were to discredit parliamentary government and party politics and strengthen the forces of military fascism.

The revival of rightist terrorism following World War II, especially the assassination of Socialist Party Chairman Asanuma Inejirō and the stabbing of Prime Minister Kishi in 1960, has aroused fears for the future of democracy and has been capitalized on by the Socialists to discredit conservative governments.

The Lifetime of Cabinets

Sixty-four cabinets have come into existence since the establishment of the cabinet system in 1885. Thus the average life of Japanese cabinets is about fourteen months.

Under the new Constitution, a general election for the lower house must be held at least once every four years, and the Cabinet must resign following a general election, so that it is legally impossible for a Cabinet to remain in office longer than four years. However, a re-appointed Prime Minister or a new Prime Minister may choose to reappoint the members of the old Cabinet, or during the middle of his term, a Prime Minister may replace nearly all of his ministers. Thus, the lives of Cabinets are poor indicators of ministerial stability.

[9] Hugh Byas, *Government by Assassination* (New York: Knopf, 1942).

Dissolution of the House of Representatives

There was once much uncertainty concerning the scope of the Government's power of dissolution. Did the Prime Minister have to wait until the House of Representatives voted no confidence before asking the Emperor to dissolve the lower house? The Constitution was unclear.

In 1948, the question arose as to whether Yoshida could advise a dissolution without there first being a vote of no confidence. His party held that Article 7 provided sufficient authorization for dissolution independently of Article 69. If Article 7 could be so construed, it would mean that the Cabinet might dissolve the House of Representatives at any time politically advantageous to the Government party (or parties), even though a majority of the house might be opposed to dissolution. The manner in which prewar Governments had bullied the Diet by too frequent dissolution was fresh in the minds of many legislators. The opposition held that the lower house could be dissolved only if the house passed a resolution of no confidence. Occupation officials arranged a compromise whereby the lower house voted no confidence in the Government and the Government then asked the Emperor for a dissolution. Thus, in principle, the supremacy of the Diet provided for in the American-drafted Constitution was upheld. The victory of the Diet in this case was largely nominal: the Cabinet got the dissolution it wanted, and in the subsequent election the Government party (Democratic-Liberals) won an absolute majority.

Four years later, when the Allied forces had withdrawn, the Yoshida Government was able to have its way completely in the matter of dissolving the lower chamber, and effected a "surprise dissolution" without a prior vote of no confidence in parliament.

In 1953, Prime Minister Yoshida insulted the Diet by calling a member a stupid fool during the course of a debate, thus provoking a vote of no confidence. This was the second and last time that the House of Representatives passed a vote of no confidence in the Cabinet. The Government immediately obtained an imperial rescript dissolving the House of Representatives. In the subsequent election, Yoshida lost his absolute majority in the lower house but managed to gain the distinction of being the only Prime Minister in Japanese history to be chosen to form a fifth Cabinet. All subsequent dissolutions were effected without votes of no confidence. The permanent parliamentary majority commanded by the governing Liberal-Democrats makes a no-confidence vote unlikely, as that party would not vote against its own Cabinet. When Prime Minister Kishi lost the support of his own party, he resigned without awaiting a no-confidence vote and made way for a fellow conservative to become Prime Minister (Ikeda). The Cabinet now has the power to dissolve the lower house at will and does so at the moment which it deems politically expedient.

In the 1960 crisis, the Socialists were in a minority and unable to vote no confidence in the Government. Nevertheless, they demanded both the resignation of the Cabinet and a dissolution of the House of Representatives. When the Kishi Government refused either to resign or dissolve the lower house, the Socialist members threatened themselves to resign from the Diet in order to deepen the crisis and thus force Kishi to do their will. They signed formal resignation papers for their party chairman, who would later submit them, if need be, to the speaker of the House. The Government, of course, could call by-elections for seats which the Socialists might vacate, rather than dissolve parliament, and as things worked out, the Socialists did not make good their threat. After a number of general strikes and mass demonstrations, Kishi announced his intention to resign, and the succeeding Ikeda Cabinet dissolved the House of Representatives without waiting for a vote of no confidence. It would almost appear that the Cabinet may be under some obligation to dissolve the lower chamber if the opposition organizes sufficiently large demonstrations and strikes.

When an especially controversial decision is made by the Government, the opposition parties are apt to demand a dissolution. The implication is, of course, that the Cabinet has disregarded the desires of the people and a new election would produce a democratically-based Government that would carry out different policies. As in the case of Satō following the enactment of the University Control Bill in 1969, the Prime Minister is apt to stick to his post and to dissolve parliament a few months later. The subsequent election results are a big disappointment for the Socialists, whose supporters among intellectuals and newsmen are highly articulate but are unable to deliver the votes necessary to dislodge the conservatives.

The Bureaucratic Spirit

The new Constitution provides that the executive branch is responsible to the Diet, which represents the people, rather than to the Emperor. The Cabinet is thus, in theory at least, a democratic rather than an oligarchic institution. Furthermore, Article 15 of the Constitution provides that "all public officials are servants of the whole community and not of any group thereof." Cabinet ministers and other officials are no longer officers of the Emperor using the authority delegated by the Throne to rule the people; they are public servants. The old attitude summed up in the motto, "Respect for officials and scorn for the people" (kanson minpi) has presumably been replaced by the egalitarian idea.

However, many historical, social, and political factors militate against democratic attitudes and behavior. Confucianism has normally exalted the role of the bureaucrat. The most promising sons of rural landlords have traditionally aspired to high position in government and the prestige that it brings to himself, his family, and his community. Many of the brightest students in the great Imperial (now National) Universities major in law and public administration in order to pass the examinations for public office.

During the Meiji period the government bureaucracy, rather than private initiative, introduced Western technology and business methods. After government enterprises were put on a paying basis they were sold to private companies. Business still depends greatly on the bureaucracy for advice and favors of all sorts. The economy as well as the politics of the country has long been under bureaucratic direction. Ordinary politicians do not enjoy the measure of respect that high government officials command. The bureaucrat is respected because of his education, technical knowledge and skill, his reputation for impartiality, and his power.

Under the new Constitution, it is necessary to be a member of the Diet in order to become Prime Minister, and half of the remaining ministers must be Diet members. Today the bureaucrat who aspires to Cabinet position must enter politics. Furthermore, when an official finds that further promotion is unlikely or that he must retire on an inadequate pension, he is apt to consider seriously a political career. He has already proved his administrative competence, and he enjoys a measure of prestige in his home community where people regard him as a home-town boy who made good, and they take a personal interest in his political career. During the long regime of Yoshida, bureaucrats streamed into the Liberal Party. Thus Japanese politics differs drastically from politics in America, for in Japan one of the best ways to begin a political career is to enter the civil service. Most of the postwar Prime Ministers in Japan have had long careers in the civil service, but never in the history of the United States has the career bureaucracy produced a president. Shidehara, Yoshida, Ashida, Kishi, Ikeda, and Satō were career civil servants before becoming Prime Minister.

Bureaucrats naturally regard their own opinion as more informed than that of the layman, and Cabinet Ministers with bureaucratic origins often take a scornful attitude towards legislators, the press, and the general public. Ikeda Hayato was notorious for his lack of tact

Table 4

Japanese Cabinets

Clan and/or party affiliations of Prime Ministers are indicated in parenthesis.

1.	December 22, 1885	Itō Hirobumi (Chōshū), *First*
2.	April 30, 1888	General Kuroda Kiyotaka (Satsuma)
3.	December 24, 1889	General Yamagata Aritomo (Chōshū), *First*
4.	May 6, 1891	Matsukata Masayoshi (Satsuma), *First*
5.	August 8, 1892	Itō Hirobumi (Chōshū), *Second*
6.	September 18, 1896	Matsukata Masayoshi (Satsuma), *Second*
7.	January 12, 1898	Itō Hirobumi (Chōshū), *Third*
8.	June 30, 1898	Ōkuma Shigenobu (Hizen, Kenseitō), *First*
9.	November 8, 1898	General Yamagata Aritomo (Chōshū), *Second*
10.	October 19, 1900	Itō Hirobumi (Chōshū, Seiyūkai), *Fourth*
11.	June 2, 1901	General Katsura Tarō (Chōshū), *First*
12.	January 7, 1906	Prince Saionji (Kimmochi (kuge [court noble], Seiyūkai), *First*
13.	July 14, 1908	General Katsura Tarō (Chōshū), *Second*
14.	August 30, 1911	Prince Saionji Kimmochi (kuge, Seiyūkai), *Second*
15.	December 21, 1912	General Katsura Tarō (Chōshū), *Third*
16.	February 20, 1913	Admiral Yamamoto Gombei (Satsuma), *First*
17.	April 16, 1914	Ōkuma Shigenobu (Hizen), *Second*
18.	October 9, 1916	General Terauchi Masatake (Chōshū)
19.	September 29, 1918	Hara Takashi (Seiyūkai)
20.	November 13, 1921	Takahashi Korekiyo (Seiyūkai)
21.	June 12, 1922	Admiral Katō Tomosaburō
22.	September 2, 1923	Admiral Yamamoto Gombei (Satsuma), *Second*
23.	January 7, 1924	Kiyoura Keigo
24.	June 11, 1924	Katō Takaaki (Kenseikai), *First*
25.	August 2, 1925	Katō Takaaki (Kenseikai), *Second*
26.	January 30, 1926	Wakatsuki Reijiro (Kenseikai), *First*
27.	April 20, 1927	General Tanaka Giichi (Seiyūkai)
28.	July 2, 1929	Hamaguchi Osachi (Minseitō)
29.	April 14, 1931	Wakatsuki Reijiro (Minseitō), *Second*
30.	December 13, 1931	Inukai Tsuyoshi (Seiyūkai)
31.	May 26, 1932	Admiral Saitō Makoto
32.	July 8, 1934	Admiral Okada Keisuke
33.	March 9, 1936	Hirota Kōki
34.	February 2, 1937	General Hayashi Senjūrō
35.	June 4, 1937	Prince Konoye Fumimaro (kuge), *First*
36.	January 5, 1939	Hiranuma Kiichirō
37.	August 30, 1939	General Abe Nobuyuki
38.	January 16, 1940	Admiral Yonai Mitsumasa
39.	July 22, 1940	Prince Konoye Fumimaro (kuge), *Second*
40.	July 18, 1941	Prince Konoye Fumimaro (kuge), *Third*
41.	October 18, 1941	General Tōjō Hideki
42.	July 22, 1944	General Koiso Kuniaki

43.	April 7, 1945	Admiral Suzuki Kantarō
44.	August 17, 1945	Prince Higashikuni Naruhiko
45.	October 9, 1945	Shidehara Kijūrō (Shimpotō)
46.	May 22, 1946	Yoshida Shigeru (Jiyūtō), *First*
47.	May 24, 1947	Katayama Tetsu (Shakaitō)
48.	March 10, 1948	Ashida Hitoshi (Minshutō)
49.	October 15, 1948	Yoshida Shigeru (Minshu-Jiyūtō), *Second*
50.	February 16, 1949	Yoshida Shigeru (Minshu-Jiyūtō), *Third*
51.	October 30, 1952	Yoshida Shigeru (Jiyūtō), *Fourth*
52.	May 21, 1953	Yoshida Shigeru (Jiyūtō), *Fifth*
53.	December 10, 1954	Hatoyama Ichirō (Minshutō), *First*
54.	March 19, 1955	Hatoyama Ichirō (Minshutō), *Second*
55.	November 22, 1955	Hatoyama Ichirō (Jiyū-Minshutō), *Third*
56.	December 23, 1956	Ishibashi Tanzan (Jiyū-Minshutō)
57.	February 25, 1957	Kishi Nobusuke (Jiyū-Minshutō), *First*
58.	June 12, 1958	Kishi Nobusuke (Jiyū-Minshutō), *Second*
59.	July 19, 1960	Ikeda Hayato (Jiyū-Minshutō), *First*
60.	December 8, 1960	Ikeda Hayato (Jiyū-Minshutō), *Second*
61.	September 9, 1963	Ikeda Hayato (Jiyū-Minshutō), *Third*
62.	November 9, 1964	Satō Eisaku (Jiyū-Minshutō), *First*
63.	February 17, 1967	Satō Eisaku (Jiyū-Minshutō), *Second*
64.	January 14, 1970	Satō Eisaku (Jiyū-Minshutō), *Third*

Note: Satō's third cabinet, as reorganized on July 5, 1971, after a House of Councillors election, was made up as follows:

Prime Minister: Satō Eisaku; Justice Minister: Maeo Shigesaburo; Foreign Minister: Fukuda Takeo; Finance Minister: Mizuta Mikio; Education Minister: Takami Saburo; Health and Welfare Minister: Saitō Noboru; Agriculture-Forestry Minister: Akagi Munenori; International Trade and Industry Minister: Tanaka Kakuei; Transport Minister: Niwa Kyoshiro; Posts and Telecommunications Minister: Hirose Masao; Labor Minister: Hara Kenzaburo; Construction Minister: Nishimura Eiichi; Home Affairs Minister (concurrently Director General, Hokkaido Development Agency): Tokai Motosaburo; State Minister (Chief Cabinet Secretary): Takeshita Noboru; State Minister (Director General, Prime Minister's Office): Yamanaka Sadanori; State Minister (Chairman, National Public Safety Commission; Director General, Administrative Management Agency): Nakamura Torata; State Minister (Director General, Science and Technology Agency; Chairman, Atomic Energy Commission): Hiraizumi Wataru; State Minister (Director General, Defense Agency): Masuhara Keikichi; State Minister (Director General, Economic Planning Agency): Kimura Toshio; State Minister (Director General, Environment Agency): Oishi Buichi; Director, Cabinet Legislation Bureau: Takatsuji Masami.

before he became Prime Minister. While Finance Minister he said in a plenary session of the Diet that "It can't be helped if five or ten small businessmen involved in blackmarketing commit suicide because of bankruptcy." This cold-hearted attitude provoked a vote of no confidence in Ikeda, forcing him to resign from the cabinet.

The Civil Service

Under the Meiji Constitution government officials were appointed and dismissed by the Emperor and acted in his name. Imperial ordinances rather than democratically enacted laws provided for the regulation of the imperial civil service. Prime Minister Yamagata deliberately placed many high positions under the merit system in order to weaken political parties by depriving them of spoils. Top bureaucrats had higher court ranks than the members of the House of Representatives. The bureaucracy alone or in combination with the military tended to dominate the state. From 1899 to 1920, of 3,126 bills introduced into the Imperial Diet, 2,856 were Government bills, and only 270 were initiated by the Diet itself.[10]

Before World War II, the Japanese government service did not base its personnel administration on the relative evaluation and classification of the duties and responsibilities of positions but conducted personnel assignments and transactions according to a rigid, complex system of assigning official rank to individual persons without particular reference to their posts of duty.

The new Constitution provided that public officials were to be the "servants"—rather than the masters—of the people. The National Public Service Law[11] enacted in 1947 was intended to subordinate the bureaucracy to the elected representatives of the people and to ensure an efficient and democratic administration.

All national government personnel are divided into two groups: the regular government service, and the special government service. The regular government service includes all of the clerical and administrative employees of the national government except those classified as belonging to the special government service. The special government service embraces the members of the Cabinet, all positions appointment to which requires Diet approval, high officials in the Imperial Court, judges, ambassadors and ministers, Diet employees, common laborers, and employees of public corporations (the Japan National Railways, the Japan Monopoly Corporation, and the Japan Telegraph and Telephone Public Corporation).

The National Public Service Law is concerned primarily with the

[10] Kiyoaki Tsuji, "The Cabinet, Administrative Organization, and the Bureaucracy," *The Annals of the American Academy of Political and Social Science,* Vol. CCCVIII (November, 1956), 10–17.

[11] Text in *Political Reorientation,* Vol. II, 1022–1035. For an extensive discussion see Harold S. Quigley and John E. Turner, *The New Japan: Government and Politics* (Minneapolis: University of Minnesota Press, 1956), pp. 212–226.

regular government service. The National Personnel Authority (Jinji-in), which administers the National Public Service Law, was modeled after the Civil Service Commission of the United States and is largely independent of both the Diet and the Cabinet. The Authority is made up of three commissioners, one of whom is the Chairman, appointed by the Cabinet with the approval of the Diet. The functions of the Authority are to supervise the preparation of civil service examinations, classify positions, promote employee training and welfare, deal with employee grievances, and recommend administrative and salary reforms to the Cabinet and Ministries. Government departments would like to regain the authority over personnel matters which they have lost to the Personnel Authority, and the government has tended to regard the Authority as a kind of internal opposition. At the same time, labor unions have frequently protested the salary recommendations advanced by the Personnel Authority. Thus, there has been pressure from both right and left to abolish the institution, which is sometimes referred to as a "love-child of the Occupation."

Regular public servants have the right to organize and may authorize their union representatives to make requests to the National Personnel Authority concerning salaries and working conditions. However, as the result of amendments in the Public Service Law insisted on by General MacArthur in 1948, neither regular public servants nor the employees of government corporations have the right to bargain collectively and to strike.

In 1968, of the total of 1,972,375 national government employees, 793,945 were in government corporations and 614,093 are carried on special accounts.[12]

In accordance with a local public service law passed by the Diet in 1950, the civil service of the prefectures and other local government units is locally administered along the same general lines as the national civil service. Prefectural and other local personnel commissions correspond in organization and function to the National Personnel Authority. National law denies the rights of collective bargaining and striking to local government as well as to national government employees.

About 2 percent of the total population, or 4 percent of the gainfully employed in Japan, are employees of the national government. They constitute a substantial voting bloc. Most of them, whether white or blue collar, vote Socialist. Although most belong to labor unions, they are forbidden by law from striking. Strikes by employees of the Japan National Railways occasionally occur. They usually take place at a time of day when a minimum of commuters will be inconvenienced

[12] Japanese Government, Bureau of Statistics, *Statistical Handbook of Japan* (Tokyo, 1969).

and last only a few hours. The legal prosecution of strikers is not a pleasant business for the government because the offense seems trifling, and the process drags out for months or years. The National Railway Workers Union reiterates the claim that the legal ban on strikes violates the constitutional rights of the workers.

Public Corporations

Although private enterprise flourishes in Japan and the economy is predominantly capitalistic, the laissez-faire theory that rigorously opposes any government intervention and participation in the economy has been much less generally accepted than in the United States. In Japan, as in most other modern states, the railways are for the most part owned and operated by the national government. In 1902, seventeen privately owned railways were nationalized. In 1949, the Japan National Railways (JNR), a public enterprise corporation, was established. Although private railways are important for local transportation, long distance transportation is almost wholly monopolized by the JNR, which owns 86 percent of all rolling stock.

Perhaps more than any other people, the Japanese are dependent on railroads for transportation. Although automobile ownership has been rapidly growing in the past few years, railways, including local rapid transit and subways, are the principal means for personal transportation. Many people employed in Tokyo commute to work daily, sometimes for a distance up to fifty miles, from the surrounding prefectures. Thus Japan ranks first in the world in number of rail passengers. The JNR's new train between Tokyo and Osaka is the world's fastest.

Since World War II, the railways have been an important political issue. In an economy move in 1949, the government reduced by 270,000 the number of railroad employees, provoking massive labor union resistance. During the bitter dispute, the president of the National Railways was killed by a train under mysterious circumstances, six people were killed by a runaway train in Mitaka, and a train was derailed in Matsukawa, resulting in the death of two trainmen. The government tried nineteen workers for conspiracy in the last mentioned incident, while labor leaders charged that there had been a frame-up. The Matsukawa affair became a cause célèbre as the case was appealed from one court to another. Twenty years after the event, there were still ideological rumblings, as the courts as well as the executive branch became involved in the controversy.

In efforts to economize, the service of many local feeder lines has been curtailed or halted, often working a severe hardship on the industries and passengers dependent on cheap transportation. In 1966, the Minister of Transportation came under severe attack for causing the National Railway to make a regular stop at a small town in his constituency while service elsewhere was being cut back.

Japan's commuting public, which is the world's largest, holds the government accountable for satisfactory rail service. At the same time, the 276,000 members of the National Railway Workers Union and the 253,000 members of the Private Railway Workers Union, both of which are affiliated with the Sōhyō labor confederation, insist upon decent wages and job security. In 1969, for example, they were strongly protesting the dismissal of assistant engineers on electric and diesel locomotives.

The state-owned JNR is the country's largest enterprise, public or private. The state also owns the Nippon Telegraph and Telephone Public Corporation, which monopolizes all telegraphic and telephonic communication in Japan. The state-owned Japan Monopoly Corporation has no competitor in tobacco and salt manufacturing and distribution.

Japan, however, is not well advanced on the road to full nationalization. Compared with Great Britain, France, Italy, and Australia, the degree of nationalization in Japan is low and private enterprise predominates in the national economy. Although the Liberal-Democratic government is committed to expand and improve public welfare and the social security system, Japan is not a socialist country. Whether or not political democracy could long exist or the economy could flourish in a society where all of the voters are employees of the state seems problematical. So long as Japan's gross national product continues to expand at the average annual rate of over 10 percent, it seems doubtful that the public will wish to discard private enterprise in order to experiment with socialism.

The Emperor System

The Emperor in History

Whether during the ancient period, the feudal era, or the modern period of successively oligarchical, parliamentary, and military ascendancy, the Japanese emperor has reigned but seldom ruled. Article I of the Meiji Constitution stated that Japan shall be "reigned over and governed by a line of Emperors . . ." but in fact His Majesty had for centuries served as the titular rather than as the effective chief executive. The Emperor, with extremely few exceptions, has not made any important political decisions in the past 750 years. He invariably follows the advice of the effective government of the time, and that government must bear the brunt of responsibility for whatever decision has been made. The Emperor, therefore, has long been a constitutional monarch who can do no wrong.

The National Structure

According to the "orthodox" interpretation of the Meiji Constitution, such as that advanced by Hozumi Yatsuka and Uesugi Shinkichi, that part of the state system arising from location of sovereignty was the national structure (kokutai), and that part of the state system arising from the manner of the exercise of sovereignty was the government structure (seitai). The national structure was monarchical or republican depending upon whether sovereignty reposed in the monarch or the people. The government structure was constitutional or absolute depending upon whether there was separation or concentration of powers. The essence of the state lay in the location of sovereignty. Although the manner of the exercise of sovereignty (the government structure) might be changed, the location of sovereignty (the national structure) could not be legally changed. So far as Japan was concerned, it might be legally permissible to alter the Cabinet or the Diet, which were matters related to the government structure, but it was absolutely impossible to alter the principle of imperial sovereignty, since that was a matter related to the national structure.[13] The Peace Preservation Law of 1925 forbade, among other things, advocating the alteration of the national structure.

In the mid-1930s, ultranationalists advocated a "Showa Restoration" which would remove the corrupt politicians from the government and restore direct rule by the Emperor. At the same time, militarists and reactionary politicians demanded a "clarification of the national structure." Professor Minobe Tatsukichi, of Tokyo Imperial University, who had long expounded the theory that the Emperor was an "organ of the state," was attacked as disloyal and forced to resign from the House of Peers. The narrow interpretation of kokutai, which held that the Emperor was sacred and ruled by mandate of his divine ancestors, became the official ideology of the state and was taught in the schools.[14] Democracy, socialism, and communism alike were held to be subversive of Japan's unique national structure. At the same time, the "Imperial Way" (Kōdō) and the theory of "eight corners of the

[13] Yamazaki Tanshō, *Tennōsei no Kenkyū* (Tokyo: Teikoku Chihō Gyōsei Gakkai, 1959), pp. 389–390.

[14] An English translation of the basic textbook is Robert K. Hall, ed., *Kokutai no Hongi: Cardinal Principles of the National Entity of Japan*, trans. J. O. Gauntlett (Cambridge, Mass.: Harvard University Press, 1949).

world under one roof," based on Shinto scriptures, were cited by statesmen to justify Japanese militarism and expansion. The Emperor system, thus exploited to justify totalitarianism and aggression, was understandably suspect in the minds of foreign observers as a rallying point of Japanese militarism.

Japan's Surrender and the Emperor System

The Potsdam Declaration

During the closing stages of World War II, Acting Secretary of State Joseph Grew urged that the Allied policy of unconditional surrender for Japan should not mean the elimination of the existing dynasty. Grew believed that the Japanese alarm lest the revered imperial institution be destroyed would deter the Japanese from giving up the struggle; unless this fear was quieted and they were able to save face, they would fight to the bitter end. Furthermore, if after victory, America banned the imperial institution, the Japanese would try to restore it, and the effort would prevent resignation to defeat and reconciliation with the United States. Besides, Grew felt that a constitutional monarchy might be the most suitable form of government for Japan.[15] Late in May, 1945, Grew submitted to the President a statement of our terms which he advocated be announced. This draft was to go through a number of versions before finally emerging as the Potsdam Proclamation.[16]

Some members of the State Department opposed the views of the Acting Secretary concerning the Japanese Emperor system. They held that the Emperor cult had enabled a coalition of aggressive military and civilian groups to control the Japanese people and to lead them to aggression and that to allow the system to survive would be to court danger for the future. Furthermore, they felt it would be unjust and illogical to eliminate and punish other elements responsible for leading Japan into war and at the same time spare the Emperor.[17]

[15] Herbert Feis, *Japan Subdued: The Atomic Bomb and the End of the War in the Pacific* (Princeton, N.J.: Princeton University Press, 1961), p. 17.

[16] U.S. Department of State, *Foreign Relations of the United States, Diplomatic Papers: The Conference of Berlin (The Potsdam Conference)*, 2 vols. (Washington, D.C.: Government Printing Office, 1960), Vol. I, 884–903.

[17] The views of Assistant Secretary of State Archibald MacLeish are set forth in *ibid.*, Vol. I, 895–897.

When the new Secretary of State, James Byrnes, left for Potsdam early in July, he took with him a draft declaration which contained the following stipulations with regard to the future of the Japanese Emperor system:

> The occupying forces of the Allies shall be withdrawn from Japan as soon as these objectives [designated in other sections] have been accomplished and there has been established a peacefully inclined, responsible government of a character representative of the Japanese people. *This may include a constitutional monarchy under the present dynasty if the peaceloving nations can be convinced of the genuine determination of such a government to follow policies of peace which will render impossible the future development of aggressive militarism in Japan.*[18] [Emphasis added.]

On July 18 at Potsdam, Admiral William D. Leahy sent Truman a memorandum indicating the view of the Joint Chiefs of Staff that the provision permitting Japan to retain "a constitutional monarchy under the present dynasty" should be clarified. The phrase might be misconstrued by extreme devotees of the Emperor as a commitment by the United Nations to depose or execute the present Emperor and install some other member of the Imperial family. To the radical elements in Japan, the phrase might be interpreted as a commitment to continue the institution of the Emperor and Emperor worship. The Joint Chiefs therefore recommended that the passage in question be deleted and the following test substituted: "Subject to suitable guarantees against further acts of aggression, the Japanese people will be free to choose their own form of government."

Leahy's memorandum concluded, "From a strictly military point of view the Joint Chiefs of Staff consider it inadvisable to make any statement or take any action at the present time that would make it difficult or impossible to utilize the authority of the Emperor to direct a surrender of the Japanese forces in the outlying areas as well as in Japan proper."[19] When the Proclamation was finally issued at Potsdam on July 26, 1945, it made no clear commitment concerning the Emperor system. It simply stated: "The occupying forces of the Allies shall be withdrawn from Japan as soon as these [elsewhere stated] objectives have been accomplished and there has been established in accordance with the freely expressed will of the Japanese people a peacefully inclined and responsible government."

[18] Feis, p. 26.
[19] *Ibid.*, Vol. II, 1268–1269.

The Surrender

On July 28 Prime Minister Suzuki announced to the Japanese press that Japan would ignore the Potsdam Declaration and resolutely fight for the successful conclusion of the war. This statement was interpreted by the Allies as an official rejection of the Potsdam ultimatum. An atom bomb was dropped on Hiroshima on August 6 and another on Nagasaki three days later. On August 8, the Soviet Government rejected a Japanese bid for Soviet mediation to end the war and declared war on Japan. There was wide disagreement within the Suzuki Cabinet as to whether the Potsdam Proclamation should then be accepted, and if so with what reservations. A principal concern of Japan's leaders was the preservation of the monarchy.

The Cabinet was hopelessly divided on the issue of peace. Under normal circumstances a Cabinet so divided on a basic issue would resign, but a resignation of the Suzuki Government at so crucial a juncture in the international situation was unthinkable. Prime Minister Suzuki, who favored peace, organized an Imperial Conference with the deliberate intention of getting the Emperor to throw his weight on the side of surrender. After a prolonged discussion at the conference Suzuki bluntly asked the Emperor, "Your Imperial Majesty's decision is requested as to which proposal should be adopted. . . ." The Emperor stated that ending the war was the only way to restore world peace and to relieve the nation from the terrible distress with which it was burdened.[20]

With the positive backing of the Emperor, it was possible for the Suzuki Cabinet to make a decision for peace despite the opposition of the Army. The Japanese Government then issued a statement to the United States indicating Japan's willingness to accept the Potsdam terms "with the understanding that the said declaration does not comprise any demand which prejudices the prerogatives of His Majesty as a Sovereign Ruler."

Secretary of State Byrnes' reply to the Japanese offer to surrender included the statements:

From the moment of surrender the authority of the Emperor and the Japanese Government to rule the state shall be subject to the Supreme Commander of the Allied Powers who will take such steps as he deems proper to effectuate the surrender

[20] J. C. Butow, *Japan's Decision to Surrender* (Stanford, Calif.: Stanford University Press, 1954), p. 176.

terms. . . . The ultimate form of government of Japan shall, in accordance with the Potsdam declaration, be established by the freely expressed will of the Japanese people.

Thus the question of the Emperor system was left in abeyance.

The Japanese Cabinet was again badly split on the question of whether to accede to the Allied surrender terms. The Foreign Minister favored acceptance, but Prime Minister Suzuki was inclined to reject the Byrnes proposal since it did not explicitly accept the Japanese condition concerning the Emperor. The Emperor favored immediate peace and obtained the support of the imperial princes for this policy. At the Imperial Conference on August 14, the Emperor indicated that he believed that the Potsdam declaration was not intended to subvert the national structure, and said, "Unless the war be brought to an end at this moment, I fear that the national polity will be destroyed and the nation annihilated."[21]

All accounts agree that Emperor Hirohito's decision for peace was decisive in overcoming the opposition of the military to making peace. Never before in modern times had the Emperor taken a crucial part in the policy-making process. The Japanese made their definitive offer to surrender on August 14.

The Japanese Foreign Office held that the national structure was not impaired by the surrender. The Emperor's surrender rescript of August 15, 1945, included the statement, "Having been able to safeguard and maintain the structure of the Imperial State (kokutai), we are always with ye, our good and loyal subjects, relying upon your sincerity and integrity." Following the surrender, rumors persisted that the Emperor would abdicate or that he would be tried as a war criminal. But General MacArthur did not order the indictment of the Emperor. To do so might provoke popular disturbances against the Occupation. Chief Prosecutor Joseph B. Keenan held that the Emperor was not considered guilty of participating in the "criminal conspiracy" for which the original panel of twenty-eight high-ranking Japanese went on trial. The head British prosecutor, Sir Arthur Comyns Carr, asked in his summation why the Emperor, who could stop the war in 1945, was unable to prevent it four years earlier. The Japanese answer was that he was permitted by tradition to vote for surrender because a deadlock had arisen in high circles; but opinion had been unanimous in favor of starting hostilities so he was "required" to remain silent.[22] Presumably, the American attitude to-

[21] *Ibid.*, p. 130.

[22] Russell Brines, *MacArthur's Japan* (Philadelphia, Pa.: Lippincott, 1948), p. 95.

wards Emperor Hirohito personally was influenced by the decision to use the Throne as a basis of control and democratization. It would have been inexpedient to destroy the prestige of the Throne by submitting its occupant to severe indignities.

The New Constitution

The position of the Emperor and the problem of the national polity were as central in the enactment of the new Constitution as they had been during the surrender negotiations. Conservative scholars held that principle of popular sovereignty ran contrary to the national structure, which vested the power to rule ultimately in the Emperor, and that it was highly undesirable, if not illegal, to amend the Constitution to provide that sovereignty resides in the people rather than the Emperor. On the day the new Constitution came into effect, Shimizu Chō, constitutional adviser to the Emperor and Chairman of the Privy Council which had approved the Constitution, drowned himself at Atami. His suicide note said, among other things: "I have decided to die so that I from the spiritual world may help to protect our national structure and wish the safe-being of His Majesty."[23]

The "Symbol of the State"

The Functions of the Emperor

Chapter I of the Meiji Constitution had provided that "The Empire of Japan shall be reigned over and governed by a line of Emperors unbroken for ages eternal," that "The Emperor is sacred and inviolable," and that "The Emperor is the head of the Empire, combining in Himself the rights of sovereignty, and exercises them according to the provisions of the present Constitution." Chapter I of the new Constitution radically altered the theoretical status of the Emperor. "The Emperor shall be the symbol of the State and of the unity of the people, deriving his position from the will of the people with whom resides sovereign power." "The advice and approval of the Cabinet shall be required for all acts of the Emperor in matters of state, and the Cabinet shall be responsible therefor." "The Emperor shall perform only such acts in matters of state as are provided for in this Constitution and he shall not have powers related to government.

[23] Kanamori Tokujirō and Yamaura Kan-ichi, eds., *Nihon Seiji Hyakunen Shi* (History of One Hundred Years of Japanese Politics) (Tokyo: Jiji Shimpō Sha, 1953), p. 457.

. . ." Thus, the Emperor no longer ruled by divine right but rather his reign was based upon the principle of popular sovereignty. He is now a constitutional monarch in theory as well as fact. It appears that the term "symbol of the State" may have been suggested by the British Statute of Westminster (1931) which provides that the British Monarch is the symbol of the British Commonwealth.

Although the Emperor "does not have powers related to government," and therefore does not make political decisions, the Constitution requires him to perform specified formal duties, or "acts in matters of state" *with the advice and approval of the Cabinet.* Article 7 lists these functions:

1. Promulgation of amendments of the constitution, laws, cabinet orders and treaties.
2. Convocation of the Diet.
3. Dissolution of the House of Representatives.
4. Proclamation of general election of members of the Diet.
5. Attestation of the appointment and dismissal of Ministers of State and other officials as provided for by law, and of full powers and credentials of ambassadors and ministers.
6. Attestation of general and special amnesty, commutation of punishment, reprieve, and restoration of rights.
7. Awarding of honors.
8. Attestation of instruments of ratification and other diplomatic documents as provided by law.
9. Receiving foreign ambassadors and ministers.
10. Performance of ceremonial functions.

The Governance of the Imperial House

Under the terms of the Meiji Constitution, the Imperial House Law of 1889[24] which determined succession to the Throne, enjoyed higher status than ordinary statutes; it could not be repealed or altered in any way by the Imperial Diet. Only the Emperor, with the advice of the Imperial Family Council and the Privy Council, could amend this law. The Emperor did not depend upon parliamentary mandate for his position as did the Kings of England under the Act of Settlement (1701).

Under the new Constitution, however, the Imperial Throne is "succeeded to in accordance with the Imperial House Law *passed by the*

[24] Text in *Political Reorientation,* Vol. II, 590–593; in Quigley, pp. 344–352; and in Itō Hirobumi, *Commentaries on the Constitution of the Empire of Japan* (Tokyo: Insetsu [*sic*] Kyoku, 1889), pp. 155–167.

Diet"[25] [emphasis added]. The changed procedure for the enactment of the Imperial House Law exemplifies the shift from divine right to popular sovereignty. The Imperial Family had lost its autonomy. The new Imperial House Law[26] passed by parliament came into effect in 1947 simultaneously with the new Constitution.

The Imperial House Law, Kōshitsu Tempan, defines membership in the Imperial Family and Imperial Household Council and provides for succession and the establishment of regencies. The Imperial Family was substantially reduced in size in 1947, when eleven princely families were reduced to the status of commoners. The Emperor and the members of the Imperial Family are not permitted to adopt children. The marriage of any male member of the Imperial Family must be approved by the Imperial House Council.

The Imperial House Law of 1947 provides that "the Imperial Throne shall be succeeded to by a male offspring in the male line belonging to the Imperial Lineage" and establishes the order of succession to the Imperial Throne within the Imperial Family. The Imperial Council may change the order of succession in case the Imperial Heir is affected with an incurable and serious disease or if there is a serious hindrance. The Imperial Heir accedes immediately to the Throne upon the demise of the Emperor.

A Regency is established by decision of the Imperial House Council when the Emperor is not of age (eighteen), when the Emperor is affected with a serious disease, or if there is a serious hindrance to his performance of acts in matters of state. Regents today must be members of the Imperial Family of age according to the order prescribed in the Imperial House Law.

The Imperial House Council is composed of ten members: two members of the Imperial Family, the speakers and vice speakers of the House of Representatives and of the House of Councillors, the Chief Judge and one other judge of the Supreme Court. The Imperial Family members are chosen by election within the Imperial Family, and the judge other than Chief Judge by the judges of the Supreme Court. Provision is made for reserve members. The Prime Minister presides over the meeting of the Imperial House Council.

The Imperial House Council of today is very different from the Imperial Family Council provided by the old Imperial House Law. The former Imperial Family Council was composed of male members of age of the Imperial Family. It was presided over by the Emperor personally or a member of the Imperial Family delegated by him. The

---

[25] The Constitution of Japan, Article 2.
[26] Text in *Political Reorientation,* Vol. II, 846–848.

Lord Keeper of the Privy Seal, the President of the Privy Council, the Minister of the Imperial Household, the Minister of Justice, and the President of the Court of Cassation took part in the deliberations. Under the present system, the members of the Imperial Family are a tiny minority in the Imperial House Council and may be outvoted by the representatives of the executive, legislative, and judicial branches of the government.

The Imperial House Council determines the exceptions from the usual order of succession to the Throne or Regency by two-thirds majority, and other questions by majority. The Council makes decisions respecting marriages of male members of the Imperial Family.

The Imperial House Agency is under the jurisdiction of the Prime Minister. It has charge of state affairs relating to the Imperial House and the Emperor's acts in matters of state provided for by government ordinance. The Imperial House Agency also has custody of the Imperial Seal and the Seal of State. The personnel of the Agency include a Grand Steward, a Vice Grand Steward, a Private Secretary to the Grand Steward, a Grand Chamberlain, Chamberlains, a Master of Ceremonies, Secretaries of the Imperial House Agency, and technical officials.

The Finances of the Imperial House

Before the Pacific War, the Imperial House owned great tracts of land and large blocks of stock in leading financial and industrial institutions. The Emperor was thus closely linked with the zaibatsu. In February, 1947, 3,330,000,000 yen of the total property of the Emperor, then amounting to 3,740,000,000 yen, was taken by the state as property tax.

Article 88 of the new Constitution provides that "All property of the Imperial Household shall belong to the State" and that "All expenses of the Imperial Household shall be appropriated by the Diet." Furthermore, no property can be given to or received by the Imperial House, nor can any gifts be made therefrom, without the authorization of the Diet. Thus, the Throne has lost the financial independence which it had enjoyed before the war when it owned property and received a fixed income from the National Treasury which could not be reduced by the Diet. The appropriation for the Imperial House is included in the budget and allocated according to the provisions of the Imperial House Economy Law,[27] other laws, and decisions of the Imperial House Economy Council and Imperial House Agency.

[27] Text in *Political Reorientation*, Vol. II, 849–850.

The Emperor Today and Tomorrow

The Imperial Family

The Peerage created by Prince Itō in the 1880s is "not recognized" in the new Constitution; there is no longer a House of Peers and the only official aristocracy remaining is the Imperial Family. The first session of the Imperial House Council was held under the terms of the new Imperial House Law in October, 1947. The Council sanctioned the decision of fifty-one Princes and Princesses of eleven princely households to renounce their membership in the Imperial Family and become commoners. Today, the Imperial Family, as formally defined, is probably the smallest it has been in history. The present Emperor (b. 1901) and Empress (b. 1903) have had two sons and five daughters, one of whom died in infancy and one of whom died in 1961. The remaining three daughters are no longer members of the Imperial Family since they are married to commoners, although their husbands are members of high-ranking former nobility.

The present Emperor, Hirohito, is 124th in a line of Emperors (and reigning Empresses), of whom the first sixteen are mythological. In the 1920s, while Crown Prince, Hirohito made a trip to Europe visiting leading statesmen and royalty. He ascended the throne in 1926 after serving as Regent for five years on behalf of his demented father, Emperor Taishō. His hobby is marine biology, and newspaper photographs sometimes show him peering through a high-powered microscope. He has published several books on the marine life in Sagami Bay and is credited with having discovered a number of new species. The present Emperor was the first monarch in Japan's history to leave the country during his reign when, in 1971, he made a visit to Europe. On the way, his airplane stopped for fuel at Anchorage, Alaska. This provided the occasion for President Nixon to fly to Alaska to greet His Majesty, reportedly in the hope that such a gesture might assuage Japanese resentments of the President's new policies on relations with China and foreign trade.

During his lifetime the Emperor is referred to as Tennō Heika (His Majesty the Emperor), and after he dies he will be referred to as the Shōwa Tennō (Shōwa Emperor), since Shōwa (Enlightened Peace) is the name of his reign. In Japan, the name of the reign is used for designating years, so that 1972 in the Western system of reckoning is referred to as Shōwa 47.

Crown Prince Akihito, eldest son of the present monarch, was born in 1933. As a boy he attended the Gakushūin (Peers School) and was tutored during the Allied Occupation by Mrs. Elizabeth Vining, an American Quaker. In 1953 he represented the Emperor at the coronation of Queen Elizabeth II and toured Europe and America. He created a sensation in 1959 when he married a commoner in violation of all historical precedent. The "love match" symbolized the right of young people in Japan to choose their own mates. The Crown Princess, *née* Shoda Michiko, is a young lady of unusual poise, charm, and intelligence, who majored in English literature at the College of the Sacred Heart in Tokyo. In 1960 and again in 1965, the couple was blessed with male progeny, so that the succession to the Throne seems well assured.

The Future of the Emperor System

The decision of the American Occupation authorities to preserve but reform the monarchy in Japan represented a compromise among conservative, moderate, and radical views on the Throne which prevailed among the Allied Powers and the Japanese people. The new status of the Emperor shocked conservative legal theorists and pious Shintoists, but conservative peasants and villagers, baffled by academic debates about the national structure, were reassured to see that the Emperor, to all appearances, still held a prominent position in the state structure. Communists and some Socialists continue to regard the Throne with suspicion but have on the whole discreetly refrained from making a frontal attack on the institution which would only result in increasing their unpopularity. The symbolic status of the Emperor is a *modus vivendi* which has thus far prevented the issue of the Throne from bedeviling the political life of the country—there is no Monarchist Party as in postwar Italy, and there is no Republican Party, albeit the Marxists are suspect. Substantive political issues have not been rendered insoluble nor has political stability been undermined by the injection of this constitutional issue.

Nevertheless, the question of the national structure remains controversial, and the political leadership, both conservative and radical, is conscious of the fundamental importance of the Throne in the ideological struggle. In Western countries, the Church has served as a basis for traditional morality and social harmony, but in Japan the moral influence exerted by Buddhism and Christianity is relatively weak. The familistic morality is based on Confucianism and ancestor worship. The Japanese state has traditionally been regarded as an enlarged family or clan, headed by the Emperor as its benevolent patriarch. Civil and military officials derived pride from exercising authority delegated to them by the Emperor. The obedience of the lower orders of the population to those higher in the hierarchy was regarded as obedience to the commands of the Emperor. Reverence for the Emperor was equated with patriotism and the moral obligations of the individual to his family and social superiors. To the Japanese conservative, the Throne represents the traditional Confucian morality and social stability; it is a bulwark against the Marxist expropriation of private property, the subversion of the family, and juvenile delinquency.

In 1954, the conservative Liberal and Progressive Parties each organized committees for the study of constitutional revision. The main issue at that time was the disarmament clause, but both committees advocated the adoption of a completely new basic law which would restore the Emperor as constitutional head of the State.[28] Within two or three years after Japan regained her independence, Cabinet ministers ceased participating in Constitution Day ceremonies. Prime Ministers Hatoyama and Kishi were both strongly committed to constitutional reform. The conservative-dominated Diet in 1955 passed a law creating the Commission on the Constitution to study the origins, operation, and possible amendment of the basic law. It is notable, however, that few conservatives today advocate the outright denial of the principle of popular sovereignty. The Socialist Party organized a People's League for the Protection of the Constitution, and thus far the parties of the left have managed to hold enough seats (slightly over one-third) in both Houses of the Diet to veto any proposal to amend the Constitution.

On the grass roots level, a movement to restore Kigensetsu gained substantial momentum in the 1960s. Kigensetsu, February 11, was the traditional anniversary of the founding of the Japanese State by the legendary first Emperor Jimmu Tennō in 660 B.C. Under the Occupation the old mythology was deleted from the textbooks and is no longer taught in the schools. Scientifically written history books have become best sellers. The younger brother of the Emperor, Prince Mikasa, who is Professor of History at Tokyo Women's College, is a strong advocate of the archeological study of Japan's origins and an outspoken opponent of the revival of Kigensetsu, which he holds to be based on erroneous conceptions of Japanese history. He shares the fear of many Japanese that the old Shinto mythology may again be exploited by ultranationalists. He has edited a book on Japanese prehistory containing contributions by leading scholars.[29]

[28] Miyazawa Toshiyoshi et al., *Kempō Kaisei* (The Amendment of the Constitution) (Tokyo: Yuhikaku, 1956), pp. 160, 226.

[29] *Nihon no Akebono* (The Dawn of Japan) (Tokyo: Kobunsha, 1959).

In sensitive situations, the officials of the Imperial Household seem determined to maintain the political neutrality of the Emperor. As the Kishi Government was making final preparations for President Eisenhower's visit to Japan, Imperial Household officials requested that the scheduled visit be called off, in the face of leftist threats to block the path of the automobile as it carried the Emperor and the President from Haneda Airport to the Imperial Palace. In 1951, students at Kyoto University had stopped the limousine bearing the Emperor and demanded that rearmament be halted.

In 1967, celebration of February 11, the old date of Kigensetsu, was revived in the form of National Foundation Day (Kenkoku Kinenbi). The following year, the one hundredth anniversary of the accession of the Emperor Meiji was observed by the government. The government's positive evaluation of the Meiji era was not shared by most of the academic community, which felt that that period of Japanese history had left a legacy of militarism and imperialism. Leading associations of historians strongly objected to the government's alleged efforts to use the anniversary to gain support for rearmament and other reactionary policies. The Meiji Centenary, lacking the support of the nation's intellectuals, was all but ignored by the public. The Olympics, held in Japan in 1964, did much more to arouse feelings of national pride and affection for the Emperor.

At the opening ceremonies, the Emperor stood with his fellow citizens (previously his subjects) as the teams paraded into the National Stadium. "The crowd cheered especially loudly as the Japanese Olympic team, holding aloft the national flag, marched into the arena and passed the reviewing stand. For perhaps the first time since the end of the war, a public event had brought together a stirring conjunction of flag, Emperor, and the people."[30]

In 1971, when the Emperor visited England and several countries in Western Europe, he was sometimes greeted with hostility by people who still had bitter memories of World War II. During the tour, a sensational book was published in the United States which charged the Emperor with personal complicity in planning Japan's aggressive policies in the 1930s.[31] Thus the Japanese were reminded that much remained to be done in order to create a more favorable international image for their country.

The existence of the Emperor, of course, has made it difficult for any other individual to capture completely the loyalty and adoration of

[30] Warren Tsuneishi, *Japanese Political Style: An Introduction to the Government and Politics of Japan* (New York: Harper & Row, 1966), p. 56.

[31] David Bergamini, *Japan's Imperial Conspiracy* (New York: William Morrow, 1971).

the people as dictators have done elsewhere. At the same time, the Emperor has served as a check against communism. He represents "the unity of the people" as opposed to class warfare. A principal reason for the unpopularity of communism is the attacks which Communists made on the Throne after the war. If the Emperor succeeds in maintaining his political neutrality and if there is no revival of Shinto fanaticism, it is probable that the Throne will continue to contribute stability to democracy in Japan.

Suggested Reading

Baerwald, Hans H. "Tento-Mura: The Making of a Cabinet," in Lucian W. Pye, ed., *Cases in Comparative Politics: Asia.* Boston, Mass.: Little, Brown, 1970, pp. 58–88.

Bergamini, David. *Japan's Imperial Conspiracy.* New York: William Morrow & Co., 1971.

Enthronement of the One Hundred Twenty-Fourth Emperor of Japan. Tokyo: *The Japan Advertiser,* 1928.

Fuji-i Shin-ichi. *Tenno Seiji* (in English, French, and German). Tokyo: Yūhikaku, 1944.

Hall, Robert K., ed. *Kokutai no Hongi: Cardinal Principles of the National Entity of Japan,* trans. J. O. Gauntlett. Cambridge, Mass.: Harvard University Press, 1949.

Kurzman, Dan. *Kishi and Japan: The Search for the Sun.* New York: Ivan Oblensky, 1960.

Miller, Frank O. *Minobe Tatsukichi: Interpreter of Constitutionalism in Japan.* Berkeley: University of California Press, 1965.

Minear, Richard H. *Japanese Tradition and Western Law: Emperor, State, and Law in the Thought of Hozumi Yatsuka.* Cambridge, Mass.: Harvard University Press, 1970.

Monnier, Claude. *Les Américains et Sa Majesté l'Empereur: Etude du Conflit Culturel d'où Naquit la Constitution Japanaise de 1946.* Neuchâtel, Switzerland: Edition de la Baconnière, 1967.

Mosley, Leonard. *Hirohito: Emperor of Japan.* Englewood Cliffs, N.J.: Prentice-Hall, 1966.

Ponsonby Fane, Richard. *The Imperial House of Japan.* Kyoto: Ponsonby Fane Memorial Society, 1959.

Ponsonby Fane, Richard. *Sovereign and Subject.* Kyoto: Ponsonby Fane Memorial Society, 1962.

Vining, Elizabeth Gray. *Windows for the Crown Prince.* Philadelphia, Pa.: Lippincott, 1952.

Tsuneishi, Warren. *The Japanese Emperor: A Study in Constitutional Change.* New Haven, Conn.: Yale University Ph.D. dissertation, 1960.

Webb, Hershel. *The Japanese Imperial Institution in the Tokugawa Period.* New York: Columbia University Press, 1968.

7

Local Government

Central Authority and Regional Subdivisions

The opposing themes of centralization and decentralization figure prominently in the development of local government in Japan. In this chapter, we shall examine how the Meiji reformers abolished feudal institutions and organized local governments as agencies of the new centralized monarchy. The Occupation shifted some of the powers of the central government to the localities, but subsequently the educational and police systems were in large measure recentralized. The problems associated with the concurrent jurisdictions of the national and local governments, the amalgamation of local government units, and the administration of Tokyo, the world's largest city, will also be discussed here.

Local Government Before and During the Pacific War

Japan is politically subdivided into forty-seven prefectures (including Okinawa). Prefectures were first established following the Meiji Restoration and the abolition of the feudal fiefs in the 1870s. The dispatch of a governor appointed by the Emperor to each of the prefectures symbolized the replacement of the authority of the daimyo by that of the Emperor. The Meiji reformers saw to it that none of the prefectures bore the names of the sixty-six provinces of the feudal era.

The reformers were determined to break down feudal particularism and establish a strong central government. The Meiji Constitution and the Law Concerning the Organization of Urban and Rural Prefectures (1890) established a unitary system rather than a federal type of government such as the American one. Consequently, the tradition of local autonomy is weak, and the constitutional theory of "states' rights" is virtually nonexistent in the Japanese political consciousness. The constitutional status of the prefectural governments is not to be compared with that of the state governments in the United States, and the governmental role of the Japanese prefecture is analogous to that of the *département* in France or the county in the United States.[1]

A number of factors account for the predominance of the unitary idea in Japan. The small area of the entire country (smaller than California) alleviates the necessity of establishing autonomous subdivisions and facilitates control from Tokyo. Whereas dissimilarities of language and religion have necessitated federalism in India and Switzerland, for centuries the Japanese have spoken the same language and have, on the whole, experienced only minor religious differences. Regional economic differences are not sufficiently great to require a large measure of regional autonomy. Since 1868, Japanese nationalism and the Emperor system have exalted national unity and centralized government over provincialism, which has usually been equated with feudalism. From the time of the adoption of Chinese political forms in the seventh century, the Emperor, until 1947, appointed territorial governors to rule in his behalf. Although many governors in ancient times never left the court and allowed local military nobles to usurp their functions, the ideal of imperial rule has persisted for well over a millennium.

During the period of the Meiji Constitution, the governor (chiji) of each prefecture was appointed by the Emperor on recommendation of the Home Minister. As "imperial appointees" (chokunin), prefectural governors were officials of the national government of rank just below that of vice ministers. The governor had the power to override decisions of the prefectural legislature and could withhold approval of candidacies for village or town head. He had the prerogative of formulating the prefectural budget, which was difficult for the prefectural assembly to veto, and had considerable control over the budgets of villages, towns, and cities. The Cabinet ministers of the central government had the authority to issue directives and instructions to governors and to suspend or cancel actions of the governors. The ministries most concerned with prefectural affairs were the Home Ministry and the Ministry of Finance. Centralization and bureaucracy rather than local autonomy and democracy were the prevailing principles of local government in prewar Japan.

In 1943 the prefectures were grouped into nine administrative and economic regions, and two years later the number was reduced to

---

[1] The student is cautioned that in English writing on Japanese government, the term *state* is often used to designate the national government, not the prefectural government.

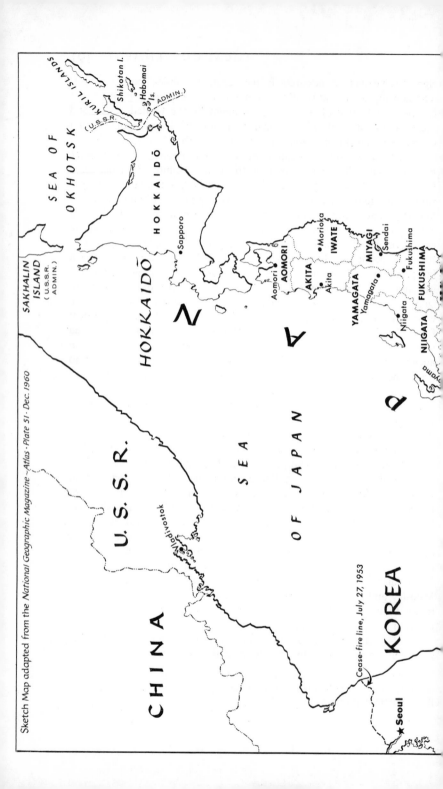

Sketch Map adapted from the *National Geographic Magazine – Atlas – Plate 51 · Dec. 1960*

FIGURE 4

Prefectures and Principal Cities of

JAPAN

★ National Capitals   ● Prefectural Capitals

0   50   100   200
STATUTE MILES

HONSHŪ

PACIFIC

OCEAN

KYŪSHŪ

SHIKOKU

KOREA STRAIT

RYUKYU ISLANDS

IZU SHICHITŌ ISLANDS
(TOKYO PREFECTURE)

OGASAWARA
(BONIN)
ISLANDS
(TOKYO PREFECTURE)

Tōkyō

eight.[2] Each region was headed by a central government appointee, usually a governor of one of the constituent prefectures. These administrative regions were not in effect during the Allied Occupation, but in the 1960s they provided a precedent for the advocates of the regional system. The eight regions in 1945 closely corresponded to the eight geographic regions often referred to in Japanese statistical and economic yearbooks. The Hokkaidō (island) and Tōhoku (northern Honshū Island) regions have long cold winters with much snow and are economically underdeveloped compared with the rest of Japan. Industry is concentrated in the four regions of Kantō (including Tokyo and Yokohama), Chūbu (including Nagoya), Kinki (including Osaka, Kobe, and Kyoto), and Kyūshū (island). The main occupations in the regions of Chūgoku (which includes Hiroshima) and Shikoku (island) have been agriculture and fishing, but they too are becoming industrialized.

Postwar Local Government

The Occupation authorities did not attempt to introduce in Japan the American type of federal system; they felt such an effort would not be successful. They were nevertheless determined to provide opportunity for more democracy and home rule. Chapter VIII of the new Constitution concerned local self-government and provided that the organization and operations of local public entities would be fixed by law "in accordance with the principle of local autonomy." The chief executive officers of all local public entities and members of their assemblies would be elected by direct popular vote. No precise functions and powers for local government units are anywhere enumerated in the Constitution, so that, notwithstanding the newly enunciated principle of local autonomy, the local governments would exercise only powers delegated to them by the Diet as had been the case before the war.

The local government system was spelled out in the Local Autonomy Law passed on April 17, 1947.[3] The Home Ministry was abolished on December 31, 1947, apparently signaling the end of domination of the local political entities by national bureaucrats.

The three principal echelons of government in Japan are, from top

[2] For a map of these eight administrative regions, see John F. Embree, *The Japanese Nation* (New York: Rinehart, 1945), p. 79.

[3] Text in Supreme Commander for the Allied Powers Government Section, of Japan: September, 1945, to September, 1948, 2 vols. (Washington, D.C.: Government Printing Office, n.d. [1949?], Vol. II, 902–959. These volumes will subsequently be cited as *Political Reorientation*.

to bottom, the national government, prefectural government, and municipal government. The term local government embraces both the prefectural and municipal levels. Of the forty-six prefectures, one is a metropolis (to, i.e., Tōkyō-to), one is a district (dō, i.e., Hokkaidō), two are urban prefectures (fu, i.e.,Ōsaka-fu and Kyōto-fu), and forty-two are rural prefectures (ken). The prefectures are collectively called todōfuken, a term which embraces all four categories of prefectures.

A forty-seventh prefecture, Okinawa-ken (the Ryukyu Islands), was under American military occupation for twenty-seven years after the war. The Japanese Peace Treaty (1951) left Okinawa under American occupation and provided that Japan would concur in any American proposal to place the Ryukyu Islands under a United Nations trusteeship to be administered by the United States. Under the American military High Commissioner and an American Civil Administrator, the Okinawans were permitted to elect their own Chief Executive and Legislature. Because of the strategic location of these islands, strung between Kyushu and Taiwan, they served as an extremely important American military base. The Korean War, the Taiwan crises in the 1950s, and the Vietnam War heightened Okinawa's strategic importance, and the American military was reluctant to give up its right to the unrestricted use of its Okinawan bases. There were more than the usual tensions between the occupying forces and the local populace concerning land leases, aircraft and automobile accidents, labor disputes, the presence of nuclear and chemical weapons, and jurisdictional controversies. From time to time there were demonstrations and riots in Okinawa in protest against American policies or actions. Prime Minister Satō repeatedly said that the postwar period for Japan would not end until Okinawa was returned to Japanese rule. In 1969, he obtained from President Nixon assurances that Okinawa would revert to Japan in 1972. In 1970, the Okinawans, still under American Occupation, were permitted to elect five Representatives and two Councillors to represent them in the Japanese Diet.

The metropolis of Tokyo (Tōkyō-to), with a population of 11,462,230 in 1969, is the world's largest city. It includes twenty-three special wards, seventeen cities, and twenty-four towns and villages. Of Tokyo's twenty-four towns and villages, fifteen are located in the three counties of Nishitama, Minamitama, and Kitatama. The remaining nine are located in the Izu Islands and the Ogasawara (or Bonin) Islands, far out in the Pacific Ocean. The subtropical Ogasawara Islands, which include Iwo Jima of World War II fame, were under American military administration from the end of the war until 1968.

The municipalities are cities (shi), towns (chō), and villages (son), and are collectively referred to as shichōson. All of the territory of a prefecture is included under the control of one or another municipal unit. Thus towns and villages, which are predominantly rural, are largely made up of fields and forests, and may include a number of separate hamlets.

Postwar legislation has encouraged the amalgamation of municipalities, and for reasons of economy and efficiency many have chosen to merge. As of October, 1970, there were 578 cities, 2,013 towns, and 684 villages.

The most notable amalgamation has been that of the cities of Moji, Kokura, Yawata, Tobata, and Wakamatsu, all in Fukuoka-ken, in the northern tip of Kyūshū. In the early 1960s they merged to become Kitakyūshū-shi, Japan's seventh largest city, with over a million inhabitants. The first mayor to be elected for this industrial city was a Socialist. The major criticism of the amalgamations is that they artificially group together separate hamlets and villages, the inhabitants of which do not identify with the enlarged municipality.

Thus far the amalgamation movement, so important on the municipal level, has not resulted in the merger of any of the prefectures, which have the same boundaries that they had before World War II. However, in the 1960s there was discussion of joining Tōkyō-to with the neighboring prefectures of Kanagawa, Saitama, and Chiba, where many of the people who work in Tokyo live. Tokyo Governor Minobe objected to the proposal on the ground that Tokyo was already too big. Other suggested possibilities have been the mergers of Osaka-fu, Nara-ken, and Wakayama-ken and of Aichi-ken, Gifu-ken, and Mie-ken. (The latter group includes the city of Nagoya.)

Much more radical are proposals to abolish the prefectures completely and to replace them with seven to nine districts (dō) or states (shū). The prefectures, it is urged, are much too small to administer efficiently, and their borders were drawn before the invention of the automobile. The proposed dō-shū system would correspond closely to Japan's natural economic and geographic regions. Some of the present functions of the prefectures would be delegated to the municipalities, and the governors and assemblies of the new districts or states would be elective. A more controversial modification of this scheme would interpose administrative units of the national government between the present prefectures and the national government. Most of these ideas are opposed by prefectural governors, who insist that the rights and interests of the people in the prefectures must be preserved, and by the opposition parties, who accuse the LDP advocates of these schemes of plotting to destroy the principle of local autonomy in favor of a centralized regime run by conservatives. Opportunities for Socialists to win prefectural governorships and assembly seats would of course be reduced by the proposals for amalgamations of prefectures.

Limitations on Local Autonomy

The functions of local government units in Japan are (1) to enforce certain national legislation and (2) to enact and enforce the legislation of the local governments themselves. In carrying out the former group of functions, the local government agencies are supervised by the competent departments of the national government, which are most frequently the Ministries of Autonomy, Finance, Education, and Welfare. In the exercise of the latter group of functions, the local unit is engaged in local self-government and exercises the legislative as well as the executive prerogative. The local governments do not possess judicial branches; justice is a function of the national government, which maintains courts on various echelons throughout the country independently of prefectural and municipal governments. The powers of the local governments are delegated to them by "law," legislation passed by the Diet. Prefectural and municipal government in Japan is both organizationally and legally quite different from state and local government in the United States, where the federal principle prevails. Nevertheless, local bodies politic are not completely at the mercy of the central government. Article 94 of the Constitution provides that local public entities "have the right to manage their property, affairs, and administration and to enact their own regulations within the law." Article 95 lays down the principle that "A special law applicable only to one local entity cannot be enacted by the Diet without the consent of the majority of the voters of the public entity concerned, obtained in accordance with law."

According to the Local Autonomy Law, the matters with which local governments may deal include maintenance of public order, protection of health and safety of the local inhabitants, establishment and management of parks, playgrounds, canals, irrigation and drainage waterways, water plants, sewage systems, electric plants, gas plants, public transportation systems, docks, piers, warehouses, schools, libraries, museums, hospitals, asylums for the aged, jails, crematories, cemeteries, disaster relief, protection of minors, indigents and the infirm, land reclamation, identification and registration of inhabitants, zoning, coordination of activities with other local bodies, and levying and collecting of local taxes. The national government, however, may also deal with these matters when it wishes. There is no enumeration of the specific powers of the local governments in the Constitution.

Because none of the functions mentioned above is constitutionally or legally assigned to the exclusive jurisdiction of any one level of government, the national, prefectural, and municipal governments are often engaged in the same activities. One level may be charged with enforcing policies made at a higher level. Furthermore, while most of the money is raised by the national government, most of it is spent by the local governments. Thus, it is in practice difficult for the concerned citizen to determine which level of government administers and finances a given operation. If something goes wrong, local authorities may blame a ministry in Tokyo for inadequate funding or guidance, while the ministry might blame the local authorities for administrative shortcomings. The muddle of functions makes it easy to pass the buck, and government, even at the local level, too often seems bureaucratic and unresponsive.[4]

Local public bodies may not deal with national affairs including judicial matters, penal punishment, national transportation and communication, post offices, and national institutions of learning and research. Local governments may not contravene laws or cabinet orders and ministerial regulations authorized by law. At the same time, a municipality may not contravene any of the by-laws of a prefecture. Unauthorized actions by a local entity are legally null and void.

Chief Executives

Governors of prefectures and mayors of municipalities are elected by the voters of their respective units for terms of four years, subject to recall by the voters and votes of no confidence by the relevant deliberative bodies. The Local Autonomy Law provides that when acting in his capacity as an organ of the national government, a governor is subject to the direction and supervision of the competent Cabinet minister. When acting for the national government, a mayor is subject to the direction and supervision of both the competent minister and the governor of the prefecture. If a governor refuses to enforce a national law or cabinet order which he is required to carry out by the national government, the competent Cabinet minister can request a court order requiring the governor to perform the function in question. In the event of continued recalcitrance by the governor, the competent minister himself may enforce the law, and the Prime Minister may remove the governor from office. Likewise, if a mayor fails to enforce

[4] For a detailed treatment of this topic, see Kurt Steiner, *Local Government in Japan* (Stanford, Calif.: Stanford University Press, 1965), pp. 231–259.

certain national or prefectural legislation, the prefectural governor may compel him to do so by means of a court order or may remove him from office.

Thus, the local chief executives must serve two masters, since they function as agents of the national government in national matters and as officers of their local governments in local matters. A Japanese governor is very different from his American counterpart, who certainly does not regard himself as a functionary of the national administration. Eighty percent of all the work handled by local government units consists of administrative affairs entrusted to them by agencies of the central government. Today the number of local government employees stands at about 1,400,000. The administrative structure of the prefectural and municipal offices is largely determined by laws enacted by the Diet.

In December, 1969, of the forty-six governors, twenty-two were independents—with notable exceptions most of these were conservatively inclined—and twenty-four were Liberal-Democrats. Of 560 city mayors, 435 were independents, 100 were Liberal-Democrats, twenty-four were Socialists, and one was a Communist. Of 2,714 town and village mayors, 2,574 were independents while only 130 were Liberal-Democrats, nine were Socialists, and one was a Communist.[5]

The elections for the governors and mayors of the metropolitan areas attract national attention and provide opportunities for the opposition parties to acquire influence and power that they are unable to achieve nationally. In 1967, the Socialists and Communists were gratified by the victory of their candidate for governor of Tokyo. These parties campaigned in 1970 for the election of Governor Ninagawa Torazō of Kyoto-fu for a sixth term against a nominee supported by the Liberal-Democrats, Democratic-Socialists, and Kōmeitō. Because the Communist vote is larger than the Socialist vote in Kyoto, Ninagawa's victory was more of a credit to the Communists than to the Socialists. The Kyoto election served to polarize the confrontation between the Communist Party and the Kōmeitō. The mayor of Yokohama has for some years been a Socialist. With the disastrous defeat suffered by the Socialists in the 1969 lower house election, local politics have assumed a special significance as an arena for a Socialist revival.

Local Assemblies

The size of prefectural assemblies is determined by law and varies from between forty and 126 members, depending on the population of

[5] *Asahi Nenkan, 1971*, p. 557.

the prefecture. The size of municipal assemblies is likewise determined by national law and varies from twelve to 100 members, depending on the population of the municipality. Assemblymen are elected for four-year terms subject to dissolution by the governor or mayor. They may be recalled by the voters, who may also demand a dissolution of the entire body.

The local legislative bodies are empowered to enact "by-laws" (jōrei) on subjects enumerated in the Local Autonomy Law. Only the national Diet can pass laws (hōritsu). The subjects within the scope of the legislative authority of the local legislative bodies include the budget of the local government, the acquisition, management, and disposal of the entity's property, levying and collecting local taxes, and matters falling under the jurisdiction of the assembly in accordance with laws and Cabinet orders.

The governor or mayor may veto a measure passed by the relevant assembly, but the assembly may pass the measure over the veto by a two-thirds vote. The assembly may vote no confidence in the chief executive provided that there is a quorum of two-thirds of the membership and that three-fourths of the legislators vote for the no confidence resolution. When a no confidence resolution is passed, the local chief executive must either resign or dissolve the legislative body. If after a dissolution the newly elected assembly immediately votes no confidence in the local chief executive, he must resign. No confidence votes occur very rarely in the local political entities. In the event that the local assembly persists in passing a resolution which the executive regards as in contravention of national laws and ordinances, he may bring a court action against the assembly.

Since World War II, political parties have played an increasingly conspicuous role in prefectural assemblies. In the late 1960s, the Kō-meitō was as significant in politics at the prefectural and municipal levels as at the national level. In December, 1969, the political composition of prefectural assemblies was as follows: Liberal-Democrats, 1,655; Socialists, 533; Kōmeitō, 104; Democratic-Socialists, 107; Communists, 54; independents, 106; others, 51. In the city assemblies the party breakdown was: Liberal-Democrats, 3,479; Socialists, 1,859; Kōmeitō, 1,202; Democratic-Socialists, 473; Communists, 650; independents, 10,052; others, 51. In the assemblies of towns and villages, 46,815 out of 52,225 assemblymen did not declare party affiliation, but among the assemblymen 2,975 were Liberal-Democrats, 1,212, Socialists, and 856 Communists, while only 214 were Kōmeitō people and 119 Democratic-Socialists.[6]

[6] *Ibid.*, p. 557.

Increasingly, local assemblies express their wishes to the central government in the form of resolutions and written opinions. In 1967 there were 902 such cases, representing an increase of 30 percent over 1965. It is no longer unusual for local assemblies to take up diplomatic and defense problems. In 1969, in Chiba prefecture, one local assembly after another adopted resolutions calling on the national government to "uphold the United States–Japan Security Treaty." While it would seem natural for local assemblies to petition the national government on matters of immediate interest to local inhabitants, some observers feared that resolutions concerning foreign policy would unnecessarily politicize local governments. The ideological issues which divide the political parties are thus entering the arena of local politics. Politics in Japan are becoming increasingly nationalized, and local assemblies could provide a supplementary forum for the debate on national issues.

In addition to the executive and legislative branches of the local government, there are, on the prefectural level and often on the municipal level, boards of education, public safety commissions, inspection (auditing) commissions, and personnel commissions, made up of members usually appointed by the governor or mayor with the approval of the deliberative organ. Local commission members, like local chief executives and assemblymen, are subject to recall by the voters.

The Local Autonomy Law provides for the exercise of initiative, recall, and referendum by the voters in local entities. If one-fiftieth of the registered voters of a locality sign a demand for the enactment of a by-law, the chief executive must present the demand together with his opinion thereon to the local assembly. Local chief executives, certain other executive officials, assemblymen, and members of the commissions may be removed from office by a recall vote held as a result of a petition signed by one third of the voters of the relevant constituency.

Perhaps nowhere more than in the field of local government has the "reverse course" been more evident. Not only has national control over the police, education, and local finance been in large measure reestablished, but in 1960, the Autonomy Agency became the Autonomy Ministry, concerned with the supervision of local governments. Conservatives have been advocating the restoration of national appointment of prefectural governors, but public opinion favors the retention of the present system of electing chief executives. A principal reason for the partial recentralization of government in Japan has been the inability of the local units to collect adequate taxes to fulfill the heavy demands placed on them.

Local Government Finance

Under present laws, 70 percent of the taxes collected go to the central government, with 30 percent retained by the local administrations. However, about 60 percent of the taxes assigned to the central government is returned to local governments in various forms. Thus, some 30 percent of all taxes is spent by the national government, and 70 percent is spent by the local administrations. However, funds returned to local governments are not distributed equally. The policy is to collect the maximum revenue from the wealthier local entities and to redistribute this wealth to the poorer entities so as to eliminate the disparity between the have and the have-not regions.

There are several much criticized defects in this system of distributing tax revenue. The local entities, deprived of adequate independent sources of revenue, are overly dependent upon the central government for their sustenance. In order to qualify for disbursements from the central government, national standards have to be met, and local autonomy is correspondingly curtailed. Another criticism is that the people in some communities receive in benefits an unduly small share of the money which they have paid into the national treasury. The government of Tokyo has complained bitterly that in 1967 taxes in Tokyo amounted to $386 per capita, while the amount spent in Tokyo came to only $161 per capita.[7]

Educational Reform

In prewar times, the Minister of Education had used the educational system to instill nationalistic doctrines in the people. The Imperial Rescript on Education of 1890[8] established the philosophy of Japanese education. In it, the "Shinto ideology of Emperor worship was combined with the Confucian ethical concepts of loyalty, filial piety, and obedience to superiors. . . . Ancestor worship, loyalty to the Emperor, duty to State, and filial piety were crystallized as State morals and absolute virtues. The Rescript tied together religion, patriotism, and the family system."[9] In 1937, the principles of the Rescript were

[7] *Sizing up Tokyo: A Report on Tokyo under the Administration of Governor Ryokichi Minobe* (Tokyo: Tokyo Metropolitan Government, 1969), p. 26.

[8] Text in Theodore McNelly, ed., *Sources in Modern East Asian History and Politics* (New York: Appleton-Century-Crofts, 1967), pp. 64–65.

[9] Ronald S. Anderson, *Japan: Three Epochs of Modern Education* (Washington, D.C.: Government Printing Office, 1959), p. 13.

elaborated upon in the *Kokutai no Hongi,* which was required reading for all school teachers. General Araki Sadao, a leading militarist, became Minister of Education in 1938.

During the Occupation, the Emperor renounced his divinity, state Shinto was disestablished, military men were forbidden to teach, ultranationalism and militarism were banned from the textbooks and the schools, and the goals of education were reformed to instill democratic attitudes, individualism, and practical citizenship. In 1947, the Diet enacted the Fundamental Law of Education[10] which declared the aims of education to be the "full development of personality," the "esteem of individual value," and "independent spirit." In 1948, the Diet passed a resolution rescinding the Imperial Rescript on Education.[11]

To break the grip of the bureaucracy on education, the administration of the school system was democratized and decentralized with the establishment of locally elected school boards patterned after those in the United States.[12] Parent-Teacher Associations were established even in the smallest communities. The new Constitution provided that all people would have the right to receive "an equal education corresponding to their ability" and that ordinary education would be without cost.[13] On the urging of Occupation authorities, the American-type 6-3-3-4 (six years elementary, three years junior high, three years senior high, and four years college) system replaced the European structure of education. The prewar ethics (shūshin) course, which had indoctrinated the students with authoritarian, undemocratic attitudes, was abolished, and history books were rewritten to make them less nationalistic. Students were to be taught to think for themselves rather than merely memorize what textbooks said. Textbooks were no longer compiled by the Ministry of Education but were published by private companies and selected by local educators. The first nine years of school (elementary and lower secondary) were made compulsory.

In the first few years of the postwar era, the post of Minister of Education was held by distinguished educators, but later appointment to the post was primarily based upon partisan political considerations. The Ministry was reorganized by the Ministry of Education Establishment Law of May, 1949, to harmonize its structure with the Occupa-

---

[10] Text in *Political Reorientation,* Vol. II, 865.
[11] Text in McNelly, ed., p. 173.
[12] Cf. The Board of Education Law in *Political Reorientation,* Vol. II, 1207–1215.
[13] Constitution, Article 26.

tion policies of democratization and decentralization. Since the administration of education would be primarily the responsibility of local and prefectural school boards, its functions were reduced to advising, coordination, and research.

The Reverse Course

The "reverse course," as the conservative policies of the government after 1949 were called, had as one of its aims the revision of the educational system to instill patriotism and love of country in the student body. Juvenile delinquency and pacifism were considered a reflection of the lack of adequate moral training in the school system. Furthermore, the powerful Japan Teachers Union (Nikkyōso), under leftist leadership, threatened to use the school system to instill Marxism in the youth of the country. Socialists and school teachers were often able to get themselves elected to local school boards. In 1956, the Diet passed a bill making the school boards appointive rather than elective. Prefectural school boards are made up of five members, and municipal school boards of three members, appointed by the governor or mayor respectively. No single political party may command a majority in the board. The Minister of Education enjoys some right of veto over the acts of the boards of education. Appointments of superintendents by prefectural boards have to be approved by the Ministry, and appointments of municipal school superintendents have to be approved by the prefectural board.

There are no specific local school taxes, and the national government collects nearly all taxes. From 1940 to 1945, the central government paid one-half the salaries of the teachers, but in 1949, the Local Finance Equalization Grant of the central government to prefectures and municipalities meant that teachers' salaries were less directly subsidized. In 1953, a more direct subsidy was provided. Today, the teachers' salaries in elementary and lower secondary schools are paid half by the prefecture and half by the national government.

The restored centralization of the educational system has been described by Kiyose Ichiro, Minister of Education in 1956. He has said that the Ministry of Education can now "positively advise, guide, and help Prefectures, and they in turn help municipalities. . . . The new legislation clarifies the lines of command in the educational structure."[14] The morals course was restored to the curriculum in 1958 over the bitter opposition of liberals and the political left, who, understand-

[14] Anderson, p. 88.

ably, fear that such a course would, as in the past, spread antidemocratic and militaristic ideology. In 1971, the Ministry of Education issued syllabi which emphasized the citizens' responsibility to check the pollution of the environment.

Higher Education

There are in Japan seventy-four colleges and universities supported by the national government, including the famous prewar Imperial Universities. There are thirty-nine "public" (i.e., prefectural or municipal) colleges and universities and 140 private colleges and universities, making a total of 256 institutions of higher learning.[15] A large number of these universities, national, public, and private, were established after World War II, and they are plagued in many instances with a lack of adequately trained staff. Salaries of professors are notoriously poor, even in the best institutions, and the economic condition of many of the students is miserable. The competition to enter universities is nevertheless extremely keen, and Japan is frequently referred to as "examination hell," where children and youths are constantly cramming for examinations to enter a university. Although it is difficult to get into a good university, once admitted, a student has an easy life because academic standards are not high, and almost anyone can graduate.

The Zengakuren, or All-Japan Federation of Student Self-Government Associations, has long been under leftist leadership.[16] In 1960, when it was distinguished for its great antigovernment demonstrations, its mainstream faction was led by elements which had been expelled from the Japan Communist Party for their "left-wing adventurism." Consequently, the term "Trotskyism" is frequently applied to the ideology of this student movement.

The turmoil on Japan's campuses in 1968 and 1969 provoked the Diet to enact the stringent Universities Control Law described in Chapter 3 of this book. This law enhanced the role of the Ministry of Education in higher education and, in a sense, may have reduced the autonomy and academic freedom so highly valued by the universities. However, so long as the academic community maintains order on the campuses, it need not fear intervention from the outside.

[15] *Statistical Handbook of Japan,* 1969, p. 121.
[16] For the history of the Zengakuren see Lawrence H. Battistini, *The Postwar Student Struggle in Japan* (Tokyo: Tuttle, 1956), and George R. Packard, III, *Protest in Tokyo: The Security Treaty Crisis of 1960* (Princeton, N.J.: Princeton University Press, 1966).

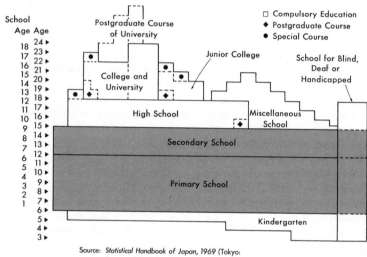

Figure 5
THE EDUCATIONAL SYSTEM OF JAPAN

Source: *Statistical Handbook of Japan, 1969* (Tokyo:
Bureau of Statistics, Office of Prime Minister, 1969), P. 121.

The Police

Occupation Reforms

Before World War II, the police were an agency of the Imperial Government, not only to maintain law and order but also to suppress internal political opposition. The Home Ministry, which supervised the police, sometimes used the officers of the law for forcibly intervening in elections. The police, like other government officers, assumed dictatorial attitudes towards the people whom they seemed more concerned to oppress than to protect. The police were responsible for the extirpation of "dangerous thoughts," i.e., liberal, democratic, and socialistic ideas. The police system thus played an important role in enforcing authoritarianism in Japan.

A principal feature of Occupation reform was the partial decentralization of the police system, so that it could no longer be used by the national government for forcing its will on the people. The Home Ministry was abolished in 1947, and a dual system of National Rural

Police and Police of Autonomous Entities was established.[17] The National Rural Police of 30,000 men were placed under the administrative control of the National Public Safety Commission and under the operational control of Prefectural Public Safety Commissions. Each municipality of over 5,000 population was responsible for the maintenance of its own police (Police of Autonomous Entities) and the enforcement of law and order. Each of these 1,600 municipalities had an independent police force functioning under the operational and administrative control of a municipal Public Safety Commission.

The Reverse Course

Fears that the decentralized police system would be inadequate to cope with large-scale leftist-led demonstrations and riots inspired General MacArthur, in 1950, to direct the formation of a National Police Reserve of 75,000 men, when American forces moved to Korea. The Police Reserve was an embryo army and has since become the Self-Defense Force.

The expense and inefficiency of the Police of Autonomous Entities proved too great a drain on the budgets of local governments, and an amendment to the Police Law, in 1951, made it possible for many local entities to relinquish the privilege of maintaining their own police and to rely on the National Rural Police.

Finally, in 1954, the Diet passed a new Police Law sponsored by the Yoshida Government.[18] Fearing a return of the prewar police state, the Socialists boycotted the deliberations. The new law abolished both the National Rural Police and the Police of Autonomous Entities and replaced them with Prefectural Police. In principle, the expense is borne by the prefecture. The police in each prefecture are under the operational control of a Prefectural Public Safety Commission composed of three or five members appointed by the governor with the approval of the prefectural assembly. The Chief of the Prefectural Police Headquarters is appointed by the National Public Safety Commission with the consent of the Prefectural Public Safety Commission.

The National Public Safety Commission is headed by a Cabinet minister (in recent years the Autonomy Minister) and has five additional members, appointed by the Prime Minister with the consent of the Diet. The National Public Safety Commission administers police

---

[17] Cf. Police Law, *Political Reorientation,* Vol. II, 1062–1071.

[18] The background of this legislation is discussed in Yoshida Shigeru, *The Yoshida Memoirs: The Story of Japan in Crisis,* trans. Yoshida Kenichi (Boston, Mass.: Houghton Mifflin, 1962), pp. 176–181.

affairs relating to state security, exercises general control over such matters as police education, communication, criminal identification, and criminal statistics, and coordinates police administration on the whole. Under its jurisdiction, the National Police Agency is concerned with criminal investigation, scientific crime detection, and police communications.

The Prime Minister may, upon recommendation of the National Public Safety Commission, proclaim a state of national emergency for all or part of the country. He may then assume control over the police in the areas involved. Such an emergency proclamation must be ratified by the Diet within twenty days. However, the Prime Minister did not avail himself of this power during the turbulent summer of 1960.[19]

In 1958, the Police Duties Act Revision Bill, sponsored by the Kishi Government, met with widespread popular opposition. It was doubtful whether the proposed legislation, which was of questionable constitutionality, was really necessary. As a result of obstruction in the Diet and mass demonstrations, the measure was not admitted to a vote in the Diet, although the Government commanded sufficient votes to pass it.

The challenges faced by the police are as formidable in Japan as in America. Mass demonstrations, riots, assassinations by rightists, narcotics traffic, smuggling, and gangsterism are acute problems. It often seems that constitutional legal limitations on the police, intended to protect the democratic rights of the individual, benefit terrorists, Communists, and criminals more than law-abiding people. Thus, constitutional and legal revisions are constantly proposed to strengthen the hands of the police, but as in the case of the 1961 Antiviolence Bill, it is virtually impossible to bring about agreement between the two major parties concerning the specific provisions of such legislation.

The Government and Politics of Tokyo

In Japan, as in France and England, the political capital is also the economic and cultural capital of the land. The factories, the port, the railways (above and below ground), the universities, the slums, the theaters, the cinemas, the large and small night clubs, and the traffic jams of Tokyo all represent the economic and cultural vitality of modern Japan, which converges on the capital. About one-fifth of Japan's population lives in Tokyo and its adjacent prefectures. The Tokyo metropolitan government is engaged in subway construction,

[19] John M. Maki, *Government and Politics of Japan: The Road to Democracy* (New York: Praeger, 1962), p. 102.

slum clearance, housing projects, control of air, water, and noise pollution, sewage and garbage disposal, and operation of water reservoirs, parks, museums, libraries, stadiums, a university, four colleges, 156 senior high schools, 504 junior high schools, 1,083 primary schools, and 135 kindergartens.

A particularly acute problem for Tōkyō-to has been the financing of the city-operated transportation systems. The slowness of the streetcars and trolley buses in Tokyo's clogged streets has greatly reduced their patronage. Faced with continuing operating deficits these forms of transportation are now being progressively eliminated. This, of course, places an increasing burden on Tokyo's famous subway system, which must be constantly expanded. The tremendous cost of subway construction requires the issuance of bonds, the interest costs of which cannot be met by the revenue from tickets. The water supply system has also operated on a deficit, as the water must be brought in from ever more distant areas and the cost of water continues to rise.[20]

The politics of the Tokyo metropolis exerts a disproportionate influence on national politics. The predominantly conservative national legislature seems under a state of siege when the Diet building is surrounded by thousands of demonstrating leftists. Conservatives have been fearful that a Socialist or Communist governor of Tokyo might show too much sympathy or leniency towards leftist demonstrators, endangering the parliamentary process.

In 1965, the Liberal-Democrats, whose image had been besmirched by a number of scandals, lost their majority in the Tokyo Metropolitan Assembly, and a Socialist was elected president of the Assembly. In 1967, Minobe Ryōkichi, an economics professor who had become popular as a television commentator, was elected governor of Tokyo. He won with the support of the Socialist and Communist Parties, and his victory was regarded as a severe blow to the conservatives. Two years later, however, the Liberal-Democrats recaptured their majority in the Tokyo Assembly, partly because an excessive number of Socialist candidates fragmented the Socialist votes. Following are the statistics:

	Before the 1969 Election	1969 Election
Socialists	43	24
Liberal-Democrats	36	54
Kōmeitō	22	25
Communists	9	18
Democratic-Socialists	4	4
Independents	1	1
Vacancies	5	

[20] *Sizing up Tokyo,* pp. 31–35.

The Tokyo delegations to the two houses of the national Diet are larger than those from any other prefecture, and their election attracts special interest. In 1969, the ten electoral districts of Tokyo elected thirty-nine members to the House of Representatives. The enormity of the Socialist defeat that year was particularly evident in Tokyo, shown by a comparison of the 1967 and 1969 lower house election results:

	1967	1969
Liberal-Democrats	16	17
Socialists	13	2
Kōmeitō	6	10
Democratic-Socialists	3	4
Communists	1	6
	39	39

The Socialist governor has taken pleasure in defending the Constitution and local autonomy against the conservative national administration. For example, in 1968 an interesting quarrel with the national government related to the establishment of a Korean special college. Recognition of the college, sponsored by Koreans oriented toward Communist North Korea, was opposed by the Ministry of Education because it would teach opposition to Japan. Opinion in Japan concerning relations with the two Koreas had been polarized during the debate on the Japan–South Korea treaty of 1965. Governor Minobe, urged on by the intellectual community, formally recognized the Korean school in 1968, insisting that the Constitution and laws, not politics, were the basis of his decision. In 1971, Governor Minobe won re-election by overwhelming the Liberal-Democratic candidate, a former police superintendent who had been hand-picked to run by Prime Minister Satō.

Evaluating Local Government in Japan

There are, of course, various criteria by which local government may be judged. Opinions are bound to differ about (1) which of these criteria are more important than others and (2) how well, in practice, an administration fulfills any given criterion. The American occupiers stressed local autonomy as the most important criterion to be achieved in reforming local government. This objective ran counter to the Japanese bureaucratic tradition of running everything from the ministries in Tokyo. Furthermore, the industrialization and urbanization of the country has largely rendered obsolete small administrative units. The reverse course since the early days of the Occupation has been to recentralize control over education, police, finance, and virtually everything else. Thus, it may be said that the Occupation's controversial objective to establish more democratic home rule in Japan has been largely frustrated by Japanese tradition and economic modernization.

A second criterion is the democratic input from local politics to the nation as a whole. Local government in Japan has made some contribution. By providing opportunities for the opposition parties (Socialist, Kōmeitō, Democratic-Socialist, and Communist) to sponsor programs and gubernatorial, mayoral, and assembly candidates on the prefectural and municipal levels, local politics provides a possibility for these parties to make positive contributions. However, because the duties of the various levels of government overlaps, it is virtually impossible to fix responsibility for things that go wrong. Who is to blame for inadequate roads or sewage systems, for example? The mayors and governors and cabinet ministers blame each other, and it is difficult for the voter to know which rascals to throw out. Furthermore, the financial dependence of local governments on the LDP-dominated central government gives an unfair advantage to LDP candidates for local offices. The local conservatives may plausibly claim that they will be more effective pleaders for local causes than the Socialists could be. Until local governments attain more financial self-sufficiency, an unlikely possibility, the opposition parties will be at an unfair disadvantage.

A third criterion is economy of operation. Here local government in Japan is so utterly dependent on the central government for funds, partly in order to meet nationally established standards, that this criterion seems almost irrelevant. More important is the fact that the modernization of roads, educational facilities, and the like, is almost open-ended. Even though few local entities are operating at a deficit, demands are not being met. Possibly the further amalgamation of local entities would result in greater economies, but this might have to be at the expense of democratic values.

A fourth criterion is the effectiveness of the Government in meeting needs which cannot be handled by the private sector. By modern standards, the sewage disposal systems in Japan are utterly inadequate. Unsafe, crowded roads, air and water pollution, and inadequate schools are continuing sources of complaint. Japan is also far behind in social security and welfare programs. It is difficult, of course, to assign responsibility for these problems, but local as well as national government is faced with formidable challenges. Japan's high productivity and the unprecedented affluence of her people somewhat mitigate the negative effect of governmental inadequacies on public morale.

A fundamental dilemma in politics is balancing the interests of the citizens of a country as a whole with the interests of the citizens of particular localities. In 1970, an extremely bitter dispute arose over the building of an international airport at Sanrizuka, in Chiba-ken, near Tokyo. Three policemen were killed and over 100 other people were injured during one of the protest demonstrations against the construction of the airport, in September, 1971. Many of the decisions concerning the new airport were made bureaucratically rather than democratically. Yet the lives of hundreds of thousands of people in the area will be greatly affected by the new airport. Its construction and operation will employ directly or indirectly many people, and land values will increase faster than ever. But roads and local services will be severely overburdened, and the traffic and noise both on the ground and in the air will endanger lives and pollute the atmosphere for the local population. How local rights and autonomy can be preserved in a densely populated industrialized country is, of course, a serious problem not unique to Japan.

Suggested Reading

Anderson, Ronald S. *Japan: Three Epochs of Modern Education.* Washington, D.C.: Government Printing Office, 1959.

Beardsley, Richard K., John W. Hall, and Robert E. Ward. *Village Japan.* Chicago, Ill.: University of Chicago Press, 1959.

Dore, R. P. *City Life in Japan: A Study of a Tokyo Ward.* Berkeley: University of California Press, 1958.

Dull, Paul S. "Maeda Shoichi: A Case Study of a Japanese Political Boss," in Ward, Robert E., ed. *Five Studies in Japanese Politics.* Ann Arbor: University of Michigan Press, 1957.

Eells, Walter Crosby, comp. *The Literature of Japanese Education, 1945–1954.* Hamden, Conn.: Shoe String Press, 1955.

Hall, Robert King. *Education for a New Japan.* New Haven, Conn.: Yale University Press, 1949.

Nagai, Michio. *Higher Education in Japan.* Tokyo: Tokyo University Press, 1970.

Passin, Herbert. *Society and Education in Japan.* New York: Teachers College, Columbia University, 1965.

Shiomi, Saburo. *Japan's Finance and Taxation, 1940–1956.* New York: Columbia University Press, 1957.

Steiner, Kurt. *Local Government in Japan.* Stanford, Calif.: Stanford University Press, 1965.

Sugihara, Yoshie and David W. Plath. *Sensei and His People: The Building of a Japanese Commune.* Berkeley: University of California Press, 1969.

8

Japan in World Politics

Economics and Foreign Policy

In the early 1970s, Japan had the world's third most prosperous economy. She is now debating her future role in world politics. Should she continue her policies of low posture and alignment with the United States? Or should she strive for a more independent role in world affairs? Will her expanding economy require an increasing involvement in political and military matters outside of Japan and the Western Pacific? As an Asian power, should she play a larger role in Asian affairs? Should she recognize Communist China? Will Japan acquire nuclear weapons? These are some of the questions with which the present chapter is concerned.

The Alignment with America

The Korean War and the Japanese Peace Treaty

As early as March, 1947, General MacArthur told American newsmen that it was time for a peace treaty with Japan. The Civil War in China and the inability of the Americans and Russians to achieve the unification of Korea, however, raised serious questions about the security of a disarmed Japan, and American military planners were unwilling to give up American bases there. In June, 1950, North Korean forces, armed and trained by the Soviet Union, invaded South Korea. American air and naval units based in Japan immediately went to the aid of the South Koreans and within a few days, United States army units, with the sanction of the United Nations Security Council,

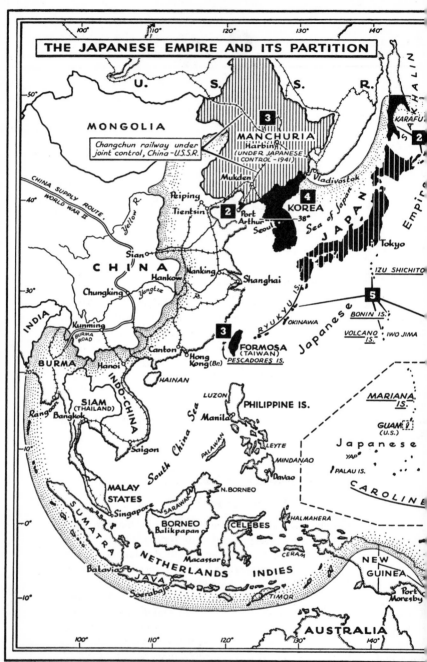

Appearing in JAPAN'S MODERN CENTURY by Hugh Borton.
Copyright 1955 The Ronald Press Company.

Figure 6

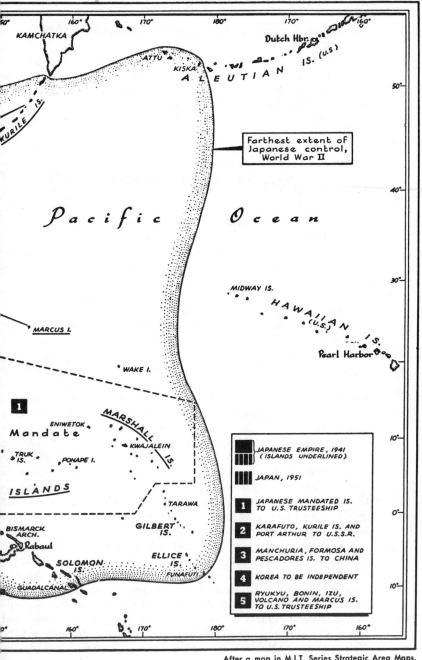

After a map in M.I.T. Series Strategic Area Maps.
Copyright by Massachusetts Institute of Technology.

moved from Japan to Korea. General MacArthur headed the United Nations Command.

To maintain internal order in Japan in the absence of the Americans who had gone to fight in Korea, Prime Minister Yoshida, acting on the instructions of MacArthur, established by cabinet order a 75,000-man Japanese Police Reserve. Through no choice of their own, the Japanese people suddenly found themselves indirectly involved in a war. Japan, only five years before at war with the United States, provided the American-led United Nations forces with air and naval bases for attacks against the Korean Communists and the Chinese Communist "volunteers." United Nations headquarters were located in Tokyo, and Japanese industry was caught up in a war boom supplying their forces with matériel and services. If General MacArthur was impatient to bomb the "privileged sanctuary" of Manchuria, where Communists mounted their air attacks on his forces, it seemed equally possible that the Chinese Communists might attack MacArthur's air bases in Japan, some of which were uncomfortably near large cities, including Tokyo.

The Americans were distressed that many Japanese seemed indifferent if not unsympathetic towards the American effort to fend off communism. American policy-makers felt that the Japanese would become more aware of their stake in the struggle against Communist imperialism if they were given their national independence. The United States proposed a formula whereby Japan would regain her sovereignty, but American forces would remain in Japan. Such an arrangement would presumably satisfy both the Japanese, who wished to see the Occupation end, and the American military, who wished to maintain their installations. The Soviet government indicated that a peace treaty with Japan should first be approved by the four chief Allied Powers, China, the United Kingdom, the Soviet Union, and the United States; and that China should be represented by the Communist Government in Peking rather than the Chiang Kai-shek regime in Taiwan. The Soviets further insisted on continuing controls to prevent the future rearmament of Japan. The Soviet views were not accepted by the United States, which refused to concede that the Soviet Union had a right to veto the conclusion by others of a peace with Japan.

The Western Allies were not in complete accord about the American proposals, which included defense arrangements vis-à-vis the Communist bloc; Australia, New Zealand, and the Philippine Republic were still fearful of Japanese aggression, and compromises had to be worked out. Three separate defense treaties were therefore devised: (1) a bilateral defense arrangement between the United States and Japan, (2) a defense treaty between Australia, New Zealand, and the United States (ANZUS), and (3) a defense agreement between the

United States and the Philippines. By midsummer of 1951, the main differences among the wartime Allies, save for the Communist states, had been ironed out, and the United States and the United Kingdom jointly invited fifty-five of the Allied Powers at war with Japan to a peace conference in September for the signing of the peace treaty with Japan. No changes were to be made in the proposed treaty after August 13.

The Peace Conference in San Francisco was attended by representatives of all of the fifty-five governments invited, except Burma, India, and Yugoslavia. China was not invited because of American objections to the Communist regime and British objections to the Nationalist regime. The Soviet delegate demanded that Communist China be invited to the conference and objected that the draft treaty did not restrict the rearmament of Japan or adequately guarantee democratic freedom. Instead, he asserted, it permitted Japan to join regional security pacts, which threatened the peace of the Far East, and its territorial provisions violated the rights of the Soviet Union and China. The Soviet proposals for changes in the treaty were defeated, and the Soviet Union, Poland, and Czechoslovakia refused to sign it.

On September 8, 1951, forty-eight Allied nations and Japan signed the peace treaty.[1] The conference was popularly regarded as a diplomatic victory over the Soviet Union. Nevertheless, the technical state of war between Japan on the one hand and the Soviet Union and Communist China on the other had not yet been brought to an end. Distrust of Japan was widespread even among those countries which adhered to the Peace Treaty.

The San Francisco treaty required Japan to recognize the independence of Korea and to renounce all claim to Formosa, the Pescadores, the Kurile Islands, and Sakhalin. Significantly, the treaty did not indicate to what states these important territories were transferred. Japan also accepted the establishment of the United Nations Strategic Trusteeship, administered by the United States, over the Pacific Islands, formerly mandated to Japan by the League of Nations. She agreed to concur with any proposal of the United States to the United Nations to place under American-administered trusteeship the Ryukyu and the Bonin (Ogasawara) Islands. In the meantime the United States would exercise all powers of administration over these areas. The Allied Powers recognized that "Japan as a sovereign nation possesses the inherent right of individual or collective self-defense referred

---

[1] Text of the Japanese Peace Treaty is given in Edwin O. Reischauer, *The United States and Japan,* 3rd ed. (Cambridge, Mass.: Harvard University Press, 1965), pp. 363–378.

to in Article 51 of the Charter of the United Nations and that Japan may voluntarily enter into collective security arrangements." Japan declared her intention to apply for membership in the United Nations and her willingness to conform to the principles of its Charter. It was provided that Japan should pay reparations to the Allied Powers for the damage and suffering she had caused during the war. "Nevertheless," the treaty stated, "it is also recognized that the resources of Japan are not presently sufficient, if it is to maintain a viable economy, to make complete reparation for all such damage and suffering and at the same time meet its other obligations." Japan would enter into negotiations with those Allied Powers who so desired to arrange for reparations.

Thus the treaty laid the groundwork for the continued American occupation of Okinawa, American military bases in Japan, Japan's rearmament, and a soft reparations policy, all of which fitted in with the American desire to establish Japan as a bulwark against communism at minimal cost to the American taxpayer.

The 1951 Security Treaty

Although the Peace Treaty recognized Japan's right of self-defense, Article 9 of the Constitution renounced war and arms, and Japan had been completely disarmed by the Allied Powers. The Korean war was still raging, and on the same day that the Peace Treaty was signed, Japan and the United States also contracted a Security Treaty, in which Japan indicated the desire that, as a provisional arrangement for its defense, the United States maintain armed forces of its own in and about Japan to deter armed attack on the latter.[2] The United States expressed its willingness to maintain armed forces in Japan "in the expectation, however, that Japan will itself increasingly assume responsibility for its own defense against direct and indirect aggression."

The Security Treaty went beyond simply allowing American forces to remain in Japan after the Occupation: it looked forward to Japanese rearmament. The signing of the Security Treaty meant that Japan became an ally of the United States on the very day that it had ceased to be an enemy. The American forces in Japan would be used to maintain "international peace and security in the Far East" as well as to protect Japan from armed attack from without. Japanese bases could presumably be employed in the pursuit of almost any policy the

[2] Text is given in John M. Maki, ed., *Conflict and Tension in the Far East: Key Documents, 1894–1960* (Seattle: University of Washington Press, 1961), pp. 219–220.

United States might follow with respect to Korea, Taiwan, and mainland China. Furthermore, American forces might assist, upon the request of the Japanese Government, in putting down large-scale internal riots and disturbances in Japan, "caused through the instigation or intervention by an outside power or powers." Thus the United States acquired a conditional right of armed intervention in Japanese internal affairs.

When the Peace and Security Treaties went into effect and the Occupation officially ended on April 28, 1952, there was little visible evidence of change in Japan. The American forces remained and enjoyed, under the terms of an administrative agreement concluded in February, 1952, essentially the same extensive extraterritorial privileges that they had enjoyed during the Occupation. The political opposition made political capital of the alleged subservience of the Yoshida regime to the American military.

In 1954, as a result of an American hydrogen bomb test in the Bikini area, men aboard the Japanese fishing vessel *Fukuryū Maru* were showered with radioactive ashes. Their catch of fish had already been partly sold and distributed throughout Japan before it was condemned as unsafe. As a consequence, there was a widespread fear that ocean fish, a staple of the Japanese diet, were unsafe to eat. The failure of American authorities to express their sympathy for the victims of the test until all the facts were in aroused widespread resentment throughout Japan. The Americans belatedly admitted that the fallout from the Bikini bomb had been on a scale and in a direction not expected by the scientists in charge, agreed that the fishing boat had been outside the danger zone, and paid a compensation to the injured fishermen.

After the end of the Occupation, Japanese magazines and newspapers were full of sensational articles concerning the moral and economic effects of American military bases. The land occupied by the bases, it was held, was sorely needed by the peasants for raising crops. The Americans left behind large numbers of illegitimate children with marked Negroid or Caucasian features. These unfortunate "mixed bloods" (konketsu) would suffer from discrimination and lack of opportunity throughout their lives. The disreputable bars and other establishments pandering to the vices of free-spending American GIs often created difficulties. Of course, leftist agitators made great capital of the "base problem," in order to hasten the withdrawal of the foreign troops. In 1957 the apparently senseless killing by an American soldier of a Japanese peasant woman salvaging shell cases at an American firing range aroused much indignation. A controversy over whether Army Specialist William Girard should be tried by a Japanese court or a United States military court aroused ill will on both sides of the Pacific Ocean. A visit by Prime Minister Kishi to President Eisenhower was followed by the announcement in June, 1957, that within a year the United States would withdraw its ground forces from Japan, with the exception of supply and administrative elements. American air and naval units in Japan, however, would remain.

The 1960 Security Pact

In 1959, the Kishi Government negotiated a new security pact with the United States which would explicitly commit the United States to defend Japan and require "previous consultation"—interpreted to mean Japanese consent—before the Americans could use their Japanese bases for military operations outside Japan or introduce nuclear weapons into the country. The new pact would not give the American forces the right to put down internal riots. Finally, the new treaty would be limited to ten years, after which it could be terminated by either party on one year's notice. Kishi and the conservatives believed that this new "Treaty of Mutual Cooperation and Security between the United States and Japan" would usher in an era of greater independence and international prestige for Japan.

Notwithstanding the advantages for Japan of the new treaty over the old, the neutralists and Socialists emphatically opposed it. They held that the pact would increase international tension in the Far East and might drag Japan into American military adventures in which Japan had no interest. They were determined that the alliance with the United States be ended and launched an all-out attack on the treaty.

In March, 1959, the Tokyo District Court ruled in the Sunakawa case that the stationing of American forces in Japan, as provided in the 1951 Security Pact, violated Article 9 of the Japanese Constitution.[3] This decision, which was not reversed by the Supreme Court until the following December, raised grave doubts about not only the status of American forces then in Japan but also the constitutionality of the new treaty. In January, 1960, student demonstrators unsuccessfully attempted to prevent Kishi and his party from taking off at Haneda Airport to sign the new treaty in the United States. Nevertheless, the Treaty of Mutual Cooperation and Security was signed in Washington on January 19, 1960.[4]

In February, the special committee on the new security pact was

[3] See Chapter 5.
[4] For the text of this treaty, see Reischauer, pp. 379–381, or Maki, pp. 220–222.

organized in the Japanese House of Representatives and debated a total of 150 hours. The Socialists evidently hoped to filibuster until the Diet session ended to prevent the passage of the pact. On May 19, at 10:25 P.M., a bell in the Diet building announced a plenary meeting of the lower house. The Socialists locked the office of the aged House Speaker from the outside, barricaded it with furniture, and staged a sit-down in the corridor of the building to prevent him from going to the chamber to call the meeting to order. Finally, he telephoned for the police, who forcibly removed the angry, kicking Socialists from the corridor. Diet guards escorted the Speaker to his rostrum, where he called the House of Representatives to order. Although Socialists, Democratic-Socialists, and some factions of the Liberal-Democratic Party were absent, the House immediately voted a fifty-day extension of the session. The meeting adjourned at 11:52 and reopened at midnight. Again, with only Liberal-Democrats present, at 0:18 the House, without forewarning and without debate, voted to approve the Security Pact.

Newspaper accounts of the night of May 19–20 emphasized the introduction of the police into the Diet and the absence of the opposition parties when the vote was taken on the pact. The press, ever hostile to the Government, played down the refusal of the Socialists to allow the House to convene peacefully and referred to the vote as a "forcible passage." The Government defended its procedure on the ground that this was the only way in which the parliamentary majority could prevail in the face of violent obstruction by the Socialists.

Many people who had not felt strongly about the Security Pact now became highly indignant towards the Government because of its role in the events of May 19–20. A wave of mass demonstrations and strikes calling for Kishi's resignation, the dissolution of the Diet, and the blocking of the Security Pact broke out in Tokyo.[5] The demonstrators were for the most part students, professors, labor unionists, and business and government employees. Over 10,000,000 people signed petitions denouncing the new Security Treaty.

It was widely asserted that Kishi had deliberately chosen May 20 as the date for the "forcible passage" of the pact in order to provide

[5] The author witnessed some of the events here described. For more complete accounts in English, see Robert A. Scalapino and Junnosuke Masumi, *Parties and Politics in Contemporary Japan* (Berkeley and Los Angeles: University of California Press, 1962), pp. 125–153, George R. Packard, III, *Protest in Tokyo: The Security Treaty Crisis of 1960* (Princeton, N.J.: Princeton University Press, 1966), and Edward P. Whittemore, *The Press in Japan Today: A Case Study* (Columbia: University of South Carolina Press, 1961).

President Eisenhower with a souvenir of his forthcoming visit to Japan. The anti-Kishi movement began to develop into an "anti-Ike visit" movement, and hostile demonstrations before the American Embassy in Tokyo became a daily occurrence. When the President's press secretary, James Hagerty, came to Tokyo on June 7, his car was blocked at Haneda airport by demonstrators, and he and the American ambassador had to be rescued by an American Marine Corps helicopter.

On June 15, a clash between students and police resulted in the hospitalization of hundreds of police and students and the death by crushing of a coed, Miss Kamba Michiko. The students charged that police brutality was the cause of Miss Kamba's death, and college students and professors throughout the country held memorial ceremonies and went on strike. Apparently fearing that the Emperor himself might become the victim of a Hagerty-type incident, imperial chamberlains urged that His Majesty, who had been scheduled to ride in an automobile from the airport to Tokyo with President Eisenhower, could not be put in a position where he might be involved in politics.[6] On June 16, Kishi asked the American Ambassador for a "postponement" of the Eisenhower visit. After the pact ratification documents were exchanged on June 23, Prime Minister Kishi announced his decision to resign.

The Socialist Party declared that the new pact was invalid and not binding on the Japanese people, alleging that its substance violated the Japanese Constitution and the United Nations Charter and that the manner of its enactment was illegal.

The new Security Pact figured as a principal issue in the subsequent November, 1960, lower house election campaign. The comfortable victory of the Liberal-Democrats, who won more votes and seats than all of the opposition parties combined, was interpreted by some observers as an indication that the Japanese people favored the American alliance; but many Japanese had voted for the Liberal-Democrats on the basis of personalities or issues other than the pact.

President Kennedy's appointment of Professor Edwin O. Reischauer in 1961 to serve as Ambassador to Japan greatly improved Japanese-American relations. Reischauer, a leading Western authority on East Asian history, had a Japanese wife and spoke the language fluently. As Ambassador, he was able to communicate effectively with Japanese intellectuals who had been generally critical of the tie with America.

After 1970, the 1960 Security Treaty could be terminated by either party on one year's notice. As 1970 approached, some conservatives,

[6] *Time Magazine,* June 27, 1960, p. 18.

fearful that a Socialist cabinet might in the future terminate the treaty urged that it be revised to provide that it remain in effect for a specified term. However, renegotiation of the pact would mean heated deliberations in the Diet and provide numerous occasions for obstruction and hostile demonstrations. The Satō Government finally chose to permit the treaty to continue automatically in force, thus hoping to avoid dramatic confrontations with the opposition as had occurred in 1960. On June 23, 1970, the tenth anniversary of the treaty, the Socialists and Communists mobilized hundreds of thousands of people in Tokyo in the largest demonstration since 1960, in opposition to the continuation of the Security Treaty, but the Government's policy of continuing the treaty in force was unaffected by this and other demonstrations.

Okinawa

The battle of Okinawa (April 1–June 21, 1945) was one of the bitterest phases of the Pacific War for both sides; tens of thousands of Japanese civilians as well as soldiers lost their lives in the struggle. Okinawa (the Ryukyu Islands) had been a prefecture since 1879. The indigenous population had originally spoken the Okinawan language, which was closely related to Japanese, and readily adopted the latter language. Unlike the Koreans, the Okinawans came to regard themselves as Japanese, although the mainland Japanese sometimes regarded them with condescension. Many Japanese families had settled permanently in Okinawa and become integrated with the local population.

During the war some Chinese had hoped that the Ryukyu (Liuchiu) Islands, before 1872 a tributary to China, would be "returned" to China, but when the war ended Okinawa was occupied by American troops. From the very beginning of the Occupation of Japan, the Ryukyus were removed from the jurisdiction of the Japanese government and placed directly under American military government. The Japanese Peace Treaty provided that Japan would concur in any United States proposals to the United Nations to place the Ryukyu and Bonin Islands and other specified islands under its trusteeship system. The United States, however, recognized Japan's "residual sovereignty" over the Ryukyus. In the meantime, the areas involved would be administered by the United States.

The conflicts and tension in Korea, Southeast Asia, and the Taiwan Strait made necessary the maintenance of strong United States bases in East Asia. At the same time, the usefulness of American bases in Japan was limited by the terms of the 1960 United States–Japan Security Pact and by political developments in Japan. The Okinawa bases, on the other hand, were located in territory under the *de facto* jurisdiction of the United States, and their use was less dependent upon local political uncertainties.

The population of the Ryukyus consists of about 945,465 Japanese[7] (Okinawans) and about 90,000 Americans, military and civilian. The Americans live in a colonial atmosphere with a standard of living higher than that of the native population, and the local economy has become largely dependent upon the military bases. At the same time, the bases have taken up much of the necessary farmland. For a number of years, the terms of the American leases on Okinawan land were a source of much dissatisfaction. The demand for the return of Okinawa to Japan became so strong that it appeared to some observers that Okinawa might become an American Cyprus. In 1959, the land problem was settled fairly satisfactorily, but the Okinawans continued to look forward to the return of Japanese rule.

While America fought in Korea and South Vietnam purportedly to protect the right of Asians to determine their own future, she denied that right to the Japanese living in Okinawa. Throughout the 1960s compromise proposals were suggested which might meet, at least part way, both the people's aspirations and the strategic needs of the United States. One possibility was the reversion of some but not all of the islands to Japan. (Actually, the Amami Oshima group in the northern Ryukyus were returned in 1953, and in 1968, the Ogasawara [Bonin] Islands [not part of the Ryukyus] were returned.) However, 90 percent of the Ryukyuans lived on Okinawa Island itself, and that island contained most of the vast American military installations. The Okinawans felt that the return of the other Ryukyu Islands would be meaningless as long as Okinawa remained in American hands, and might result in the further delay of Okinawa's reversion. It was proposed that certain administrative functions (such as social security or education) revert to Japan, while leaving the bases in American hands. The proposals for partial functional reversion were unacceptable to the American military, which evidently felt that their absolute freedom to use Okinawa should in no way be compromised as long as Americans were fighting in Southeast Asia.

The Ryukyu legislature repeatedly passed resolutions demanding reversion to Japan, and in 1968, Yara Chōbyō, a progressive, became the first Ryukyuan chief executive to be popularly elected, and demanded immediate, unconditional, and complete reversion of the islands to Japan.

[7] *Asahi Nenkan, 1971,* p. 601.

The political opposition in Japan exploited the Okinawan issue with increasing effectiveness against the pro-American conservative Government, which was accused of indifference to the welfare and patriotic and democratic aspirations of the citizens of Okinawa prefecture. There was a possibility that if the United States did not substantially alter its position on Okinawa, the pro-American Government in Tokyo might be replaced with a less friendly regime. In that case, the usefulness of American bases in Japan proper might be jeopardized. Furthermore, after 1970, either party to the Security Pact could terminate it on one year's notice, and this possibility doubtless gave Tokyo leverage in its negotiations with Washington.

In November, 1969, President Nixon and Prime Minister Satō, meeting in Washington, issued a joint communiqué announcing that Okinawa would be returned to Japanese administration in 1972. The use of American bases in Okinawa would be subject to the same restrictions as those in the rest of Japan. Without admitting the presence of nuclear weapons in Okinawa, the carefully worded communiqué implied that any such weapons would be removed by 1972. Satō made it clear that peace and stability in the Far East were important to Japan and that Japan would take a positive attitude in future consultations concerning the use of American bases. Thus, in case of a flare-up in Korea or the Taiwan Straits, the Americans could probably make full use of their bases in Japan. Japan would, it was promised, increase her own defense capacity and play a larger role in the economic development of the Far East.

On June 17, 1971, Foreign Minister Aichi Kiichi and Secretary of State William Rogers signed the Okinawa reversion treaty, which embodied the provisions of the Satō-Nixon communiqué.[8] The treaty remained to be approved by the legislatures of the two countries. Some Japanese expressed fears that some American senators might, as a price for their support of the reversion treaty, require that Japan impose severe restrictions on textile exports to the United States. (In November, after Nixon had announced his new economic policy and the Japanese government had agreed to restrict textile exports, the United States Senate approved the treaty by a vote of 84 to 6.)

The opposition bitterly criticized the reversion agreement on several grounds. American military bases would remain in Okinawa after the reversion to the disadvantage of the inhabitants and the detriment of peace in Asia. Japan was committed to more rearmament. Finally, Satō's references to the importance of peace and stability in Korea, Taiwan, and the Far East seemed to reduce restrictions on the use of

[8] For text of the treaty, see *New York Times,* June 18, 1971, p. 10.

American bases in Japan. Thus the Japan bases would be "Okinawa-ized," and Japan would become a more active partner of the United States in the latter's military ventures in Asia.

Economic Ties with America

During the Occupation, the United States extended very substantial economic aid to Japan. Japan's yearly imports amounted to about a half-billion dollars more than her exports, and American assistance made good the trade deficit. The Korean War touched off a boom for the Japanese economy, and by 1968, Japan's GNP was the world's third largest. The Vietnam War stimulated Japanese export trade to Southeast Asia.

In 1969, the United States bought 30.0 percent of Japan's exports and supplied Japan with 27.2 percent of its imports.[9] For over a decade the United States has been Japan's best customer, and Japan, after Canada, has been the United States' best customer. Japan's close economic ties with the United States since World War II have been a decisive factor in Japan's remarkable industrial revival.

There is, unfortunately, a negative side to the picture. Because Japan's prosperity is so closely linked with America's, a recession in the United States or a change in American tariff policies could prove disastrous for the Japanese. In order to lessen Japan's excessive economic dependence on the United States, the government has made strong efforts to increase trade with Europe, mainland China, and Southeast Asia.

Japan's textile exports to the United States intermittently strained relations between the two countries during the 1960s. The fact that Japan was a major importer of American agricultural goods did not inhibit American textile manufacturers from complaining vociferously about Japanese competition. A crisis was reached in 1970, when the Japanese textile industry refused to accept the voluntary quota on exports of woolen and synthetic textiles demanded by the United States. Other Japanese industries and the Japanese government desired such a quota in order to ensure continued good relations with America and to avoid provoking a massive protectionist reaction in America that could hurt all of Japan's exporting industries. President Nixon, evidently for domestic political reasons, indicated his willingness to support legislation restricting textile imports.

When the United States–Japan talks on textile quotas completely

[9] *Asahi Nenkan, 1971*, p. 375.

broke down in June, 1970, some observers noted that this was the first time that Japan had rejected an American demand since World War II. Late in 1970, the textile negotiations between the two countries were resumed. The bitterness over the textile issue threatened to undo much of the goodwill achieved by the promise of Okinawa's reversion. Ironically, as some economists have pointed out, it would make better sense if technologically advanced countries like the United States and Japan concentrated on the production of sophisticated goods and left textile manufacturing to the less developed nations.

Japan's slowness in opening her own country to the importation of American goods and capital has been the source of much complaint from American business. In 1971, the problem of unemployment in the United States coincided with a flood of Japanese imports and exaggerated accounts of the revival of Japanese militarism. Japan's growing economic power and a more independent foreign policy suggested that her economic and political partnership with the United States might conceivably break up.

On August 15, 1971, President Nixon announced a dramatic new economic policy. Gold payments for the dollar would be suspended, and a 10 percent surcharge on imports would be imposed. These measures were intended primarily to halt the rapidly growing deficit in America's balance of payments and to force other leading countries to revalue upward their currencies. Americans singled out Japan for special criticism for exporting large quantities of automobiles, television sets, radios, and textiles to the United States while severely restricting imports into Japan. Nixon hoped that by making the dollar cheaper in relation to the yen and other foreign currencies, more foreigners, as well as Americans would be induced to buy American goods.

The Japanese government, wishing to retain the advantage of its cheap currency in international trade, had, for some months before the Nixon announcement, resisted an upward revaluation of the yen. After Nixon announced his new economic policy, the Japanese government for nearly two weeks maintained the old ratio of 360 yen to one dollar. But as more and more yen flowed out in exchange for the weak dollar, it finally gave up and let the yen "float." The value of the dollar began to decline, thus making Japanese products relatively more expensive for Americans to buy. At the same time, the 10 percent surcharge put Japanese imports at a further disadvantage in the United States.

Nixon's radical measures respecting the dollar and tariffs were in clear violation of existing international agreements on currency and tariffs. They apparently marked a sharp reversal of America's policy of free trade. Japan appeared to be the chief loser, but the Japanese government had been given no prior warning, even though it was a principal trading partner and military ally. The pro-American Satō administration and its conservative precedessors had been faithful in carrying out Japan's obligations as an ally of the United States in the face of violent criticism from those in Japan who had favored closer ties with Communist China, North Korea, and North Vietnam. Because Nixon had reversed American policies on Communist China and international trade without consulting Japan, the Japanese felt that their closest friend had let them down and could no longer be completely relied upon. Still distrusted in Asia because of her aggressions in World War II, Japan felt isolated.

When the Japanese Emperor and Empress stopped at Anchorage, Alaska, in September, 1971, on their way to Europe, they were greeted by President Nixon. The president had reportedly proposed the meeting early in August, before the announcement of his new economic policy. The meeting was widely interpreted as an effort to strengthen the ties between America and Japan which had been shaken by Nixon's new policy towards China. Later it was announced that Prime Minister Satō would visit President Nixon in San Clemente in January, 1972.

New Strategic Patterns

In the early 1970s, America's relations with Japan appeared to be destined for rapid change. At the same time that China's nuclear threat to Japan was increasing, the United States was withdrawing from Vietnam and Okinawa. Japanese conventional land, air, and sea forces were replacing American conventional forces in Japan and the Ryukyus, but the American nuclear umbrella would remain as a protection for Japan. Many Japanese, however, began to doubt the credibility of the American nuclear commitment. A military conflict in Korea or the Taiwan Strait could result in a clash between Communist Chinese forces and American forces based in Japan. If China then launched a nuclear attack on Japan, could America be relied upon to retaliate, thus provoking a nuclear attack on American cities? Would the reduction of American conventional forces in Japan or the United States–Soviet strategic arms limitations talks (SALT) undermine the American nuclear deterrent in Japan? Many Japanese wondered if Japan, already building up her conventional capacity, might not be wise to develop her own nuclear capability. "A posture that would maximize the possibility for continued Japanese disengagement from Asia, avoid the uncertainties of American nuclear support, and meet immediate, narrow security needs would consist of nuclear weapons and limited conventional forces."[10]

The Chinese Communists and others of Japan's neighbors, threatened by the possibility of a Japan with nuclear weapons, might begin to regard the American-Japanese alliance as a desirable restraint on Japan. Thus the improvement of Peking's relations with Washington may be predicated upon the continuance, rather than the withdrawal, of American conventional and nuclear power in East Asia. Conceivably a Washington-Peking rapprochement could be at the expense of Japan's strategic independence.

The power distribution in East Asia since World War II has moved successively from a bipolar pattern (United States and the Soviet Union) to a tripolar pattern (with the addition of Communist China), and to a quadripolar pattern (with the addition of a powerful, more independent Japan). The Free World versus Communist bloc confrontation thus had given way in the early 1970s to a complex balance of power, in which China and Japan had become largely independent actors, willing to deal with each other and with states of opposing as well as similar ideologies. In this situation, it seems most probable that, with the gradual reduction of American power and the rise of Japanese trade in East Asia, Japan will find it both necessary and possible to exercise a foreign policy which is less dependent on the United States.

Japan and Asia

Japan and Nationalist China

It was anticipated at the end of the Pacific War that Nationalist China would play a leading role in the maintenance of peace and security in the Far East. China was a permanent member of the United Nations Security Council and one of the four veto-holding powers in the Far Eastern Commission and was represented in the four-power Allied Council for Japan. The prestige of the Nationalist regime, however, was enormously damaged by its retreat to Taiwan and the loss of mainland China to the Communists in 1949. The United States and Great Britain were unable to agree on which of the rival Chinese regimes, Nationalist or Communist, should be invited to the Japanese Peace Conference, and, as a result, China was not represented at all.

[10] Donald C. Hellmann, "The United States and Japan," in Steven L. Spiegel and Kenneth N. Waltz, eds., *Conflict in World Politics* (Cambridge, Mass.: Winthrop, 1971), pp. 357–374.

The Cairo Declaration of November 1943 had promised the return of Taiwan to China. In September 1945, the Allies specifically directed that Japanese forces in Taiwan surrender to "Generalissimo Chiang Kai-shek." However, Nationalist maladministration of Taiwan, which provoked a rebellion there in 1947, gave rise to suggestions that Taiwan be placed under some kind of United Nations trusteeship or that a plebiscite be held to determine its status. In the Japanese Peace Treaty, the Japanese renounced all claim to Taiwan and the Penghu Islands, but the treaty did not indicate to whom sovereignty over the islands would be assigned.

The Yoshida Government, acting under strong United States pressure,[11] signed a peace treaty with the Nationalist regime on April 28, 1952, the day that Japan regained its sovereignty.[12] This treaty, which recognizes Nationalist sovereignty over Taiwan and the Penghu Islands, is of great importance to the Nationalists in maintaining their claim to be the de jure government in Taiwan. However, the Japanese Government encourages trade between Japanese firms and both Nationalist and Communist China, and Japanese recognition of the Nationalist Government is largely dependent upon United States policy.

The Taiwanese people, as distinguished from the Nationalist officials, were under Japanese rule for fifty years, and the older ones speak Japanese in addition to the Fukienese dialect. After the 1947 revolt, a number of Formosans in Japan organized a Formosa independence movement, which would give the Taiwanese self-government free of Nationalist or Communist domination. The movement has a headquarters in Tokyo and is, of course, illegal in Formosa itself.[13] In 1971, as the reversion of Okinawa neared, a bitter dispute arose between China and Japan over the control of the Tiao Yu Tai (Senkaku) Islands, 120 miles northeast of Taiwan. These islands, which are near reported offshore oil reserves, are regarded by both Japan and the United States, but not by China, as belonging to the Ryukyu chain, which is to be returned to Japan in 1972.

[11] Sir Esler Dening, *Japan* (New York: Praeger, 1961), pp. 207–208. Mr. Dening was British Ambassador in Tokyo from 1952 to 1957.

[12] The text of the treaty between the Republic of China and Japan is given in *The Japan Yearbook, 1949–1952* (Tokyo: The Foreign Affairs Association of Japan, 1952), pp. 485–488.

[13] For a sympathetic recent account of the movement, see Douglas Mendel, *The Politics of Formosan Nationalism* (Berkeley: University of California Press, 1970).

Relations with Communist China

The Peking regime (Central People's Government of the People's Republic of China) was scarcely four months old when, on February 14, 1950, it contracted with the Soviet Union its famous Treaty of Friendship, Alliance, and Mutual Assistance. The two parties agreed to adopt all necessary measures at their disposal to prevent the resumption of aggression and violation of peace on the part of Japan or any other state that might collaborate with Japan directly or indirectly in acts of aggression. "In the event of one of the Contracting Parties being attacked by Japan or any state allied with her and thus being involved in a state of war, the other Contracting Party shall immediately render military and other assistance by all means at its disposal." This Sino-Soviet alliance was aimed explicitly at Japan and implicitly at the United States.

In the same year, the North Korean Government launched its invasion of South Korea. When the Chinese Communists sent "volunteers" into the war, United Nations Commander Douglas MacArthur urged that the Chinese Communist coast be blockaded, that Chiang Kai-shek be "unleashed" to invade the mainland, and that United Nations forces be authorized to bomb Communist bases in Manchuria, i.e., in China. MacArthur was dismissed from his command purportedly in order to keep the war limited, and in 1953 a truce brought an end to the Korean hostilities.

By 1971 Communist China had not yet negotiated peace treaties with Japan to settle World War II, nor had diplomatic relations been established between the two countries. So long as Japan permits the United States to maintain bases on Japanese territory from which an attack upon China may be launched, and so long as the Chinese Communists retain their anti-Japanese alliance with the Soviet Union and encourage internal subversion in Japan, a substantial improvement in the relations between the Peking regime and the Tokyo government will be difficult.

The attitude of the Japanese toward Communist China generally has differed from the prevailing American attitude. Japanese intellectuals tend to feel remorse for Japan's aggression against China in the 1930s and are prone to forgive Chinese expressions of distrust for Japan. Furthermore, many Japanese share with the Chinese their fear of a revival of Japanese militarism and fascism.

In many respects, the Japanese and Chinese economies are complementary: China needs Japanese heavy machinery, ships, telecommunications equipment, and steel; Japan needs Chinese coal, iron ore, and soy beans. Many Chinese leaders were educated in Japan and speak Japanese, and thousands of Japanese have served at one time or another as soldiers, officials, businessmen, or technicians in China and Manchuria. Renewed trade and cultural exchange with mainland China are desired by most Japanese, and the present lack of official relations between the two countries is regarded as abnormal and undesirable.

The Peking Government has fostered the development of "people's diplomacy" in order to capitalize on the desire of many Japanese for more contacts and to increase internal pressure on the Japanese Government for official recognition. Since Japan regained her independence in 1952, many delegations of Japanese, including leading conservative politicians and businessmen, have visited Communist China in an unofficial capacity. Some have made unofficial and quasi-official "trade agreements" with the Communists.[14] Although Japan, as a member of the United Nations and a loyal ally of the United States, has conformed with the rules of the United Nations embargo on strategic goods for China, substantial trade has grown up between China and Japan.

Peking's trade relations and "people's diplomacy" with Japan since 1952 have of course been disturbing to the Nationalist regime in Formosa. If they led to Japanese diplomatic recognition of the Peking Government, the Nationalist hold on Taiwan would be seriously undermined. A trade agreement in 1958 between some private Japanese groups and the Chinese Communists provided that the consent of the Japanese Government would be obtained for the right of the Chinese Communist trade agency in Japan to enjoy diplomatic immunities. As a result of vigorous Nationalist protests and a brief suspension of Nationalist trade with Japan, Japanese officials announced that they would not recognize the right of the Chinese Communists to fly their flag or enjoy official status in Japan. Because the volume of Japan's trade with Taiwan was almost equal to that with mainland China, Nationalist threats to boycott Japanese goods are not taken lightly. It was next the turn of the Peking Government to protest furiously. When a Japanese rightist tore down the unauthorized flag of the Peking trade agency in Nagasaki, the Chinese Communists, after unsuccessfully demanding an apology, denounced the Kishi Government, completely halted all trade with Japan, and canceled existing trade contracts.

In 1960 trade was resumed between Japan and Communist China.

[14] English translations of some of the agreements are given in James William Morley, *Soviet and Communist Chinese Policies toward Japan, 1950–1957: A Comparison* (New York: Institute of Pacific Relations, 1958).

The Sino-Soviet dispute disrupted mainland China's commercial intercourse with the Soviet Union, and China's modest trade with Japan rapidly rose to $475 million in the first nine months of 1966, so that Japan became Peking's principal trading partner. This commerce dropped during the Great Proletarian Cultural Revolution, but revived in 1969. In 1970, trade in both directions between mainland China and Japan reportedly amounted to $800 million.[15] The threat of protection in the United States and Europe has increased the relative importance of Japan's trade with other countries, including the Communist bloc.

The Ikeda and Satō Administrations have called their policy towards Peking "the separation of politics and economics." This means that Japanese firms may trade with the mainland even though Tokyo does not recognize the Peking government. The recognition of China's Communist regime by France in 1964 and by Canada in 1970 and the announced arrangement for President Nixon to visit China have thrown in doubt the appropriateness of the Japanese policy of political aloofness from the Chinese Communists. A continuing nightmare of Japanese Foreign Ministry officials is that the United States would recognize the Peking regime without giving Japan a chance to do so beforehand. Such an American surprise would mean that Tokyo's subsequent recognition of Peking would corroborate charges that the conservative government slavishly follows orders from Washington.

In 1971, Japan was a cosponsor with the United States of a resolution in the United Nations which would retain Nationalist China in the world organization while admitting the Chinese Communists. The proposed resolution was defeated; the Nationalists were forced out and the Communists were admitted. Japan was the only one of America's major allies which had wholeheartedly supported the United States on this issue.

Japan and Korea

Japan has from ancient times been much interested in Korea. Japanese influence there was at its height between 360 and 390, when the Japanese established a protectorate over Mimana (Imna) and made an alliance with Paekche, whence Buddhism came to Japan. In about 562, the kingdom of Silla conquered all of Korea, driving out the Japanese. The Mongols used Korea in the thirteenth century as a staging platform for the attempted invasion of Japan. In the 1590s, the Japanese invaded Korea in preparation for the conquest of China,

---

[15] *The New York Times,* January 18, 1971.

which was not accomplished. In 1895, Japan defeated China in a war fought primarily over Korea, and in 1904–1905 Japan fought with Russia for dominance in Korea, the "dagger pointed at the heart of Japan." The Japanese annexation of the peninsula in 1910 was impelled by strategic and commercial, as well as political, motives. At the close of World War II, the Soviet Union and the United States occupied north and south Korea respectively, and in 1950 the Korean War broke out.

From 1945 to 1965, relations between Japan and Korea were notoriously bad. Many Koreans still resented Japanese imperialism. After Korea was liberated from Japan in 1945, the South Korean Government confiscated Japanese industrial and agricultural holdings in Korea and sold them to Korean private enterprisers and farmers. The Syngman Rhee regime also demanded, without success, reparations from Japan. About 930,000 Koreans living in Japan at the end of the war chose to return to Korea with what few possessions they could carry and a very limited amount of money. Thousands of returnees soon found life in Korea so difficult that they reentered Japan illegally. The Japanese are prone to regard the some 600,000 Koreans living in their midst with a measure of contempt, and the proportion of Korean residents who are in jail, on relief, or making a living by illegal methods is much higher than that of the Japanese.

After the Occupation, the principal sources of contention between Japan and Korea were the "Rhee Line" and the repatriation of the North Koreans. In 1952, Republic of Korea (ROK) President Syngman Rhee announced an extension of South Korean control over large parts of the Sea of Japan, the Korean Strait, and the Yellow Sea, averaging some sixty miles from the Korean coast. The purposes of this "Peace Line" were to prevent the entry of Communist agents and smugglers and to conserve fishery resources from "rapacious Japanese exploitation." A truce halted the Korean War in 1953, but in that year, the Rhee administration undertook to enforce the ban on Japanese fishing in the area by capturing Japanese vessels, confiscating the boats and their catches, and imprisoning the crew members. From 1953 to 1960, over two thousand Japanese fishermen were captured and detained by the South Koreans on the charge of crossing what had become known as the Rhee Line. It was hoped that the overthrow of Syngman Rhee in 1960 would result in more friendly policies towards Japan; however, the Korean National Assembly reaffirmed its strong support of the Rhee Line in 1961.

About half of the Koreans living in Japan are affiliated with a political organization sympathetic to North Korea while about one-fifth of the Korean residents are in a political group favorable to South

Korea. The Government of the Republic of (South) Korea claims to be the protector of *all* Koreans, both in Korea and abroad. In 1959, arrangements were made between the Japanese and North Korean Red Cross organizations for the repatriation of Koreans wishing to return to North Korea. The ROK Government, the only Korean regime formally recognized by Japan, protested the "shipment into slavery" of its nationals, even though the repatriation was voluntary. Seoul cut off trade and diplomatic talks with Tokyo but did not carry out its threat to intercept the chartered Soviet repatriation ships. By December, 1961, 76,655 Koreans had returned to North Korea.

The "Normalization" of Relations with South Korea

Japan had, of course, renounced in the Peace Treaty all claim to Korea. However, neither the Democratic People's Republic of Korea (North Korea) nor the Republic of Korea (South Korea) was a party to the treaty, which had been negotiated when war was raging on the peninsula. For thirteen years following the restoration of Japan's sovereignty in 1952, the Japanese government had only indirect contacts with the North Korean regime and only intermittent official contacts with the South Korean government.

The principal issues between Japan and Korea were economic and moral, and these were closely interrelated. There were problems relating to Japanese-owned property in Korea and Korean-owned property in Japan. There were Korean claims that during the period of colonial rule, the Japanese had removed cultural treasures from Korea. Koreans felt that they, like the other victims of Japanese aggression and oppression, were entitled to reparations. Some Japanese felt that Korea, an underdeveloped country before its annexation by Japan, had benefited, rather than suffered, from Japanese administration. Japanese indirect negotiations with North Korea had been primarily concerned with the repatriation of Koreans. That country was a member of the Communist block, and Japan was an ally of the United States, which had fought North Korea in 1950–1953. South Korea, on good terms with the United States, was outraged by Japan's policy of repatriating Koreans to Communist enslavement in North Korea and by Japan's implied recognition of the Pyongyang regime. Leftists in Japan opposed strong ties with the Republic of Korea because it was an ally of the United States and might drag Japan into war. They alleged that a normalization of Japan–South Korea relations would be a part of an American scheme to bring Japan into a NEATO (Northeast Asia Treaty Organization) with South Korea and Taiwan.

Finally, in 1962, two years after the removal of Syngman Rhee from power, President Park Chung-hee of South Korea opened serious negotiations with the Japanese government to settle outstanding differences and establish permanent diplomatic missions in Tokyo and Seoul. The Japan–Korea Treaty, which was signed and ratified in 1965, accomplished these purposes. Without mentioning Korea's former colonial status, the treaty referred to "the historical background of relationships between their peoples and their mutual desire for good neighborliness." Treaties made on or before August 22, 1910, between the Japanese and Korean Empires were declared void, thus nullifying the Korean Annexation Treaty. The Seoul regime was recognized as the only lawful government of Korea. Important supplementary agreements concerned the thorny fisheries question, property claims, and economic and cultural cooperation. The territorial dispute over Takeshima (Dakto), an island, was left for future determination. Japan would give Korea, as an outright grant, $300 million worth of Japanese goods and services and $200 million in long-term and low-interest loans, all to be conducive to Korea's economic development.[16]

The Japan–Korea Treaty provoked the greatest outpouring of vituperation against the Japanese government since the Security Pact crisis in 1960. There were massive organized demonstrations and riots in both Japan and Korea in opposition to the treaty. The Diet was thrown into a turmoil. The conservative Government obtained lower house approval of the treaty only by resorting to a surprise midnight vote, strongly reminiscent of the "forced passage" of the United States–Japan Security Pact five years earlier.

The Japan–South Korea Treaty will not, of course, solve for all time the multitude of problems which will arise in the future between the two countries. Their close economic, cultural, and strategic interests bind the two neighbors closely together. But problems relating to Japan's commercial ties with North Korea, the residence in Japan of over a half-million Koreans (many owing allegiance to North, rather than to South, Korea), and differing views about the nature of the Communist threat in Asia, will no doubt continue to plague relations between Seoul and Tokyo in the years ahead. For example, South Korea, like Nationalist China, has not been altogether happy about reversion of Okinawa, so ardently desired by Japan, because that might entail a weakening of the American military ability to come to the aid of Korea. Conversely, Japan has prevented the Koreans and Chinese

---

[16] For the text of the treaty and summaries of the accompanying agreements and a lively account of the Diet debate concerning them, see Hans Baerwald, "Nikkan Kokkai," in Lucian Pye, ed., *Cases in Comparative Politics: Asia* (Boston, Mass.: Little, Brown, 1970), pp. 19–57.

Nationalists from transforming the Asian and Pacific Council (ASPAC) into an anti-Communist military alliance.

Relations with the Soviet Union

The Soviet Union honored its Neutrality Pact of April 13, 1941, with Japan until August 9, 1945, when it declared war on the island empire only five days before the final Japanese offer to surrender. The top secret Yalta Agreement of February, 1945, had provided that the Soviet Union would enter the war against Japan two or three months after the war in Europe ended. In return for this help, Churchill, Roosevelt, and Stalin agreed that Japan would return to the Soviet Union the Manchurian ports and railroads and the southern half of Sakhalin Island which she had conquered from Russia in the Russo-Japanese War. In addition, the Kurile Islands, which reached from the eastern tip of Hokkaido northward to the Kamchatka peninsula of Siberia, were to be turned over to the Soviets.[17] At the end of the war, the Soviet Union occupied southern Sakhalin and the Kuriles. By terms of the San Francisco Peace Treaty, Japan renounced all claims to these northern territories without, however, stipulating that they were being transferred to Russian control.

The Kurile Islands (Chishima Rettō) had long stood as a Japanese barrier between much of Soviet Siberia and the Pacific Ocean. They were used as a base for launching the attack on Pearl Harbor in 1941. Their strategic relation to Japan, the Soviet Union, the Aleutian Islands, and the northern sea and air routes from Japan to the United States is readily evident from a glance at a polar map. Possession of the Kurile Islands is important to the Soviet Union today not only strategically but also diplomatically. The Soviets can make their partial or complete return to Japan dependent upon the removal of American bases from Japan, or some other valuable diplomatic *quid pro quo*. The Japanese eagerly desire the return of the Kurile Islands, although they have been less concerned with them than with Okinawa, where many more of their countrymen reside. A particularly touchy problem has been that of Shikotan and the Habomai Islands, which the Soviet occupies, notwithstanding Japanese assertions that these are not actually part of the Kuriles.

The Soviet Union refused to sign the San Francisco Treaty and bitterly protested the termination without her consent of the Occupation and the demise of the Far Eastern Commission and the Allied

---

[17] Text in Theodore McNelly, ed., *Sources in Modern East Asian History and Politics* (New York: Appleton-Century-Crofts, 1967), pp. 155–156.

Council for Japan, where Russia could influence Occupation policies. The Soviet Union persistently vetoed Japanese entrance into the United Nations. Following the death of Stalin and the end of the Korean War, there were indications of a more friendly Russian attitude.

Formal talks to prepare a Soviet-Japanese peace settlement began in London in 1955. Among their more extreme demands, the Russians insisted that the Sea of Japan be closed to warships of all countries except the Soviet Union, Korea, and Japan. The discussions continued sporadically for ten months but broke down, primarily because of the failure of the two sides to agree on the future of the Kurile Islands. Immediately the Soviet Union announced stringent restrictions on fishing by the Japanese in northern waters. Kōnō Ichirō, Minister of Agriculture and Forestry, obtained a ten-year fishing agreement with Russia which would go into effect either when a peace treaty was signed or when diplomatic relations were resumed. As a result, the fishing industry in Japan put great pressure on the Japanese government to arrive at an understanding with Russia.

Foreign Minister Shigemitsu Mamoru renewed peace negotiations in Moscow, but again was unable to get the Russians to renounce their claim to the Kuriles. Finally, Prime Minister Hatoyama went to Moscow. He too was unable to achieve a settlement of the territorial dispute, and no peace treaty emerged from the talks. Finally, on October 19, 1956, Japanese and Soviet leaders (including Hatoyama and Bulganin) signed a Joint Peace *Declaration* which formally ended the war, restored diplomatic and consular relations between the two countries, brought the fisheries agreement into force, and committed the Soviet Union to support Japan's application for membership in the United Nations. On December, 1956, Japan entered the world organization.[18]

By 1971, Japan and the Soviet Union had still failed to sign a peace *treaty*, largely because of the dispute over the Kuriles. The Japanese asserted that their renunciation of the island chain in the San Francisco Peace Treaty in no way affected their dispute with the Russians, because the Soviet Union had not signed that Peace Treaty. In any case, they argued, Shikotan, the Habomai, and the Southern Kuriles were not part of the Kurile Islands, which Japan gave up at San Francisco.

Unquestionably an important factor in Japanese-Soviet relations is

[18] For the text of the Declaration, see Maki, pp. 147–151. For an analytical discussion of the negotiations, see Donald C. Hellmann, *Japanese Foreign Policy and Domestic Politics: The Peace Agreement with the Soviet Union* (Berkeley: University of California Press, 1969).

the alliance between Japan and the United States and the presence of American bases in Japan which might conceivably be used against the Soviet Union. At the same time, the great cities of Japan are extremely vulnerable to air attack from the Soviet Union. The Russians may continue to exploit the fisheries and the territorial issues in the hope of weakening the Japanese-American alliance.

During the 1960s trade between Japan and the Soviet Union increased about tenfold. Economic leaders in the two countries have recently been making plans for the introduction of Japanese technology and capital in the development of the Soviet Far East. In 1967, direct air service between Tokyo and Moscow was established, and in 1970, the trans-Siberian route between Tokyo and Western Europe was opened with the participation of Japan Air Lines, Air France, BOAC, and the Soviet Aeroflot.

On the whole, the attitude of the Japanese towards Russia has been antipathetic. The two nations have been rivals for power in northeast Asia for decades and have been at war twice within this century. Conservatives are not the only Japanese who dislike Communist Russia. Many Japanese leftists (especially the "Trotskyite" students) hold that the Soviet Union has become bureaucratic and betrayed the principles of Karl Marx.

The Military

Civil-Military Relations Before the Surrender

In prewar Japan, the Army was the virtual basis of state authority. The political importance of the Imperial Army was dramatically demonstrated in Satsuma in 1877, when samurai rebels under the leadership of Saigo Takamori were subdued by conscript troops loyal to the Imperial Government. In 1882, the Meiji Emperor issued his famous "Rescript to Soldiers and Sailors," in which he proclaimed:

> Our relations with you will be most intimate when We rely upon you as our limbs and you look up to Us as your head. Whether We are able to guard the Empire, and so prove Ourself worthy of Heaven's blessings and repay the benevolence of Our Ancestors, depends upon the faithful discharge of your duties as soldiers and sailors.[19]

The Emperor also pointed out, "The supreme command of Our forces is in Our hands, and though We may entrust subordinate

[19] Full text in McNelly, ed., pp. 53–57.

commands to Our subjects, yet the ultimate authority We Ourself shall hold and never delegate to any subject." Articles XI and XII of the 1889 Constitution provided that the Emperor had the supreme command of the Army and Navy and determined the organization and peace standing of the Army and Navy. The imperial command prerogative was interpreted to mean that the military was independent of control by the Diet or the Cabinet. Military policies were formulated by the Board of Field Marshals and Fleet Admirals and the Supreme War Council, rather than by the Prime Minister and his Cabinet.

The Ministers of Army and Navy had to be generals or admirals respectively. When one of the services disagreed with the policies of the prime minister, the service minister could resign or threaten to resign, bringing about a cabinet crisis. Furthermore, the service ministers, unlike other members of the cabinet under the prime minister, had direct access to the Throne. Not only was the military branch largely independent of the civilian branch of the government, it could and often did dominate the civilian side.

The abolition of armed forces provided for in the new Constitution stands in striking contrast to the militaristic philosophy of the Imperial Rescript to Soldiers and Sailors. The new basic law further ensures civilian supremacy by providing that only civilians may become ministers of state.

Rearmament

The present Constitution outlaws war and arms but is now interpreted by the government to mean that defensive armament is permissible. Article 9 reads:

> Aspiring sincerely to an international peace based on justice and order, the Japanese people forever renounce war as a sovereign right of the nation and the threat or use of force as means of settling international disputes.

> In order to accomplish the aim of the preceding paragraph, land, sea, and air forces, as well as other war potential, will never be maintained. The right of belligerency of the state will not be recognized.

The first paragraph apparently does not renounce all kinds of war, only war and threat or use of force *as means of settling international disputes.* It has been argued that war and the threat or use of force *as means of self-defense* are permissible. One of the Japanese drafters of the Constitution states that he had inserted the phrase "in order to accomplish the aim of the preceding paragraph" to qualify the prohibition on armament, so that armaments for certain purposes, such as self-defense, might be permitted.[20] Nevertheless, when the Diet was deliberating on the draft Constitution in 1946, Prime Minister Yoshida asserted that although Article 9 did not renounce the right of self-defense, armaments, even for purposes of self-defense, would be illegal. The full implications of the Ashida amendment were not made evident to the public until after the outbreak of the Korean War.

In 1950, when American troops in Japan were transferred to Korea, General MacArthur suggested to Prime Minister Yoshida the creation of a National Police Reserve. Yoshida created the Reserve by means of a Cabinet Order (i.e. without the authorization of the Diet) in the fall of 1950 "for the purpose of supplementing the strength of the National Rural Police and the Local Autonomous Police Forces to the extent necessary to maintain peace and order within the country and to guarantee the public welfare."[21] Many Japanese regarded the establishment of the Police Reserve as a move to centralize and strengthen the police for the purpose of suppressing left-wing violence. American policy-makers from the beginning intended that the Reserve be the nucleus for an army.

The Peace Treaty recognized Japan's "inherent right of individual or collective self-defense," and the accompanying Security Treaty stated the "expectation" that Japan would itself increasingly assume responsibilities for its own defense against direct and indirect aggression.

The National Police Reserve received equipment and training from American Forces in Japan. In August, 1952, the Police Reserve was reorganized as the National Safety Agency. In 1954, the Security

---

[20] Ashida Hitoshi, "Japan: Communists' Temptation," *Contemporary Japan*, Vol. XX, Nos. 1–3 (January-March, 1951), 15–24. For accounts in English of the history and interpretation of the disarmament clause see David Sissons, "The Pacifist Clause of the Japanese Constitution: Legal and Political Problems of Rearmament," *International Affairs*, Vol. XXXVII (January, 1961), 45–59; Grant Jiro Hirabayashi, "Renunciation of War and the Japanese Constitution" (unpublished Master's thesis, University of Southern California, 1957); Theodore McNelly, "The Renunciation of War in the Japanese Constitution," *Political Science Quarterly*, Vol. LXXVII, No. 3 (September, 1962), 350–378; Nishijima Yoshiji, "The Peace Constitution Controversy" in Betty B. Burch and Allan B. Cole, eds., *Asian Political Systems* (Princeton, N.J.: Van Nostrand, 1968), 141–149; and "The Story of Article Nine," *Newsweek*, Vol. LXXVIII, No. 14 (October 4, 1971), 38–43.

[21] Text of Cabinet Order 260, in Harold S. Quigley and John E. Turner, *The New Japan: Government and Politics* (Minneapolis: University of Minnesota Press, 1956), pp. 435–437.

Agency and Security Force became the Defense Agency and Self-Defense Force respectively. Each step in the conversion of the Police Reserve into a military force was accompanied by bitter disputes centering on Article 9 of the Constitution and the dangers of the revival of militarism in Japan and of the alliance with the United States. As one astute observer noted in 1957, "The ban on armed forces has already been turned by sheer casuistry into an open fraud."[22]

The Defense Agency

The supreme control over the new defense forces is vested in the Prime Minister. The Prime Minister has the power to appoint and dismiss the Director General of the Defense Agency, who is a Minister of State and therefore a civilian. By 1956, the National Defense Council was established, which included the Prime Minister, Deputy Prime Minister, Ministers of Foreign Affairs and Finance, Director General of the Defense Agency, and the Head of the Economic Planning Board. All of these are members of the Cabinet. The Council's duties are to discuss and decide: (1) formulation of a basic plan for national defense, (2) adjustment of defense plans with related industries, (3) activation of national defense, and (4) all other matters that the prime minister considers necessary from the standpoint of defense.

In late 1970, the Defense Agency published its Fourth Defense Build-Up Plan to cover the five-year period beginning in 1972. A general strengthening of the Ground, Air, and Maritime Self-Defense Forces was planned, but the number of servicemen would not be increased significantly beyond its 1970 figure of 179,000 for the Ground SDF and 37,800 for the Maritime SDF.

The budget for the five-year build-up plan totaled 5.8 trillion yen, or $16.1 billion. This would amount to about 0.92 percent of Japan's estimated GNP for that period. The Ground SDF, while not increasing its manpower, planned to adopt the 120 new-type tank, capable of carrying 105-mm cannon, and the total number of tanks would be about 1,000. The number of ground-to-air missiles would be increased. The Ground SDF would add 240 antitank missiles, 850 armored cars, and 380 helicopters. The Air SDF, with 970 aircraft in 1970, would have only 880 in 1972. The Air SDF intended to create three Mobile Aircraft Control and Warning Squadrons as well as an Airborne Early Warning System using radar to detect airplanes infiltrating Japan's air space at low altitudes. A total of 158 F4EJ Phantom Jet fighters equipped with Vulcan machine guns, Sidewinder (infrared-homing)

[22] Reischauer, p. 251.

and Sparrow (radar-homing) missiles would comprise six flight squadrons. Twenty all-weather reconnaissance RF4E Phantoms would replace all the F86F reconnaissance planes used in 1970 by the Air SDF.

The largest build-up in the Maritime SDF would be devoted to antisubmarine operations. Two 8,000-ton destroyer helicopter carriers capable of carrying large antisubmarine helicopters to locate and destroy nuclear submarines would be built. The Maritime SDF would also add thirty PSI antisubmarine flying boats and fourteen small high-speed hydrofoil missile boats carrying surface-to-surface missiles. In 1970, the Maritime SDF had 210 ships with a total of 133,000 tons. The fourth build-up would increase the size of the fleet to around 245,000 tons by 1976.

The Japanese government's 1970 National Defense White Paper[23] emphasized that Japan would remain a nonnuclear nation whose military forces would be used purely for self-defense. Therefore Japan could not maintain such potentially offensive weapons as strategic bombers, attack aircraft carriers, or intercontinental ballistic missiles. Also, the military could not be sent overseas. Small nuclear weapons for defensive purposes would not be forbidden under the Constitution, and Japan has the capacity to produce them. However, Japan maintains the three principles that the nation will not (1) manufacture nuclear weapons, (2) possess them, or (3) allow such weapons into her territory. The ban on such weapons, of course, reflects the "nuclear allergy" of the people.

In the event of direct aggression, Japan would rely on American forces for defense against nuclear and large-scale wars and for strategic operations outside Japanese territory. Japan would try to secure air and naval supremacy around its territory in order to limit damage to the country. The White Paper refers to quick action that would be taken to prevent the prolongation and expansion of "indirect aggression," which has increased "in the guise of support of national liberation struggles." Since such struggles are widespread in Southeast Asia, where Japan is a principal trading partner for all of the countries, one wonders whether or not the Dullesian concept of indirect aggression might not involve Japan in a foreign war. In this connection, however, the importance of nonmilitary preventive efforts is strongly emphasized. The Japanese have made it abundantly clear that they do not want to become involved in Vietnam-type wars.

[23] This was the first defense white paper issued by the government. Summarized in *Japan Report*, Vol. XVI, No. 23 (December 1, 1970), 1–3.

For fiscal 1970, 570,000 million yen ($1.58 billion), were allocated for national defense. This amounted to only 7.16 percent of the national budget, or less than 1 percent (0.79 percent) of the gross national product. Thus Japan's military establishment, when viewed in relation to its economy, is extraordinarily modest. Military expenditures are expected to rise to .92 percent of the GNP during the five years beginning in 1972, and in light of the expected great expansion of the economy, this will be the seventh largest defense expenditure in the world—the largest in Asia except for Communist China.

Although labor shortages and high pay in civilian occupations have made it difficult to recruit volunteers—there is no military draft—into the Defense Forces, the quality of personnel has been high. There is now a substantial pool of civilians who formerly served in the forces and are available for mobilization in time of emergency. The technical skill and fine discipline of the Japanese military forces suggest that, if need be, they could give a good account of themselves. A would-be aggressor would probably think twice before taking them on.

In the late 1960s, a question arose about the possible involvement of the SDF in the suppression of riots. Plans for public security training for the SDF were often debated in the Japanese Diet, and the Defense Agency was temporarily forced to abandon draft plans and manuals designed as guides in such training. However, in October, 1969, the SDF for the first time openly conducted public security training with artillery units using helicopters and tanks. The Tokyo police insisted that they were able to cope with rioting and that they had no intention of asking for SDF help in the 1970 struggles. Socialists charged that the purpose of this SDF training was to intimidate the political left. Thus the training and purposes of the SDF are a highly charged political issue.

Japan's Foreign Policy in the 1970s

The reversion of Okinawa to Japan in 1972 terminates foreign rule in Japanese territory and brings an end to the "postwar period." With the world's third most productive economy and one of the strongest armed forces in Asia, Japan is in a position to play a much more active role in world politics than was possible in the 1950s and 1960s, when she was militarily disarmed and struggling to rebuild her war-damaged industries. The rise of Japan coincides with President Nixon's Guam doctrine and the gradual withdrawal of American fighting forces from Asia.

Many Americans, weary of the role of world policeman and of

Figure 7

THE SELF DEFENSE FORCES OF JAPAN

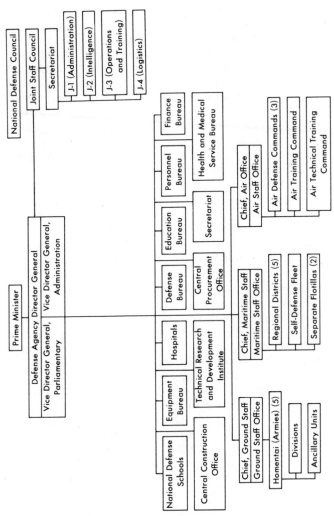

Source: *Area Handbook for Japan* (Washington, D. C.:
U. S. Government Printing Office, 1969), P. 583.

fighting Asian wars, have hoped that the Japanese might be induced to carry some of the burden of resisting communism in Asia. These hopes are, this writer believes, illusory for several reasons.

First, the Japanese trade with mainland China, North Korea, and North Vietnam, as well as with Soviet Asia and the anti-Communist and neutral nations in Asia. They want to expand their trade, and a policy of coexistence rather than anti-Communist crusade seems better suited to this. They take the long view concerning mainland China, and for several years have been that country's principal trading partner. History and geography seem to dictate this important commercial relationship.

Second, the Japanese do not perceive Asian communism as the threat that the Americans often do. They seem to think that, after the Vietnam War ends, a sympathetic understanding of the nationalistic aspirations of Asians and enlightened diplomacy on Japan's part will suffice to protect Japan's interests. Japan's insular geographic position and effective defense forces supplemented by the American nuclear shield should be adequate to protect the country. Japan has no aspirations to conquer militarily or rule politically other peoples.

Thirdly, Japan sees herself as a world economic power and in the future may play a role in world politics more commensurate with her gross national product. Her trade with North America, like her trade with Europe, exceeds her trade with Asia. The Japanese may not wish to divert their efforts in creating an anti-Communist East Asian Co-Prosperity Sphere when they can play a leading role in global affairs.

In 1971, China was increasingly fearful that Japan might acquire nuclear weapons, but Japan insisted upon protection for its homeland and the Ryukyu Islands. The obvious solution would be the continuance of a substantial American nuclear and conventional presence in the western Pacific. Such was the expressed desire of the Japanese government: "We assume that the nuclear power balance—and the security of Japan from nuclear war—will continue to rest on the American deterrent. It is for this reason that my government favors continuing in force the United States–Japan Security Treaty, which places Japan under the American nuclear umbrella and provides the United States with forward military bases on Japanese soil."[24]

As Japan assumes a more independent posture, misunderstandings and resentments are bound to result. The American bases in Japan and Okinawa will close down as the Japanese Self-Defense Forces take over. The tie with America may weaken at the same time that eco-

[24] Speech of Japan's Ambassador to the United States, Ushiba Nobuhiko, at Annapolis Naval Academy, April 20, 1971, printed in *Japan Report,* Vol. XVII, No. 11 (June 1, 1971), 1–5.

nomic and political intercourse with the Soviet Union and mainland China expand.

There will be many problems for Japan in the years ahead. The former victims of Japan's aggressions still fear her and suspect that her economic penetration of Southeast Asia may prove to be a prelude to conquest. New flare-ups in Korea, Southeast Asia, and the Taiwan Strait could cause the Americans to re-escalate their military activities in East Asia to the detriment of Japan's independence and security. There is a knotty territorial dispute with the Soviet Union over the northern islands. There are still no diplomatic relations with Communist China. The rise of protectionism in America and Europe could be disastrous to Japan's economy. There may be difficulties in preventing the proliferation of nuclear weapons, and the Japanese may feel constrained to develop their own nuclear arsenal, with serious consequences for her relations with neighbors and allies. Japan appears to be entering a new era of a quadrilateral balance of power in East Asia, in which Japan, Communist China, the Soviet Union, and the United States each exert equal and independent influence in that important area of the world.

Suggested Reading

Barnett, A. Doak, and Edwin O. Reischauer, eds. *The United States and China: The Next Decade.* New York: Praeger, 1970.

Buck, James H., "Japan's Defense Options for the 1970's." *Asian Survey,* Vol. X, No. 10 (October, 1970), 890–899.

Burnell, Elaine H., ed. *Asian Dilemma: United States, Japan and China.* Santa Barbara, Calif.: Center for the Study of Democratic Institutions, 1969.

Cary, James. *Japan: Reluctant Ally.* New York: Praeger, 1962.

Chapin, Emerson, ed. *Japan and the United States in the 1970's.* New York: Japan Society, 1970.

Chinese People's Institute of Foreign Affairs, ed. *Oppose the Revival of Japanese Militarism: A Selection of Important Documents and Commentaries.* Peking: Foreign Languages Press, 1960.

Cohen, Bernard C. *The Political Process and Foreign Policy: The Making of the Japanese Peace Settlement.* Princeton, N.J.: Princeton University Press, 1957.

Curtis, Gerald L., ed. *Japanese-American Relations in the 1970's.* Washington, D.C.: Columbia Books, 1970.

Emmerson, John Kenneth. *Arms, Yen and Power: The Japanese Dilemma.* Cambridge, Mass.: Dunnellen, 1971.

Halloran, Richard. *Japan: Images and Realities.* New York: Knopf, 1969.

Hellmann, Donald C. *Japanese Foreign Policy and Domestic Politics: The Peace Agreement with the Soviet Union.* Berkeley: University of California Press, 1969.

Hellmann, Donald C. "The United States and Japan," in Spiegel, Steven L., and Kenneth N. Waltz, eds., *Conflict in World Politics.* Cambridge, Mass.: Winthrop, 1971.

Hersey, John. *Hiroshima.* New York: Knopf, 1946.

Higa, Mikio. *Parties and Politics in Postwar Okinawa.* Vancouver: University of British Columbia Press, 1963.

Jan, George P., ed. *International Politics of Asia: Readings.* Belmont, Calif.: Wadsworth, 1969.

Jones, F. C., Hugh Borton, and B. R. Pearn. *Survey of International Affairs, 1939–1946: The Far East, 1942–1946.* London: Oxford University Press, 1955.

Kahn, Herman. *The Emerging Japanese Superstate: Challenge and Response.* Englewood Cliffs, N.J.: Prentice-Hall, 1970.

Kerr, G. H. *Okinawa: The History of an Island People.* Tokyo: Tuttle, 1958.

Kojima, Kiyoshi. *Japan and a Pacific Free Trade Area.* Berkeley, Calif.: University of California Press, 1971.

Leng Shao Chuan. *Japan and Communist China.* Kyoto: Doshisha University Press, 1958.

McNelly, Theodore, "The Renunciation of War in the Japanese Constitution," *Political Science Quarterly,* Vol. LXXVII, No. 3 (September, 1962), 350–378.

Maki, John M. *Conflict and Tension in the Far East: Key Documents, 1894–1960.* Seattle: University of Washington Press, 1961.

Mendel, Douglas H., Jr. *Formosan Nationalism at Home and Abroad.* Berkeley: University of California Press, 1970.

Mendel, Douglas H., Jr. *The Japanese People and Foreign Policy: A Study of Public Opinion in Post-Treaty Japan.* Berkeley and Los Angeles: University of California Press, 1961.

Mendel, Douglas H., Jr. "Japanese Policy and Views Toward Formosa," *The Journal of Asian Studies,* Vol. XXVIII, No. 3 (May, 1969), pp. 513–534.

Morley, James W. *Japan and Korea: America's Allies in the Pacific.* New York: Walker, 1965.

Morley, James W., ed. *Forecast for Japan: Security in the 1970s.* Princeton, N.J.: Princeton University Press, 1972.

Morley, James William. "Japan's Image of the Soviet Union, 1952–1962," *Pacific Affairs,* Vol. XXXV, No. 1 (Spring, 1962), 51–58.

Morley, James William. *Soviet and Communist Chinese Policies Toward Japan, 1950–1957: A Comparison.* New York: Institute of Pacific Relations, 1958.

Neumann, William L. *America Encounters Japan.* Baltimore, Md.: Johns Hopkins University Press, 1963.

Olson, Lawrence. *Japan in Postwar Asia*. New York: Praeger, 1970.

Osgood, Robert E., George R. Packard III, and John H. Badgley. *Japan and the United States in Asia*. Baltimore, Md.: Johns Hopkins University Press, 1968.

Packard, George R., III. *Protest in Tokyo: The Security Treaty Crisis of 1960*. Princeton, N.J.: Princeton University Press, 1966.

Passin, Herbert, ed. *The United States and Japan*. Englewood Cliffs, N.J.: Prentice-Hall, 1966.

Reischauer, Edwin O. *Beyond Vietnam: The United States and Asia*. New York: Vintage Books, 1967.

Reischauer, Edwin O. *The United States and Japan,* 3rd ed. Cambridge, Mass.: Harvard University Press, 1965.

Rosecrance, R. N. *Australian Diplomacy and Japan, 1945–1951*. New York: Cambridge University Press, 1962.

Sebald, William J., and C. Nelson Spinks. *Japan: Prospects, Options, and Opportunities*. Washington, D.C.: American Enterprise Institute for Public Policy Research, 1967.

Scalapino, Robert A. "The Foreign Policy of Modern Japan," in Macridis, Roy C., ed. *Foreign Policy in World Politics,* 3rd ed. Englewood Cliffs, N.J.: Prentice-Hall, 1967, pp. 270–313.

Schwantes, Robert S. *Japanese and Americans: A Century of Cultural Relations*. New York: Harper and Brothers, 1955.

Stockwin, J. A. A. *The Japanese Socialist Party and Neutralism: A Study of a Political Party and Its Foreign Policy*. London: Cambridge University Press, 1969.

Thorp, Willard L., ed. *The United States and the Far East,* 2nd ed. Englewood Cliffs, N.J.: Prentice-Hall, 1962.

United States–Japanese Political Relations. Washington, D.C.: Georgetown University Center for Strategic and International Studies, 1968.

Van Adouard, Baron E. J. Lewe. *Japan: From Surrender to Peace*. New York: Praeger, 1954.

Velen, Elizabeth, and Velen, Victor A., eds. *The New Japan*. New York: H. W. Wilson, 1958.

Weinstein, Martin. *Japan's Defense Policy, 1945–1968*. New York: Columbia University Press, 1971.

Wilcox, Wayne Ayres. *Asia and United States Policy*. Englewood Cliffs, N.J.: Prentice-Hall, 1967.

9

Democracy in Japan: An Assessment

This concluding chapter discusses how prosperity and a prudent foreign policy have contributed to the stability of the Japanese political system, reviews the prospects for the political parties in the 1970s, and, finally, in light of the revolutionary critique of liberal institutions, explores the question of whether or not Japan is a democracy.

Economic Prosperity

In Japan, as in Western Europe, the primary concern in the postwar period was the restoration of the war-devastated economy. Following the Korean War boom, Japan's gross national product grew at an average annual rate of over 10 percent. By 1960, Japan had entered the stage of high mass consumption. The gross national product in the financial year ending March 31, 1969, exceeded $147.4 billion, representing a nominal increase of 18.3 percent, or a real increase of 14.3 percent over the previous year. This meant that Japan's economic production had surpassed West Germany's and was the third largest in the world, after those of the United States and the Soviet Union.

Whatever one's ideological preference concerning the distribution of goods, the fact remains that, unless adequately high productivity is achieved and maintained, poverty will be widespread no matter how the goods are divided up. The contempt for materialism, reportedly widespread among affluent American and Japanese youth today, is itself made possible by high productivity. The hard working and thrifty Japanese, who on the average save or invest over 20 percent of what they earn, have remained rather loyal to the Liberal-Democratic

Party, the party of free enterprise and high productivity, ever since it was founded in 1955. Capitalism has worked in Japan; socialism has never been tried, and its appeal is limited to intellectuals.

However, in the 1970s, now that Japan's struggle for high productivity has been won, public attention is focusing on other priorities. The per capita income remains lower than that of Western Europe. Consumers suffer from inflation. The narrow streets and highways are grossly inadequate to handle the great increase of trucks and private automobiles. City dwellers suffer from air and water pollution, inadequate sewage and garbage disposal systems, and an acute housing shortage. Schools are overcrowded, and the quality of instruction leaves much to be desired. Social security is niggardly. The Japanese hope that the worst imbalances in the economy and the widespread damage to the ecology may be corrected in the 1970s.

Resource Allocation

The usual indicator of the effectiveness of a political system is the quality of public policy that it is able to formulate and to enforce.[1] Largely by means of taxation, the state deprives its members of some of their money, and with the expenditure of this money the state provides its members with certain benefits. Statesmen therefore are prudent to make taxes as painless as possible and to emphasize to their constituents the benefits that they receive from the state. It would, of course, be a gross distortion of reality to evaluate public policies solely by examining the revenues and expenditures of the state. Yet these are concrete indicators of actual commitments and can be expressed in terms of dollars and cents. Where does the Japanese government get its money and how does it spend it?

The main sources of revenue for the Japanese government are the individual income tax, the corporation tax, and the liquor tax.

A comparison of the 1971 budget with that of the preceding year is instructive. The 18.4 percent overall increase was no doubt greatly facilitated by the substantial increase in the GNP in 1970. The 1971 budget gave priority to sustaining the nation's economic growth, price stabilization, pollution control, and improvement of the social environment. The ceilings were raised on government indebtedness and reserves were increased in order to permit fiscal flexibility in the possibility of an economic decline. There would be a great expansion of

---

[1] On the comparative analysis of the outputs of political systems, see Alexander Groth, *Comparative Politics: A Distributive Approach* (New York: Macmillan, 1971), pp. 1–22.

Table 5

Budget for 1971 *(General Account in millions of yen)*

Major items	Fiscal 1970	Fiscal 1971	Increase
Revenues			
Taxes (including stamps)	6,938,417	8,296,258	1,357,841
Others	558,306	592,257	33,951
Bonds	430,000	430,000	0
Surplus from previous year	23,041	95,800	72,759
Total	7,949,764	9,414,315	1,464,551
Expenditures			
Social security	1,140,768	1,344,080	203,312
Education, science	925,901	1,078,875	152,974
Government debt servicing	290,897	319,340	28,443
Pensions	299,128	366,002	36,877
Grants to local governments	1,662,872	2,054,424	391,552
Defense	569,518	670,902	101,384
Public works	1,409,881	1,665,591	255,710
Trade promotion, economic cooperation	92,847	101,103	8,256
Small business measures	50,318	57,907	7,589
Food control account	383,007	463,372	80,365
Transfer to industrial investment account	93,600	80,300	*13,300
Others	921,027	1,102,416	181,389
Reserves	110,000	140,000	30,000
Total	7,949,764	9,414,315	1,464,551

* Indicates decrease.

new housing, sewage systems, harbors, and airports. Spending on antipollution measures was to be increased by 38 percent over 1970, and 50 million yen was earmarked for the development of a pollution-free automobile. Tariff rebates would be given corporations which provided facilities for the removal of sulfur from fuel oil. A cut-back in government purchasing of rice was planned so as to eliminate the continued overproduction of rice, and bounties would be paid to farmers to induce them to switch from rice to other crops.

As usual, the opposition charged that the 1971 budget disregarded the welfare of the people in favor of business. The emphasis on industrial growth and military expansion meant that the people's hopes for lower taxes and lower prices and better social welfare would be disappointed.

Since 1955, the Cabinets, all of which have been conservative, have been able to count on the permanent conservative majorities in both houses to pass the Cabinet-sponsored budget. The annual budgets represent the combined view of the Cabinet ministries, agency heads, and Liberal-Democratic Party leaders. The Budget Committees of the two houses of the Diet are perhaps the most prominent of the standing committees, and they debate basic questions of policy, such as foreign relations, not directly relevant to the budget. In the final analysis, the budget largely reflects the views of the Japanese business community. Priority is given to the encouragement of business expansion and increasing the national income. However, Japan has long been far behind other advanced countries in the area of social security, and it appears that more funds must be appropriated there. Air, water, and sound pollution have attracted the attention of both the local and national levels of government, and it may be expected that increasing appropriations will relate to this problem.

The heavy taxes imposed on agriculture during the Meiji era were at that time the principal grievance voiced by the political parties against the government. Excessive taxes may deprive the businessmen of necessary capital and the consumers of money with which to buy things. In the prewar period of 1934 to 1936, taxes in Japan amounted to only 13 percent of the national income, but in 1949, taxes rose to supply 29 percent. This figure subsequently dropped to 19.1 percent in 1967.[2] Of course, with the phenomenal growth of the national product since 1950, the absolute amount of taxes collected has greatly increased.

To an American observer, the most notable feature of the Japanese budget is the small percentage devoted to national defense: less than 8 percent since 1968. The corresponding figure for the United States (1971 estimate) was 36 percent. The Japanese spend less than 1 percent of their national income on defense.

The Political System and Foreign Policy

One of the most important aspects of governmental performance is the quality of the foreign policy. Some American observers have praised the effectiveness of the Japanese government in fostering economic development but have deplored the inability of the pro-American government (immobilism, in the current jargon) to carry out a strong anti-Communist policy in Asia. Such an interpretation evidently assumes that, if it were not for neutralist demonstrators and factionalism in the ruling party, the Government would be a more enthusiastic and effective enforcer of Pentagon policies. However, it is this author's view that the foreign policy of Japan has been remarkably

[2] The corresponding figure for the United States was 28.3 percent.

successful. With less than 1 percent of the gross national product appropriated to the military, Japan has managed both to preserve the national security and to avoid costly military involvements. The Communist threat which Americans perceive in Asia does not frighten the Japanese, who appreciate that Asian Communists do not have the naval power necessary directly to threaten Japan with an invasion. Even if such a threat existed, the readiness of American policy-makers to intervene on the Asian continent with American troops, as they have done in Korea and Vietnam, would make it unnecessary for the Japanese to become actively involved in Asian military affairs.

The Japanese learned in the 1930s the danger and futility of fighting a war on the Asian mainland. The Japanese now see the United States embroiled in a military and diplomatic morass in Southeast Asia, and they prudently want no part of it. The articulate and at times violent pacifist movement in Japan provides the Japanese government with a convenient pretext for begging off American invitations to "play a greater role" in the "defense of the free world." By assuming a live-and-let-live attitude towards the Communist as well as the non-Communist governments of Asia, Japan keeps open her lines of communication. She trades with the Communist parts of China, Korea, and Vietnam as well as with the non-Communist parts, notwithstanding the protestations of Red and anti-Red crusaders who wish to see imposed, by massive military invasion if necessary, alien concepts of freedom or totalitarianism on Asian peoples. It would seem to this observer that Japan's foreign policy has been remarkably well conceived for the advancement of Japan's national interest.

The Politics of the 1960s and 1970s

During the 1960 crisis, in which the Kishi Cabinet was forced to resign primarily as the result of mass demonstrations, it appeared to many that the country was being ruled by the mob rather than by a legitimate government. The demonstrations seemed to be under the control of leftist extremists who were manipulating people for the purpose of destroying democratic government. However, public opinion overwhelmingly supported parliamentary government even though it deserted Kishi. The demonstrators and the government both emphatically proclaimed their loyalty to parliamentarianism; a principal demand of the demonstrators was new parliamentary elections. The demonstrators dispersed after Kishi resigned and was replaced by another conservative prime minister; the movement was not fundamentally revolutionary, notwithstanding the radicalism of some of its leadership. Furthermore, if constitutional government in Japan had really been threatened by the mob, the police could have suppressed the demonstrators in short order. The conservative "establishment" preferred to avoid bloodshed by letting Kishi, whose hard-line parliamentary tactics had provoked the demonstrations in the first place, resign. Analysis seems to disclose that the situation was not as uncontrollable as it appeared at that time.

As noisy as the left is in Japan, it is much weaker than the forces of conservatism. The left is divided into three political parties: Socialist, Democratic-Socialist, and Communist. These parties are internally and externally divided on both the means and the ends of socialist transformation. Their relative lack of administrative experience in government and their political irresponsibility mean that their programs lack appeal to most voters, who are more concerned with bread-and-butter issues than Marxist doctrine. Trotskyite and Maoist student radicals who engage in violent activities have proved a severe embarrassment to the parties of the left. In the 1960s the middle-of-the-road Kōmeitō made impressive inroads into the constituencies of the leftist parties.

Conservatives have never seriously tried to mobilize mass demonstrations in support of their causes. This is partly because the conservatives are supported by responsible people who do not have time to engage in demonstrations, but do find the time to vote for conservative candidates. These are the "koe naki koe" (voices without voices), or "silent majority," to whom Kishi referred to during the 1960 Security Pact demonstrations. Until a few years ago, half of the voters were farmers and villagers. Ninety percent of the farmers are landowners as a result of the land reform, and the countryside has been pretty staunchly antisocialist. Never in history has the left obtained a majority in the Diet. Although the conservatives failed to win a majority of the popular votes in the general election in 1967, the middle-of-the-road Kōmeitō rather than the parties of the left has profited from the conservative slippage.

Some observers fear that the Kōmeitō may sometime try to use its political power to establish the Nichiren Shōshū form of Buddhism as the official religion of the state. In an apparent effort to calm these apprehensions and broaden its appeal, in 1970 the Kōmeitō stressed its organization's separation from its religious sponsor, the powerful Sōka Gakkai. If the Kōmeitō political power peaks out fairly soon, or if the party is genuinely sincere in its commitment to religious freedom, the Kōmeitō will not be as great a threat to democracy as some observers fear. Indeed, the idealism and energy of the Kōmeitō leaders could make a constructive contribution to Japanese politics, which suffers from cynicism and fatigue.

If the Kōmeitō loses its appeal to the lower-middle class, and if the Liberal-Democrats fail to take up the slack, there might be a drift towards the Socialists, as there was in the 1950s. In order to acquire power, however, the Socialists would have to broaden their appeals by moderating their platform. Since the conservative party is already committed to the welfare state and may be expected to enact more welfare legislation, the differences between the socialist and conservative camps in Japan might ultimately prove to be more illusory than real. Japan might then have a two-party system not greatly different from that of Great Britain and the United States, in which both parties are committed to the democratic form of government and to welfare policies.

On the other hand, the beginnings of a trend towards multipartyism in the late 1960s suggest that the Japanese polity might not evolve into a two-party system after the English model. If the Liberal-Democratic Party loses its majority in the Diet, it might not have to step down from power, because there might not be any other single party that could command a parliamentary majority. We might then see a return to coalition cabinets such as occasionally existed during the Occupation. The LDP might be the leading party in such a coalition. Its most plausible partner would be the Democratic-Socialists, in view of the DSP's support for many of the LDP's policies. However, the DSP might not command sufficient seats in the Diet to make it a worthwhile partner. The larger Kōmeitō might be a stronger partner but might wish to assume the leadership in the opposition rather than play second fiddle in a coalition government.

A Grand Coalition of the conservatives and the Socialists would seem to be very unlikely. The two parties are ideologically too far apart. The passage of time and the lure of ministerships, however, might in a decade or so reconcile some Socialists to a coalition with the LDP. Many Socialists would no doubt regard such a union with the establishment as a betrayal. The Socialist Party would then split, as did the Labour Party under such circumstances in England in the 1920s. The Communists, who made something of a comeback in 1969, are probably too far to the left to enter a coalition with the conservatives. If, as some observers suspect, the LDP will soon be seeking a coalition partner, the politics of the 1970s will be very interesting to watch.

Democracy and Revolution

In prewar Japan, democracy was often equated with opposition, because the government was authoritarian and oppressive. After the war, the thought persisted among many Japanese that democracy meant opposition to the government. When the majority of the population voted for the governing conservative party, this was taken as evidence that Japan was not a democracy. Others interpreted the same event as evidence that the people had democratically chosen the conservatives in preference to the Socialists.

Is Japan now, and will Japan in the future be, a democracy? Answers to this question first require a definition of terms. Democracy means rule by the people. In the sense that government officials are regularly elected by the people and the people enjoy freedom of expression, Japan is certainly a democracy. However, some people are not satisfied with that simple—but perfectly valid—statement. They expect democracy to provide some kind of utopia, and here we enter a very controversial area.

In Japan, the revolutionary New Left emerged over a decade before it appeared in the United States, France, and West Germany. Its votaries protest that the government in a capitalist system cannot possibly be responsive to human needs, and they condone or advocate violence as a legitimate weapon with which to enforce governmental responsibility and transfer power to the people. When the government fails to enforce love, peace, and justice, they are quick to accuse it of being fascist and call for a "revolution." However, when the people on whose behalf the revolutionaries claim to act, fail to respond to the activists' call, the revolution deteriorates into bloody clashes between students and police, and the people side with the police. The vaunted revolution deteriorates into a puberty rite, and the detached observer finds it difficult to distinguish revolutionary from nonrevolutionary violence. Revolutionary rhetoric (the litany of a counterculture) is exposed as irrelevant to the solution of social problems in the real world, the generation gap widens, and alumni or legislators cut the salaries of the university professors. This has been the story of the revolution and power-to-the-people movements in Japan and the other leading industrialized democracies.

It seems to the author that the basic reason for the failure of this revolution is that it is antithetical to democracy. In democratic states, revolutionaries are a self-appointed elite who arrogate to themselves the right to impose their will forcibly on the majority, which elected the government. Revolutionary activities are symptoms of frustration and alienation rather than of political strength. If the revolutionaries really had the support of the masses in a democracy, their candidates could win elections and make public policy, and a revolution would be unnecessary.

When the revolutionaries are intellectuals, there may be a cultural gap between them and the rest of the population. Most people are normally indifferent to politics except where their own interests seem to be involved. Intellectuals, on the other hand, often make a religion of political ideology. They sometimes profess a willingness to make great sacrifices (or to force others to make great sacrifices) for the revolution and have only scorn for the materialism of the majority. The revolutionaries despise the police as defenders of the materialistic establishment, but the majority regard the police as the protectors of lives and hard-earned property. When the revolutionaries attack the police, the majority regard this as an attack upon their own interests and side with the police.

Intellectuals among the revolutionaries are usually of upper-class background (either by birth or by education), and this fact provokes distrust among the working class, whose support is essential if the revolution is to succeed. The enthusiasm of university students for violent confrontations with the police or other authorities is regarded by the workers as an aberration of affluent adolescents. If their revolutionary acts result in arrests, these children will be defended by their upper-class parents and professors, but a working man engaged in revolution does not enjoy the immunities of the young and rich. The workers come to see revolution as a kind of game that children play. When the children grow up, they will become the managers of capitalist enterprises like their daddies, sitting on the other side of the table from the workers when wages are negotiated. The class barrier between the workers and the students is difficult, if not impossible, to surmount, and the attempts of revolutionary students to link up with the workers usually meet with failure. Thus the objective conditions necessary for revolution are not present, and today's left-wing communism is, in Lenin's words, an infantile disease.

Conclusion

To the foreign observer, democracy appears to flourish in Japan today. Advocates of totalitarianism, either of the left or right, are unable to generate mass support for the establishment of a dictatorship. The parliamentary-cabinet system of government, in which the executive branch is formally responsible to the legislative branch and indirectly to the people—the form of government which prevails in Great Britain and many other democratic countries—is operating effectively in Japan. All classes of society are enjoying unprecedented material prosperity.

The monarchy may be expected to continue to play an inconspicuous but significant role in Japanese politics. By sponsoring the postwar democratic Constitution, the Emperor legitimized it among the public. Conservatives have learned that democracy is not necessarily inimical to their revered monarchy. At the same time, the Emperor, by maintaining scrupulous neutrality in politics, has made it clear to the moderate left that republicanism is not a prerequisite of social reform. By 1970, the issue of constitutional revision, which involved the Emperor's status, was virtually dead.

The human rights provisions of the postwar Constitution have made a great impression in Japan. Students and intellectuals especially concern themselves with the rights guaranteed by the third chapter of the basic law. In spite of its irregular origin and disputes over its interpretation, the new Constitution is almost universally recognized as legitimate and binding. There appears to be a widening dedication to and understanding of democratic values. Since 1945, labor, universities, press, and political parties have enjoyed and come to cherish their new rights and freedoms. It seems doubtful that they would give them up as they did in the 1930s. At the same time, the expansion of the Japanese economy makes for greater social stability and strengthens the commitment of most major groups to the liberal democratic system.

To summarize, in terms of form of government, Japan is a democracy. The criticism of the government is as a rule focused on the policies of the government rather than on its constitutional structure. Japan's leftist as well as conservative parties work within this system and try to win seats in parliament, although the Socialists and Communists have sometimes tolerated extralegal political tactics. The Trotskyite and Maoist revolutionaries (to the left of the Japan Communist Party) who charge that the Japanese state is not a democracy are not being completely honest. Precisely because Japan is a democracy, they are unable to establish a leftist dictatorship against the will of the sovereign majority.

In 1971, twenty-five years after the adoption of the democratic Constitution, the prospects for the future of democracy in Japan appeared good. Only a depression or a war could upset the political stability of the country.

THE CONSTITUTION OF JAPAN

We, the Japanese people, acting through our duly elected representatives in the National Diet, determined that we shall secure for ourselves and our posterity the fruits of peaceful cooperation with all nations and the blessings of liberty throughout this land, and resolved that never again shall we be visited with the horrors of war through the action of government, do proclaim that sovereign power resides with the people and do firmly establish this Constitution. Government is a sacred trust of the people, the authority for which is derived from the people, the powers of which are exercised by the representatives of the people, and the benefits of which are enjoyed by the people. This is a universal principle of mankind upon which this Constitution is founded. We reject and revoke all constitutions, laws, ordinances, and rescripts in conflict herewith.

We, the Japanese people, desire peace for all time and are deeply conscious of the high ideals controlling human relationship, and we have determined to preserve our security and existence, trusting in the justice and faith of the peace-loving peoples of the world. We desire to occupy an honored place in an international society striving for the preservation of peace, and the banishment of tyranny and slavery, oppression and intolerance for all time from the earth. We recognize that all peoples of the world have the right to live in peace, free from fear and want.

We believe that no nation is responsible to itself alone, but that laws of political morality are universal; and that obedience to such laws is incumbent upon all nations who would sustain their own sovereignty and justify their sovereign relationship with other nations.

We, the Japanese people, pledge our national honor to accomplish these high ideals and purposes with all our resources.

CHAPTER I. THE EMPEROR

Article 1. The Emperor shall be the symbol of the State and of the unity of the people, deriving his position from the will of the people with whom resides sovereign power.

Article 2. The Imperial Throne shall be dynastic and succeeded to in accordance with the Imperial House Law passed by the Diet.

Article 3. The advice and approval of the Cabinet shall be required for all acts of the Emperor in matters of state, and the Cabinet shall be responsible therefor.

Article 4. The Emperor shall perform only such acts in matters of state as are provided for in this Constitution and he shall not have powers related to government.

The Emperor may delegate the performance of his acts in matters of state as may be provided by law.

Article 5. When, in accordance with the Imperial House Law, a Regency is established, the Regent shall perform his acts in matters of state in the Emperor's name. In this case, paragraph one of the preceding article will be applicable.

Article 6. The Emperor shall appoint the Prime Minister as designated by the Diet.

The Emperor shall appoint the Chief Judge of the Supreme Court as designated by the Cabinet.

Article 7. The Emperor, with the advice and approval of the Cabinet, shall perform the following acts in matters of state on behalf of the people:

Promulgation of amendments of the constitution, laws, cabinet orders and treaties.

Convocation of the Diet.

Dissolution of the House of Representatives.

Proclamation of general election of members of the Diet.

Attestation of the appointment and dismissal of Ministers of State and other officials as provided for by law, and of full powers and credentials of Ambassadors and Ministers.

Attestation of general and special amnesty, commutation of punishment, reprieve, and restoration of rights.

Awarding of honors.

Attestation of instruments of ratification and other diplomatic documents as provided for by law.

Receiving foreign ambassadors and ministers.

Performance of ceremonial functions.

Article 8. No property can be given to, or received by, the Imperial House, nor can any gifts be made therefrom, without the authorization of the Diet.

CHAPTER II. RENUNCIATION OF WAR

Article 9. Aspiring sincerely to an international peace based on justice and order, the Japanese people forever renounce war as a sovereign right of the nation and the threat or use of force as means of settling international disputes.

In order to accomplish the aim of the preceding paragraph, land, sea, and air forces, as well as other war potential, will never be maintained. The right of belligerency of the state will not be recognized.

CHAPTER III. RIGHTS AND DUTIES OF THE PEOPLE

Article 10. The conditions necessary for being a Japanese national shall be determined by law.

Article 11. The people shall not be prevented from enjoying any of the fundamental human rights. These fundamental human rights guaranteed to the people by this Constitution shall be conferred upon the people of this and future generations as eternal and inviolate rights.

Article 12. The freedoms and rights guaranteed to the people by this Constitution shall be maintained by the constant endeavor of the people, who shall refrain from any abuse of these freedoms and rights and shall always be responsible for utilizing them for the public welfare.

Article 13. All of the people shall be respected as individuals. Their right to life, liberty, and the pursuit of happiness shall, to the extent that it does not interfere with the public welfare, be the supreme consideration in legislation and in other governmental affairs.

Article 14. All of the people are equal under the law and there shall be no discrimination in political, economic or social relations because of race, creed, sex, social status or family origin.

Peers and peerage shall not be recognized.

No privilege shall accompany any award of honor, decoration or any distinction, nor shall any such award be valid beyond the lifetime of the individual who now holds or hereafter may receive it.

Article 15. The people have the inalienable right to choose their public officials and to dismiss them.

All public officials are servants of the whole community and not of any group thereof.

Universal adult suffrage is guaranteed with regard to the election of public officials.

In all elections, secrecy of the ballot shall not be violated. A voter shall not be answerable, publicly or privately, for the choice he has made.

Article 16. Every person shall have the right of peaceful petition for the redress of damage, for the removal of public officials, for the enactment, repeal or amendment of laws, ordinances or regulations and for other matters; nor shall any person be in any way discriminated against for sponsoring such a petition.

Article 17. Every person may sue for redress as provided by law from the State or a public entity, in case he has suffered damage through illegal act of any public official.

Article 18. No person shall be held in bondage of any kind. Involuntary servitude, except as punishment for crime, is prohibited.

Article 19. Freedom of thought and conscience shall not be violated.

Article 20. Freedom of religion is guaranteed to all. No religious organization shall receive any privileges from the State, nor exercise any political authority.

No person shall be compelled to take part in any religious act, celebration, rite or practice.

The State and its organs shall refrain from religious education or any other religious activity.

Article 21. Freedom of assembly and association as well as speech, press and all other forms of expression are guaranteed.

No censorship shall be maintained, nor shall the secrecy of any means of communication be violated.

Article 22. Every person shall have freedom to choose and change his residence and to choose his occupation to the extent that it does not interfere with the public welfare.

Freedom of all persons to move to a foreign country and to divest themselves of their nationality shall be inviolate.

Article 23. Academic freedom is guaranteed.

Article 24. Marriage shall be based only on the mutual consent of both sexes and it shall be maintained through mutual cooperation with the equal rights of husband and wife as a basis.

With regard to choice of spouse, property rights, inheritance, choice of domicile, divorce and other matters pertaining to marriage and the family, laws shall be enacted from the standpoint of individual dignity and the essential equality of the sexes.

Article 25. All people shall have the right to maintain the minimum standards of wholesome and cultured living.

In all spheres of life, the State shall use its endeavors for the promotion and extension of social welfare and security, and of public health.

Article 26. All people shall have the right to receive an equal education correspondent to their ability, as provided by law.

All people shall be obligated to have all boys and girls under their protection receive ordinary education as provided for by law. Such compulsory education shall be free.

Article 27. All people shall have the right and the obligation to work.

Standards for wages, hours, rest and other working conditions shall be fixed by law.

Children shall not be exploited.

Article 28. The right of workers to organize and bargain and act collectively is guaranteed.

Article 29. The right to own or to hold property is inviolable.

Property rights shall be defined by law, in conformity with the public welfare.

Private property may be taken for public use upon just compensation therefor.

Article 30. The people shall be liable to taxation as provided by law.

Article 31. No person shall be deprived of life or liberty, nor shall any other criminal penalty be imposed, except according to procedure established by law.

Article 32. No person shall be denied the right of access to the courts.

Article 33. No person shall be apprehended except upon warrant issued by a competent judicial officer which specifies the offense with which the person is charged, unless he is apprehended, the offense being committed.

Article 34. No person shall be arrested or detained without being at once informed of the charges against him or without the immediate privilege of counsel; nor shall he be detained without adequate cause; and upon demand of any person such cause must be immediately shown in open court in his presence and the presence of his counsel.

Article 35. The right of all persons to be secure in their homes, papers and effects against entries, searches and seizures shall not be impaired except upon warrant issued for adequate cause and particularly describing the place to be searched and things to be seized, or except as provided by Article 33.

Each search or seizure shall be made upon separate warrant issued by a competent judicial officer.

Article 36. The infliction of torture by any public officer and cruel punishments are absolutely forbidden.

Article 37. In all criminal cases the accused shall enjoy the right to a speedy and public trial by an impartial tribunal.

He shall be permitted full opportunity to examine all witnesses, and he shall have the right of compulsory process for obtaining witnesses on his behalf at public expense.

At all times the accused shall have the assistance of competent counsel who shall, if the accused is unable to secure the same by his own efforts, be assigned to his use by the State.

Article 38. No person shall be compelled to testify against himself.

Confession made under compulsion, torture or threat, or after prolonged arrest or detention shall not be admitted in evidence.

No person shall be convicted or punished in cases where the only proof against him is his own confession.

Article 39. No person shall be held criminally liable for an act which was lawful at the time it was committed, or of which he has been acquitted, nor shall he be placed in double jeopardy.

Article 40. Any person, in case he is acquitted after he has been arrested or detained, may sue the State for redress as provided by law.

CHAPTER IV. THE DIET

Article 41. The Diet shall be the highest organ of state power, and shall be the sole law-making organ of the State.

Article 42. The Diet shall consist of two Houses, namely the House of Representatives and the House of Councillors.

Article 43. Both Houses shall consist of elected members, representative of all the people.

The number of the members of each House shall be fixed by law.

Article 44. The qualifications of members of both Houses and their electors shall be fixed by law. However, there shall be no discrimination because of race, creed, sex, social status, family origin, education, property or income.

Article 45. The term of office of members of the House of Representatives shall be four years. However, the term shall be terminated before the full term is up in case the House of Representatives is dissolved.

Article 46. The term of office of members of the House of Councillors shall be six years, and election for half the members shall take place every three years.

Article 47. Electoral districts, method of voting and other matters pertaining to the method of election of members of both Houses shall be fixed by law.

Article 48. No person shall be permitted to be a member of both Houses simultaneously.

Article 49. Members of both Houses shall receive appropriate annual payment from the national treasury in accordance with law.

Article 50. Except in cases provided by law, members of both Houses shall be exempt from apprehension while the Diet is in session, and any members apprehended before the opening of the session shall be freed during the term of the session upon demand of the House.

Article 51. Members of both Houses shall not be held liable outside the House for speeches, debates or votes cast inside the House.

Article 52. An ordinary session of the Diet shall be convoked once per year.

Article 53. The Cabinet may determine to convoke extraordinary sessions of the Diet. When a quarter or more of the total members of either House makes the demand, the Cabinet must determine on such convocation.

Article 54. When the House of Representatives is dissolved, there must be a general election of members of the House of Representatives within forty (40) days from the date of dissolution, and the Diet must be convoked within thirty (30) days from the date of the election.

When the House of Representatives is dissolved, the House of Councillors is closed at the same time. However, the Cabinet may in time of national emergency convoke the House of Councillors in emergency session.

Measures taken at such session as mentioned in the proviso of the preceding paragraph shall be provisional and shall become null and void unless agreed to by the House of Representatives within a period of ten (10) days after the opening of the next session of the Diet.

Article 55. Each House shall judge disputes related to qualifications of its members. However, in order to deny a seat to any member, it is necessary to pass a resolution by a majority of two-thirds or more of the members present.

Article 56. Business cannot be transacted in either House unless one-third or more of total membership is present.

All matters shall be decided, in each House, by a majority of those present, except as elsewhere provided in the Constitution, and in case of a tie, the presiding officer shall decide the issue.

Article 57. Deliberation in each House shall be public. However, a secret meeting may be held where a majority of two-thirds or more of those members present passes a resolution therefor.

Each House shall keep a record of proceedings. This record shall be published and given general circulation, excepting such parts of proceedings of secret session as may be deemed to require secrecy.

Upon demand of one-fifth or more of the members present, votes of the members on any matter shall be recorded in the minutes.

Article 58. Each House shall select its own president and other officials.

Each House shall establish its rules pertaining to meetings, proceedings and internal discipline, and may punish members for disorderly conduct. However, in order to expel a member, a majority of two-thirds or more of those members present must pass a resolution thereon.

Article 59. A bill becomes a law on passage by both Houses, except as otherwise provided by the Constitution.

A bill which is passed by the House of Representatives, and upon which the House of Councillors makes a decision different from that of the House of Representatives, becomes a law when passed a second time by the House of Representatives by a majority of two-thirds or more of the members present.

The provision of the preceding paragraph does not preclude the House of Representatives from calling for the meeting of a joint committee of both Houses, provided for by law.

Failure by the House of Councillors to take final action within sixty (60) days after receipt of a bill passed by the House of Representatives, time in recess excepted, may by determined by the House of Representatives to constitute a rejection of the said bill by the House of Councillors.

Article 60. The budget must first be submitted to the House of Representatives.

Upon consideration of the budget, when the House of Councillors makes a decision different from that of the House of Representatives, and when no agreement can be reached even through a joint committee of both Houses, provided for by law, or in the case of failure by the House of Councillors to take final action within thirty (30) days, the period of recess excluded, after the receipt of the budget passed by the House of Representatives, the decision of the House of Representatives shall be the decision of the Diet.

Article 61. The second paragraph of the preceding article applies also to the Diet approval required for the conclusion of treaties.

Article 62. Each House may conduct investigations in relation to government, and may demand the presence and testimony of witnesses, and the production of records.

Article 63. The Prime Minister and other Ministers of State may, at any time, appear in either House for the purpose of speaking on bills, regardless of whether they are members of the House or not. They must appear when their presence is required in order to give answers or explanations.

Article 64. The Diet shall set up an impeachment court from among the members of both Houses for the purpose of trying those judges against whom removal proceedings have been instituted.

Matters relating to impeachment shall be provided by law.

Chapter V. The Cabinet

Article 65. Executive power shall be vested in the Cabinet.

Article 66. The Cabinet shall consist of the Prime Minister, who shall be its head, and other Ministers of State, as provided for by law.

The Prime Minister and other Ministers of State must be civilians.

The Cabinet, in the exercise of executive power, shall be collectively responsible to the Diet.

Article 67. The Prime Minister shall be designated from among the members of the Diet by a resolution of the Diet. This designation shall precede all other business.

If the House of Representatives and the House of Councillors disagree and if no agreement can be reached even through a joint committee of both Houses, provided for by law, or the House of Councillors fails to make designation within ten (10) days, exclusive of the period of recess, after the House of Representatives has made designation, the decision of the House of Representatives shall be the decision of the Diet.

Article 68. The Prime Minister shall appoint the Ministers of State. However, a majority of their number must be chosen from among the members of the Diet.

The Prime Minister may remove the Ministers of State as he chooses.

Article 69. If the House of Representatives passes a non-confidence resolution, or rejects a confidence resolution, the Cabinet shall resign en masse, unless the House of Representatives is dissolved within ten (10) days.

Article 70. When there is a vacancy in the post of Prime Minister, or upon the first convocation of the Diet after a general election of members of the House of Representatives, the Cabinet shall resign en masse.

Article 71. In the cases mentioned in the two preceding Articles, the Cabinet shall continue its functions until the time when a new Prime Minister is appointed.

Article 72. The Prime Minister, representing the Cabinet, submits bills, reports on general national affairs and foreign relations to the Diet and exercises control and supervision over various administrative branches.

Article 73. The Cabinet, in addition to other general administrative functions, shall perform the following functions:

Administer the law faithfully; conduct affairs of state.

Manage foreign affairs.

Conclude treaties. However, it shall obtain prior or, depending on circumstances, subsequent approval of the Diet.

Administer the civil service, in accordance with standards established by law.

Prepare the budget, and present it to the Diet.

Enact cabinet orders in order to execute the provisions of this Constitution and of the law. However, it cannot include penal provisions in such cabinet orders unless authorized by such law.

Decide on general amnesty, special amnesty, commutation of punishment, reprieve, and restoration of rights.

Article 74. All laws and cabinet orders shall be signed by the competent Minister of State and countersigned by the Prime Minister.

Article 75. The Ministers of State, during their tenure of office, shall not be subject to legal action without the consent of the Prime Minister. However, the right to take that action is not impaired hereby.

Chapter VI. Judiciary

Article 76. The whole judicial power is vested in a Supreme Court and in such inferior courts as are established by law.

No extraordinary tribunal shall be established, nor shall any organ or agency of the Executive be given final judicial power.

All judges shall be independent in the exercise of their conscience and shall be bound only by this Constitution and the laws.

Article 77. The Supreme Court is vested with the rule-making power under which it determines the rules of procedure and of practice, and of matters relating to attorneys, the internal discipline of the courts and the administration of judicial affairs.

Public procurators shall be subject to the rule-making power of the Supreme Court.

The Supreme Court may delegate the power to make rules for inferior courts to such courts.

Article 78. Judges shall not be removed except by public impeachment unless judicially declared mentally or physically incompetent to perform official duties. No disciplinary action against judges shall be administered by any executive organ or agency.

Article 79. The Supreme Court shall consist of a Chief Judge and such number of judges as may be determined by law; all such judges excepting the Chief Judge shall be appointed by the Cabinet.

The appointment of the judges of the Supreme Court shall be reviewed by the people at the first general election of members of the House of Representatives following their appointment, and shall be reviewed again at the first general election of members of the House of Representatives after a lapse of ten (10) years, and in the same manner thereafter.

In cases mentioned in the foregoing paragraph, when the majority of the voters favors the dismissal of a judge, he shall be dismissed.

Matters pertaining to review shall be prescribed by law.

The judges of the Supreme Court shall be retired upon the attainment of the age as fixed by law.

All such judges shall receive, at regular stated intervals, adequate compensation which shall not be decreased during their terms of office.

Article 80. The judges of the inferior courts shall be appointed by the Cabinet from a list of persons nominated by the Supreme Court. All such judges shall hold office for a term of ten (10) years with privilege of reappointment, provided that they shall be retired upon the attainment of the age as fixed by law.

The judges of the inferior courts shall receive, at regular stated intervals, adequate compensation which shall not be decreased during their terms of office.

Article 81. The Supreme Court is the court of last resort with power to determine the constitutionality of any law, order, regulation or official act.

Article 82. Trials shall be conducted and judgment declared publicly.

Where a court unanimously determines publicity to be dangerous to public order or morals, a trial may be conducted privately, but trials of political offenses, offenses involving the press or cases wherein the rights of people as guaranteed in Chapter III of this Constitution are in question shall always be conducted publicly.

CHAPTER VII. FINANCE

Article 83. The power to administer national finances shall be exercised as the Diet shall determine.

Article 84. No new taxes shall be imposed or existing ones modified except by law or under such conditions as law may prescribe.

Article 85. No money shall be expended, nor shall the State obligate itself, except as authorized by the Diet.

Article 86. The Cabinet shall prepare and submit to the Diet for its consideration and decision a budget for each fiscal year.

Article 87. In order to provide for unforeseen deficiencies in the budget, a reserve fund may be authorized by the Diet to be expended upon the responsibility of the Cabinet.

The Cabinet must get subsequent approval of the Diet for all payments from the reserve fund.

Article 88. All property of the Imperial Household shall belong to the State. All expenses of the Imperial Household shall be appropriated by the Diet in the budget.

Article 89. No public money or other property shall be expended or appropriated for the use, benefit or maintenance of any religious institution or association, or for any charitable, educational or benevolent enterprises not under the control of public authority.

Article 90. Final accounts of the expenditures and revenues of the State shall be audited annually by a Board of Audit and submitted by the Cabinet to the Diet, together with the statement of audit, during the fiscal year immediately following the period covered.

The organization and competency of the Board of Audit shall be determined by law.

Article 91. At regular intervals and at least annually the Cabinet shall report to the Diet and the people on the state of national finances.

Chapter VIII. Local Self-Government

Article 92. Regulations concerning organization and operations of local public entities shall be fixed by law in accordance with the principle of local autonomy.

Article 93. The local public entities shall establish assemblies as their deliberative organs, in accordance with law.

The chief executive officers of all local public entities, the members of their assemblies, and such other local officials as may be determined by law shall be elected by direct popular vote within their several communities.

Article 94. Local public entities shall have the right to manage their property, affairs and administration and to enact their own regulations within law.

Article 95. A special law, applicable only to one local public entity, cannot be enacted by the Diet without the consent of the majority of the voters of the local public entity concerned, obtained in accordance with law.

Chapter IX. Amendments

Article 96. Amendments to this Constitution shall be initiated by the Diet, through a concurring vote of two-thirds or more of all the members of each House and shall thereupon be submitted to the people for ratification, which shall require the affirmative vote of a majority of all votes cast thereon, at a special referendum or at such election as the Diet shall specify.

Amendments when so ratified shall immediately be promulgated by the Emperor in the name of the people, as an integral part of this Constitution.

Chapter X. Supreme Law

Article 97. The fundamental human rights by this Constitution guaranteed to the people of Japan are fruits of the age-old struggle of man to be free; they have survived the many exacting tests for durability and are conferred upon this and future generations in trust, to be held for all time inviolate.

Article 98. This Constitution shall be the supreme law of the nation and no law, ordinance, imperial rescript or other act of government, or part thereof, contrary to the provisions hereof, shall have legal force or validity.

The treaties concluded by Japan and established laws of nations shall be faithfully observed.

Article 99. The Emperor or the Regent as well as Ministers of State, members of the Diet, judges, and all other public officials have the obligation to respect and uphold this Constitution.

CHAPTER XI. SUPPLEMENTARY PROVISIONS

Article 100. This Constitution shall be enforced as from the day when the period of six months will have elapsed counting from the day of its promulgation.

The enactment of laws necessary for the enforcement of this Constitution, the election of members of the House of Councillors and the procedure for the convocation of the Diet and other preparatory procedures necessary for the enforcement of this Constitution may be executed before the day prescribed in the preceding paragraph.

Article 101. If the House of Councillors is not constituted before the effective date of this Constitution, the House of Representatives shall function as the Diet until such time as the House of Councillors shall be constituted.

Article 102. The term of office for half the members of the House of Councillors serving in the first term under this Constitution shall be three years. Members falling under this category shall be determined in accordance with law.

Article 103. The Ministers of State, members of the House of Representatives and judges in office on the effective date of this Constitution, and all other public officials who occupy positions corresponding to such positions as are recognized by this Constitution shall not forfeit their positions automatically on account of the enforcement of this Constitution unless otherwise specified by law. When, however, successors are elected or appointed under the provisions of this Constitution, they shall forfeit their positions as a matter of course.

INDEX

271